Hamlet

edited by Elizabeth Seely and Ken Elliott

Series Editor: John Seely

Heinemann

Heinemann Educational Publishers
Halley Court, Jordan Hill, Oxford OX2 8EJ
Part of Harcourt Education

Heinemann is a registered trademark of .
Harcourt Education Limited

First published in the *Heinemann Shakespeare Plays* series 1996
Second edition 2000

Reprinted 2005

07 06 05
10 9 8 7 6

10-digit: ISBN 0 435193 10 4
13-digit: ISBN 978 0 435193 10 2

Cover Design by Miller Craig and Cocking

Cover illustration by Nigel Casseldine R. W. A.

Produced by Celia Floyd, Basingstoke

Additional typesetting by TechType, Abingdon, Oxon

Printed and bound in Great Britain by Biddles Ltd, King's Lynn, Norfolk

CONTENTS

iv   How to use this book
vii   The plot
xii   Hamlet and the tradition of revenge
xiv   The text of Shakespeare's plays
xv   The text of *Hamlet*

Hamlet
1   Characters
3   Act one
69   Act two
123   Act three
189   Act four
243   Act five

Explorations
295   Drama activities
299   Character
305   Relationships
307   Some issues and themes
314   Contexts
322   Preparing for an examination
325   Writing an essay
332   Essay questions

333   Glossary

How to use this book

This edition of *Hamlet* has been prepared to provide you with several different kinds of information and guidance.

The introduction

Before the text of the play there is:
- a summary of the plot
- an explanation of how *Hamlet* fits in to the literary theme of revenge which was so popular in Shakespeare's day
- a brief explanation of Shakespeare's texts.

The text and commentary

On each right-hand page you will find the text of the play. On the facing left-hand pages there are three types of support material:
- a summary of the action
- detailed explanations of difficult words, phrases and longer sections of text
- suggestions of points you might find it useful to think about as you read the play.

End-of-act activities

After each act there is a set of activities. These can be tackled as you read the play. Many students, however, may want to leave these until they undertake a second reading. They consist of the following.

Keeping track: straightforward questions directing your attention to the action of the act.

Drama: practical drama activities to help you focus on key characters, relationships and situations.

The key elements: a short section listing important elements in the act.

Key scene: a focus on an important scene in the act. This is intended to help you combine an understanding of the characters and broader themes of the play with the ability to comment on the text in detail.

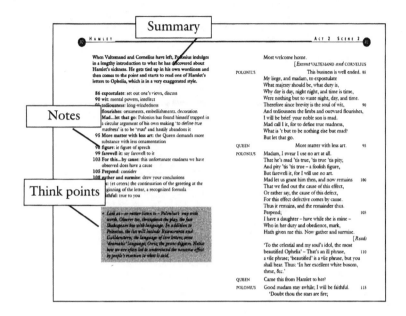

Close study: work on the text of selected extracts from the play, designed to help you tackle Shakespeare's language in detail.

Writing: progressive activities throughout the book help you to develop essay writing skills.

Explorations

At the end of the book there are a variety of different items designed to draw together your thoughts and insights about the play as a whole:

- how to approach thinking about the whole play
- work on character
- work on the themes and issues
- guidance on how to tackle practical drama activities
- advice on preparing for an examination
- advice on essay writing, together with a sample essay written by an A-level student, with comments
- practice essay questions
- glossary of technical terms.

The plot

Act 1

On the battlements of Elsinore castle at midnight the relief guard, consisting of **Barnardo** and **Marcellus**, takes over from **Francisco**. **Horatio** is to join them. The atmosphere of dark and cold and the midnight hour is deepened by mention of a **Ghost** which has now appeared for two nights in succession. It looks like the late **King Hamlet**, father of **Hamlet, Prince of Denmark**. Horatio, the young Hamlet's fellow-student and friend, whom the sentries have told about the Ghost, has come to see whether it will appear again.

The Ghost, armed from head to foot, does appear and Horatio, visibly shaken, claims that this apparition means there is some threat to the State of Denmark. Although only recently returned from university in Germany, he seems to be very well-informed about the reasons for the preparations for war they have all observed. The Ghost appears again but, although challenged, it will not speak. They decide to tell Prince Hamlet what has happened.

The new king, **Claudius**, brother of the late King Hamlet, has married **Gertrude**, the dead man's widow. To the whole court he explains that **Fortinbras, Prince of Norway** is laying claim to land that his father, **old Fortinbras**, once forfeited to King Hamlet. Claudius is sending ambassadors to try to deal with the matter before it comes to war.

Claudius then grants permission to **Laertes** to leave the court and return to France. Laertes is the son of **Polonius**, counsellor to the king. Hamlet is then reproached by Claudius, his uncle, and by Gertrude, his mother, for what seems to them an excessive period of mourning for his father. Hamlet protests that his grief is very real, agrees not to return to university at Wittenberg and, when he is left alone, gives expression to his depression and his misery.

Horatio tells Hamlet about the appearance of what seems to be his father's ghost and it is decided that Hamlet too will keep watch that night.

Laertes, about to leave for France, says goodbye to his sister **Ophelia**. Their talk has clearly turned on the subject of Hamlet's affection for her. Laertes warns her to keep him at arm's length, as Hamlet will not be allowed a free choice in love because he is still a potential heir to the throne. Polonius, their father, loads Laertes with advice on the way he should behave. Once Laertes has left, Ophelia becomes the object of Polonius's recommendations. He warns her not to believe Hamlet's protestations of love and not to talk to him.

When the Ghost next appears, Hamlet speaks to it as though it is his dead father. Against his friends' advice he follows when it beckons: the Ghost tells him that he is his father's spirit, at present suffering the torments of purgatory. He was murdered, he claims, by Claudius and is grieved that Gertrude, his widow, so swiftly gave her affections to his murderer. The Ghost knows that his son will seek to avenge his murder, but tells him to leave Gertrude to the torments of her conscience, and above all to remember him. This Hamlet swears to do. He also swears his friends to secrecy.

Act 2

Polonius sends an acquaintance to spy on his son Laertes in Paris and to report back to him. Ophelia has been carrying out her father's instructions to ignore Hamlet and in some distress tells Polonius of Hamlet's apparently crazed behaviour in her presence. The King and Queen have become increasingly concerned at the changes in Hamlet and call upon old school friends of his, **Rosencrantz** and **Guildenstern**, to try to find out the cause of his strange moods.

The ambassadors sent to Norway return with news of the success of their mission – young Fortinbras is to be prevented by his uncle from raising an army to fight with Denmark. Polonius tells Claudius and Gertrude that he has discovered the reason for Hamlet's madness – he is in love with Ophelia. Hamlet is pointedly rude to Polonius and demonstrates his 'craziness' to him and to Rosencrantz and Guildenstern, deliberately misleading all three. When Hamlet learns that a troupe of actors is about to arrive, he has the idea of trying to prove to himself that Claudius is guilty of the Ghost's accusations. He will ask the players to act out a similar story to the alleged murder of his father by his uncle.

Act 3

Rosencrantz and Guildenstern report back to Claudius and
Gertrude. Ophelia is set to walk, reading her prayer book,
where Hamlet may meet her, while Claudius and Polonius
listen to their conversation. Hamlet contemplates suicide, but
is concerned that there may be something worse after death.
This hesitation causes indecision, he claims. Ophelia speaks of
returning Hamlet's gifts and he maintains he has never loved
her. He rejects her quite brutally and tells her to go to a
convent where she will not be tempted to give birth to another
generation. Ophelia mourns his descent into madness.

Claudius, increasingly alarmed by what he has heard, decides
to bring forward the journey to England he has apparently
already planned for Hamlet in the care of Rosencrantz and
Guildenstern.

Hamlet takes Horatio into his confidence over his plan to
trap Claudius into showing his guilt as he watches the murder
played out on the stage. The mime which precedes the spoken
play shows the affectionate king and queen parting in the
garden. When the king is asleep, a man approaches him, shows
that he covets the crown and pours poison in the king's ears.
Although the queen is distressed at the king's death she soon
responds to gifts from the poisoner and accepts his love.
Claudius reacts when the spoken play is under way. He rises
hastily and leaves. Hamlet and Horatio agree about the guilty
reaction they have observed. Gertrude sends for Hamlet by
Rosencrantz and Guildenstern. Hamlet shows them that he is
suspicious of them. He reminds himself that he must keep
himself in check when he talks to his mother.

Claudius has become aware of the danger he runs while
Hamlet is at court and speeds up the arrangements for him to
go under Rosencrantz and Guildenstern's guard to England.
On his way to his mother's room – where, by arrangement
with Claudius, Polonius has already hidden to hear what
mother and son will say – Hamlet comes across Claudius,
apparently at prayer. He is full of remorse for the murder he
committed, but is unable to repent or pray properly because he
will not give up what his crime has secured for him. Hamlet,

assuming that Claudius is confessing his sins to God and receiving forgiveness, will not kill him.

Hamlet speaks aggressively to the Queen, frightening her. She calls for help and Polonius answers. Hamlet draws his sword and kills whoever is hiding behing the arras, possibly thinking it is Claudius. Hamlet goes on to contrast his father with Claudius until Gertrude sees what she has done and begs him to stop. The Ghost enters again, unseen by Gertrude who sees her son apparently talking to the empty air, confirming his madness. He is being rebuked by the Ghost for not turning his energies to vengeance. Hamlet assures her he is not mad and begs her not to tell Claudius this, and to stop sleeping with Claudius.

Act 4

Gertrude reports the death of Polonius to Claudius. He arranges to have the body taken to the chapel and to speed up Hamlet's departure for England. Rosencrantz and Guildenstern have letters to the King of England instructing him to arrange for Hamlet's death. Before Hamlet leaves, he meets some of Fortinbras's troops who are crossing Denmark on their way to fight in Poland. The sight of his resolution makes Hamlet again reproach himself for his own lack of action in avenging his father. Ophelia, deeply distressed by Hamlet's rejection of her, now has to face the fact that he has killed her father. She has been driven mad with grief. Laertes, already angered and hurt by his father's murder and unceremonious burial, is now forced to face his sister's madness.

Horatio learns from a letter, delivered to him by a sailor, that when the ship in which he was travelling with his gaolers was attacked by pirates, Hamlet did a deal with his captors and escaped on the pirate ship, which is shortly to return to Denmark. When Claudius learns this, he plots with Laertes to rid themselves of Hamlet for good. They plan a fencing match between Laertes and Hamlet where Laertes's blade will be sharp, not blunted as for an exhibition bout, and will also have been smeared with a poison to which there is no antidote. In addition, Claudius will poison a goblet of wine to be offered to Hamlet as refreshment. No sooner has all this been agreed, than Gertrude brings news of Ophelia's death by drowning.

Act 5

While two grave-diggers prepare Ophelia's grave, Horatio and Hamlet look on. Before Hamlet realizes whose funeral is about to take place he is made to consider the reality of death and the fact that human flesh and blood return to earth. The funeral procession arrives and Laertes and Hamlet fight over the grave, competing in their love for the dead girl. Horatio is given charge of Hamlet and then learns that while at sea Hamlet discovered Claudius's death plot against him and managed to substitute a letter instructing the English king to execute Rosencrantz and Guildenstern.

Bets are laid on the planned fight between Hamlet and Laertes. Hamlet scores the first two hits and, before Claudius can stop her, Gertrude celebrates with a drink from the poisoned goblet. As Laertes wounds Hamlet with the poisoned foil, they exchange rapiers in the scuffle and Laertes is wounded with his own foil. As Gertrude dies she tells Hamlet that it is the drink which has poisoned her and Hamlet orders the door to be locked, crying 'treachery'. Laertes falls, admitting to Hamlet that the blade which has wounded them both was poisoned, and that there is no hope for either of them. He puts the blame on Claudius. Hamlet wounds the king with the poisoned rapier and then forces him to drink from the poisoned cup. He dies. Laertes and Hamlet forgive each other. Hamlet dissuades Horatio from committing suicide, placing on him the duty of explaining all the recent events, so that Hamlet will not appear to be an unprincipled murderer and traitor.

The sound of Fortinbras's army returning from Poland is heard in time for Hamlet to give him his dying vote as future King. Fortinbras, promising to listen to Horatio's account, has the bodies removed and Hamlet's corpse raised up. Hamlet shall have the funeral rites due to a soldier and a prince.

Studying the play

When you study a play, you need to be able to see it from two different perspectives simultaneously. You need to be able to imagine and experience the text line by line, sharing the thoughts and feelings of the characters as they go through the events of the play, but at the same time you need to be able to 'look down on' the play as a whole and see the patterns of character and relationship, of language and imagery, of themes and issues.

A play is essentially an audio-visual experience. No two members of the audience see quite the same 'play' and no two performances are ever exactly the same. Two important lessons should be learned from this. The first is that the printed text is not the play; the play is what you see when you go to the theatre. The text is a set of instructions to be interpreted by the director and the actors, artists and technicians. The second lesson is that there is no one 'right answer' to the play, only a range of possible interpretations. Your view can be just as valid as any one else's, but only if you can present it clearly and support it by valid arguments derived from the text. For this purpose you need, again, to see it as a whole and as a set of details.

Thinking about the play

By the time you have discussed the text carefully you should be beginning to clarify and organize your response to the play as a whole. Most examination questions concentrate on content and form, and these are useful terms which offer you an approach and a framework within which you can prepare to write successfully.

Your first task is to establish clearly in your mind the broad issues raised by the text and the possible areas for discussion, including major characters. You need to consider and discuss some of the possible views and interpretations of these issues and lay down a sensible framework within which personal response can be convincing and well–considered. You also need to get close to the text and identify the key incidents, scenes or even quotations which will form the basis of any essay. When you come to write essays on the whole text, or even a specified passage, the appropriate textual evidence and illustrations should be noted and easily available.

The text of Shakespeare's plays

Shakespeare's work is generally treated with such immense respect
that it may seem strange to admit that we cannot be certain exactly
what he wrote. The reasons for this mystery lie in the
circumstances of the theatre and publishing in the sixteenth and
seventeenth centuries.

Shakespeare was a professional actor and shareholder in a
company of actors, the Lord Chamberlain's Men, for whom he
wrote his plays. Since copyright and performing rights did not
exist before the eighteenth century there was the risk that, if a
play was successful, other companies would perform it and reap
the financial rewards. To avoid this, acting companies guarded
the handwritten copy of a completed work. It was their most
valuable resource and was kept by the prompter: each actor was
given only his own lines and cues. None of these manuscripts
survives to the present day. The lack of printed texts may seem
strange but, like the work of other playwrights of his time,
Shakespeare's plays existed essentially as oral, not written, texts.
His concern was with what they looked and sounded like on stage.

However, there was money to be made from printed plays
and during his lifetime nearly half of Shakespeare's plays were
printed in what are known as quartos: paperback editions of
single plays. Some of these, called 'bad' quartos, are pirated
editions based on the memories of actors and audience. Others
are much more accurate and may have been authorised by
Shakespeare or the shareholders in his company, perhaps to
capitalize on a popular success which was about to go out of
repertory or to forestall a pirate edition. None, however, seems
to have been supervised by the playwright and all differ, often
considerably, from the key text of Shakespeare's plays, the *First
Folio*.

The *First Folio*, published in 1623, is a collected edition of
all Shakespeare's plays (with the exception of *Pericles*). It was
edited by John Hemming and Henry Condell, two
shareholders in the Lord Chamberlain's Men, using 'good'
quartos, prompt copies and other company papers to provide
an accurate text as a fitting memorial to their partner. They did
not start the editing process until after Shakespeare died and
apparently based their editorial decisions on what had
happened in the theatre. We cannot be certain how far they

represent what Shakespeare's ultimate intentions might have been. Even if Shakespeare had approved the text which went to the printer, it was the custom of writers to leave much of the detail of spelling and punctuation to the printer or to a scribe who made a fair copy from the playwright's rough drafts. The scribe and the printer thus introduced their own interpretations and inaccuracies into the text. The *First Folio* was reprinted three times in the seventeenth century and each edition corrected some inaccuracies and introduced new errors. A modern editor tries to provide a text which is easy to read and close to Shakespeare's presumed intentions. To do this the editor may modernize spelling and change punctuation, add stage directions and scene divisions, and make important decisions about which of several readings in quarto and folio editions is most acceptable. If you are able to compare this edition of the play with other editions, you are likely to find many minor variations between them as well as occasional major differences which could change your view of a character or situation.

The text of *Hamlet*

The earliest published text of Shakespeare's *Hamlet*, as opposed to versions of the story which appeared in the late 1580s, is dated 1603. We cannot be certain when Shakespeare wrote this play but it seems highly unlikely that it was any earlier than the beginning of the seventeenth century. This is also suggested by the internal evidence of references to *Julius Caesar*, which was being performed in 1599. Only two copies have survived of this first 'quarto' (Q1) and most critics regard it as an unreliable and unauthorized version of the play.

The second version of the play is another quarto (Q2) which is dated either 1604 or 1605. This publication is widely accepted as being based on Shakespeare's own manuscript.

The third version is to be found in the first folio (F) which was published in 1623 after Shakespeare's death. This version omits passages which were in the second quarto but it contains new passages and some 'variant' readings. For example, Hamlet's first soliloquy in Act 1 scene 2 includes the best known of these variant readings as the first folio gives us *'solid flesh'* while the quartos give us *'sallied flesh'*.

What all this means is that we have no definitive version of the play: no original manuscript has survived.

HAMLET, PRINCE OF DENMARK

CHARACTERS

HAMLET, Prince of Denmark, son of the dead King Hamlet

CLAUDIUS, King of Denmark, Hamlet's uncle

GERTRUDE, Queen of Denmark, formerly wife of King Hamlet, mother of Hamlet

GHOST of King Hamlet

POLONIUS, chief councillor to Claudius

LAERTES, son of Polonius

OPHELIA, daughter of Polonius

REYNALDO, servant of Polonius

HORATIO, friend and fellow-student of Hamlet

MARCELLUS
BARNARDO } officers of the watch
FRANCISCO

VALTEMAND } ambassadors to Norway
CORNELIUS

ROSENCRANTZ } former schoolfellows of Hamlet
GUILDENSTERN

OSRIC } courtiers
GENTLEMAN

FORTINBRAS, Prince of Norway

CAPTAIN in the Norwegian army

PLAYERS

First CLOWN, the sexton and gravedigger

Second CLOWN, his mate

PRIEST

English AMBASSADORS

Lords, Ladies, Officers, Soldiers, Sailors, Messengers, and Attendants

SCENE *The Danish royal castle at Elsinore*

At the castle of Elsinore, at midnight, the guard is being changed. It is a bitterly cold night. Barnardo takes over from Francisco. Horatio and Marcellus join him for the watch.

2 Nay, answer me: the newcomer should prove who he is
   unfold yourself: declare who you are, identify yourself
3 Long live the King!: Francisco recognizes Barnardo's voice
6 carefully upon your hour: punctually
8 relief: Barnardo is relieving him of his guard duty
9 sick at heart: in low spirits
13 rivals of my watch: my opposite numbers on guard duty
15 ground: country
   liegemen to the Dane: loyal subjects of the King of Denmark

- *What is the atmosphere of this opening scene and how is it created on the page?*

Act one

Scene 1

Elsinore

Enter BARNARDO *and* FRANCISCO, *two sentinels*

BARNARDO	Who's there?
FRANCISCO	Nay, answer me. Stand and unfold yourself.
BARNARDO	Long live the King!
FRANCISCO	Barnardo?
BARNARDO	He.

5

FRANCISCO	You come most carefully upon your hour.
BARNARDO	'Tis now struck twelve, get thee to bed Francisco.
FRANCISCO	For this relief much thanks, 'tis bitter cold,
	And I am sick at heart.
BARNARDO	Have you had quiet guard?
FRANCISCO	Not a mouse stirring. 10
BARNARDO	Well, good night.
	If you do meet Horatio and Marcellus,
	The rivals of my watch, bid them make haste.

Enter HORATIO *and* MARCELLUS

FRANCISCO	I think I hear them. Stand ho, who is there?
HORATIO	Friends to this ground.
MARCELLUS	And liegemen to the Dane. 15
FRANCISCO	Give you good night.
MARCELLUS	O, farewell honest soldier.
	Who hath relieved you?
FRANCISCO	Barnardo has my place.
	Give you good night. [*Exit*

Horatio has been asked to join the watch because, having
been told that Barnardo and Marcellus have seen a ghost, he
insists it is their imagination. They tell him they have seen it
for two nights. As they start to give him the details, the
Ghost appears. It looks like the dead king. They ask Horatio
to speak to it.

19 **A piece of him**: either he does not feel that all his body is
   there, because he is numb with cold, or he is joking that
   because it is dark and misty the others can see him only
   fitfully, as he can see them. In Shakespeare's day, plays were
   performed in daylight, so the language and the acting had to
   indicate the time of day and the weather in the scene being
   played.
21 **thing**: creature
23 **fantasy**: imagination
24 **will not...seen of us**: (Horatio) cannot persuade himself to
   believe in this terrible sight we have now seen twice
25 **dreaded**: terrible
26 **entreated him along**: asked him to come with us
27 **watch...night**: keep watch throughout the night
29 **approve our eyes**: confirm what we have seen
31 **assail your ears**: tell you. The words '*assail*' (attack) and
   '*fortified*' (defended) suggest that Horatio is strongly resisting
   their story.
36 **pole**: the pole star. The star to the west of this has been held
   to be the bright star Capella.
37 **t'illume**: to light up
39 **The bell then beating one**: as the clock was striking one
40 **break thee off**: stop speaking
41 **same figure like**: same form as
42 **scholar**: Horatio has been a student and so would not only
   be quick-witted and clever enough to talk to the Ghost, but if
   it seemed to be evil, he might know the religious form of
   words in Latin to exorcize it

MARCELLUS	Holla, Barnardo!
BARNARDO	Say,

What, is Horatio there?

HORATIO	A piece of him.
BARNARDO	Welcome Horatio, welcome good Marcellus. 20
HORATIO	What, has this thing appeared again tonight?
BARNARDO	I have seen nothing.
MARCELLUS	Horatio says 'tis but our fantasy,
	And will not let belief take hold of him
	Touching this dreaded sight twice seen of us. 25
	Therefore I have entreated him along,
	With us to watch the minutes of this night,
	That if again this apparition come,
	He may approve our eyes and speak to it.
HORATIO	Tush, tush, 'twill not appear.
BARNARDO	Sit down awhile, 30

And let us once again assail your ears,
That are so fortified against our story,
What we have two nights seen.

HORATIO	Well, sit we down,

And let us hear Barnardo speak of this.

BARNARDO	Last night of all, 35

When yond same star that's westward from the
    pole
Had made his course t'illume that part of
    heaven
Where now it burns, Marcellus and myself,
The bell then beating one –

Enter GHOST

MARCELLUS	Peace, break thee off. Look where it comes
	again! 40
BARNARDO	In the same figure like the King that's dead.
MARCELLUS	Thou art a scholar, speak to it Horatio.

Horatio speaks to the Ghost, but it turns away and goes
without a word. Horatio is shaken by what he has seen. He
agrees the apparition is the image of the dead king and
suggests that he is warning them of some calamity to come.

43 **'a**: he. The word is scarcely pronounced. The apparition is
usually referred to as 'it'.
44 **harrows me**: distresses me
45 **It would be spoke to**: it wants me to speak to it
46 **What art thou that usurp'st**: what are you, you who are
trespassing on
47 **Together with**: also assuming, taking on
48 **the majesty of buried Denmark**: the late King of Denmark
49 **sometimes**: in former times, previously
50 **stalks away**: walks haughtily away
51 **I charge thee**: I order you
57 **Without...eyes**: without the knowledge that my eyes saw this
and are my guarantee for what happened
61 **Norway**: King of Norway
combated: fought
62 **parle**: talk, conversation, or more specifically 'a meeting to
discuss terms under a truce'
63 **He smote...on the ice**: the reading of this line has been
much discussed. The question is whether to accept (a) the Q1
and Q2 version '*sleaded pollax*' or (b) the F version '*sledded
Pollax*' (see Introduction page xv for an explanation of these
terms). In (a) the weapon 'poleaxe' seems to be meant, with
which King Hamlet struck the ice; (b) suggests that he fought
with the Poles (Polacks) who had come in sledges.
65 **jump**: precisely
66 **martial stalk**: a slow and stately walk, like a soldier
67 **In what...opinion**: in detail I do not know what to think,
but as far as my general opinion goes
69 **bodes...to our state**: threatens our state with some disastrous
outbreak
70 **Good now sit down**: do please sit down now

> • *What early indications do we gain of Horatio's
> character and the role he will play?*

BARNARDO	Looks 'a not like the King? Mark it Horatio.
HORATIO	Most like. It harrows me with fear and wonder.
BARNARDO	It would be spoke to.
MARCELLUS	Question it Horatio. 45
HORATIO	What are thou that usurp'st this time of night,
	Together with that fair and warlike form
	In which the majesty of buried Denmark
	Did sometimes march? By heaven I charge thee
	speak.
MARCELLUS	It is offended.
BARNARDO	See it stalks away. 50
HORATIO	Stay, speak, speak, I charge thee speak.
	[*Exit* GHOST
MARCELLUS	'Tis gone and will not answer.
BARNARDO	How now Horatio, you tremble and look pale.
	Is not this something more than fantasy?
	What think you on 't? 55
HORATIO	Before my God I might not this believe,
	Without the sensible and true avouch
	Of mine own eyes.
MARCELLUS	Is it not like the King?
HORATIO	As thou art to thyself.
	Such was the very armour he had on 60
	When he the ambitious Norway combated;
	So frowned he once, when in an angry parle
	He smote the sledded Polacks on the ice.
	'Tis strange.
MARCELLUS	Thus twice before, and jump at this dead hour, 65
	With martial stalk hath he gone by our watch.
HORATIO	In what particular thought to work I know not,
	But in the gross and scope of my opinion,
	This bodes some strange eruption to our state.
MARCELLUS	Good now sit down, and tell me he that knows, 70

Marcellus asks about the state of alert. Horatio tells of a
challenge to battle between the King of Norway and of
Denmark, with land as the prize. King Hamlet won, killing
Fortinbras. Now his son wants to reclaim the land, fairly
won.

71 Why...land: why the subjects of this nation have the burden
of this present strict and careful watch imposed upon them
73 daily cast...war: brass cannons are being produced every
day and arms deals are made abroad
75 impress of shipwrights: conscription of shipbuilders
whose sore task...the week: whose heavy work goes on day
and night, seven days a week
77 toward: (stress on first syllable) about to happen
78 Doth...the day: the work goes on at night as well
80 whisper: rumour
81 even but now: just a few moments ago
82 by Fortinbras...the combat: challenged by Fortinbras –
who was led on by a most ambitious pride – to do battle
83 Thereto pricked on: incited to it
85 For...him: this was the western world's opinion of him
86 sealed compact: formal agreement
87 ratified: confirmed
heraldry: a code of chivalrous behaviour between monarchs
89 stood seized of: possessed
90 moiety competent: similar amount
91 gaged: pledged
had: would have
93 cov'nant...designed: contract and understanding of these
terms
96 unimproved mettle: undisciplined spirit
97 skirts: border territories
98 Sharked up: hastily assembled a random crowd (as a shark
might gobble up a shoal of fish) of lawless men, committed
to action. The soldiers will only get their keep, so 'stomach'
puns on 'food' and 'stomach' for the fight.

> • *The Fortinbras story begins – a framework device*
> *completed in the final scene of the play. Note where he*
> *reappears.*

Why this same strict and most observant watch
So nightly toils the subject of the land,
And why such daily cast of brazen cannon,
And foreign mart for implements of war,
Why such impress of shipwrights, whose sore
    task   75
Does not divide the Sunday from the week,
What might be toward that this sweaty haste
Doth make the night joint-labourer with the day,
Who is't that can inform me?

HORATIO   That can I.
At least the whisper goes so; our last King,   80
Whose image even but now appeared to us,
Was as you know by Fortinbras of Norway,
Thereto pricked on by a most emulate pride,
Dared to the combat; in which our valiant
    Hamlet –
For so this side of our known world esteemed
    him –   85
Did slay this Fortinbras, who by a sealed compact,
Well ratified by law and heraldry,
Did forfeit, with his life, all those his lands
Which he stood seized of to the conqueror.
Against the which a moiety competent   90
Was gaged by our King, which had returned
To the inheritance of Fortinbras,
Had he been vanquisher; as by the same
    cov'nant
And carriage of the article designed,
His fell to Hamlet. Now sir, young Fortinbras, 95
Of unimproved mettle hot and full,
Hath in the skirts of Norway here and there
Sharked up a list of lawless resolutes
For food and diet to some enterprise
That hath a stomach in't; which is no other,   100
As it doth well appear unto our state,
But to recover of us, by strong hand

Horatio considers that the possibility of invasion by young Fortinbras may be the reason for putting the state on a warlike footing. Barnardo agrees. Horatio goes on to explain that there were natural warnings of disaster in Rome before Julius Caesar was murdered. As Horatio finishes, the ghost appears again, and Horatio tries to find out why it has appeared.

103 terms compulsatory: compelling means
106 head: origin, cause
107 post-haste and rummage: hasty preparation and commotion
109 Well may it sort: that may well be the reason
portentous: ominous, warning of some calamity
112 mote: speck of dust
113 palmy: triumphant
115 tenantless: empty
116 gibber: jabber, babble
117–118 some words appear to have been left out here. The sense should either continue the idea of line 116 or introduce that of line 117.
117 stars...fire: comets
118 Disasters: an unfavourable aspect of a star or planet. Sunspots may be meant here.
the moist star...empire stands: the moon which influences the tides. Neptune is the god of the sea.
121 And even the like...countrymen: just such warnings of terrible happenings have been given to our people in this country
121 precurse: heralding
122 harbingers: forerunners, messengers
123 omen coming on: the approaching disaster
125 climatures: regions
127 cross it: cross its path
133 If thou art privy to: if you have some secret knowledge of
134 happily: possibly

And terms compulsatory, those foresaid lands
So by his father lost; and this I take it
Is the main motive of our preparations,   105
The source of this our watch, and the chief head
Of this post-haste and rummage in the land.

BARNARDO   I think it be no other but e'en so.
Well may it sort that this portentous figure
Comes armed through our watch so like the
        King   110
That was and is the question of these wars.

HORATIO   A mote it is to trouble the mind's eye.
In the most high and palmy state of Rome,
A little ere the mightiest Julius fell,
The graves stood tenantless, and the sheeted
        dead   115
Did squeak and gibber in the Roman streets;
As stars with trains of fire and dews of blood,
Disasters in the sun; and the moist star,
Upon whose influence Neptune's empire stands,
Was sick almost to doomsday with eclipse.   120
And even the like precurse of feared events,
As harbingers preceding still the fates,
And prologue to the omen coming on,
Have heaven and earth together demonstrated
Unto our climatures and countrymen.   125

Enter GHOST

But soft, behold, lo where it comes again.
I'll cross it, though it blast me. Stay illusion,
If thou hast any sound or use of voice,
                              [*It spreads its arms*
Speak to me.
If there be any good thing to be done   130
That may to thee do ease and grace to me,
Speak to me.
If thou art privy to thy country's fate
Which happily foreknowing may avoid,

As Horatio puts his third point to the Ghost, the cock
crows. They move to prevent the Ghost leaving, but at the
sound, and just as it appeared about to speak, the Ghost goes
away. Horatio explains that at cockcrow spirits have to
return to their place. Marcellus explains that some people
believe that towards Christmas the cock crows all day and
people are safe from spirits.

136 **uphoarded**: hoarded up, saved up
137 **Extorted**: taken by force, or some other unfair means
140 **partisan**: a long-handled spear with short, sharp blades
    projecting from the end of it
143 **being so majestical**: since it seems so like a king
145 **it is...invulnerable**: like empty air it cannot be hit or injured
    by us
148 **started**: took fright
149 **fearful**: terrible
150 **trumpet**: (here) trumpeter, announcing the arrival of an
    important person
152 **the god of day**: Phoebus Apollo
    at his warning...confine: there was a belief that at
    cockcrow all ghosts and spirits had to return to their place,
    on pain of punishment
154 **extravagant...hies to his confine**: the spirit, straying
    beyond its limits, returns to its own territory; The word
    'confine' also carries the play on words of 'imprisoned'.
156 **probation**: proof
158 **'gainst**: (against) just before
162 **no planets strike**: no evil influence of planets has power to
    harm
163 **takes**: strikes (with misfortune or disease)
164 **So hallowed and so gracious**: so blessed

O speak.   135
Or if thou hast uphoarded in thy life
Extorted treasure in the womb of earth,
For which they say you spirits oft walk in
    death,

                      [*The cock crows*

Speak of it; stay and speak. Stop it Marcellus.

MARCELLUS Shall I strike at it with my partisan?   140

HORATIO Do, if it will not stand.

BARNARDO   'Tis here.

HORATIO   'Tis here.

MARCELLUS 'Tis gone.   [*Exit* GHOST
We do it wrong, being so majestical,
To offer it the show of violence;
For it is as the air invulnerable,   145
And our vain blows malicious mockery.

BARNARDO It was about to speak when the cock crew.

HORATIO And then it started like a guilty thing
Upon a fearful summons. I have heard
The cock, that is the trumpet to the morn,   150
Doth with his lofty and shrill-sounding throat
Awake the god of day, and at his warning,
Whether in sea or fire, in earth or air,
The extravagant and erring spirit hies
To his confine; and of the truth herein   155
This present object made probation.

MARCELLUS It faded on the crowing of the cock.
Some say that ever 'gainst that season comes
Wherein our Saviour's birth is celebrated,
The bird of dawning singeth all night long,   160
And then they say no spirit dare stir abroad;
The nights are wholesome, then no planets strike,
No fairy takes, nor witch hath power to charm,
So hallowed and so gracious is that time.

HORATIO So have I heard and do in part believe it.   165

Dawn is breaking. Hamlet's friends will tell him what they
have seen. They are sure the Ghost will speak to him.

166 **russet**: the name given to a coarse woollen homespun cloth,
worn by country people. The colour was reddish-brown
(today's meaning) grey or neutral. (Compare modern
French 'roux, rousse' which, among other uses, describes
auburn hair.)
169 **impart**: tell
173 **As needful...fitting our duty?**: it is appropriate because we
love him as a friend and owe him duty as crown prince

Claudius is holding court beside his queen, Hamlet's
mother. He comments on the mixture of joy and grief that
has accompanied the funeral and his marriage.

Flourish: Fanfare of trumpets
2 **green**: fresh
it us befitted: it was right for us
4 **To be...woe**: the whole country is united in one sorrowing
expression
5 **discretion**: rational judgement
6 **wisest sorrow...ourselves**: our sorrow is tempered with
wisdom and we have also thought of ourselves
8 **sometime**: former
9 **imperial jointress**: a jointress held property in common with
her husband and had a right to it after his death. Gertrude's
status as Queen has not changed.
11 **With...eye**: one eye shining with happiness, the other with
tears
12 **mirth...marriage**: merriness at the funeral and mournfulness
in marriage
13 **dole**: misery, grief
14 **barred**: refused to consider
15 **Your better wisdoms**: your best counsels

> • *How would you describe the language of Claudius's*
> *first speech? What are the political and personal aims*
> *here?*

But look the morn in russet mantle clad
Walks o'er the dew of yon high eastward hill.
Break we our watch up, and by my advice
Let us impart what we have seen tonight
Unto young Hamlet; for upon my life,   170
This spirit dumb to us will speak to him.
Do you consent we shall acquaint him with it,
As needful in our loves, fitting our duty?

MARCELLUS   Let's do't I pray, and I this morning know
Where we shall find him most convenient.   175

[Exeunt

Scene 2

Flourish. Enter CLAUDIUS *King of Denmark,*
GERTRUDE *the* QUEEN, COUNCILLORS, POLONIUS
and his son LAERTES, VALTEMAND, CORNELIUS,
HAMLET, *and others*

KING   Though yet of Hamlet our dear brother's death
The memory be green, and that it us befitted
To bear our hearts in grief, and our whole
     kingdom
To be contracted in one brow of woe,
Yet so far hath discretion fought with nature,   5
That we with wisest sorrow think on him,
Together with remembrance of ourselves.
Therefore our sometime sister, now our Queen,
Th' imperial jointress to this warlike state,
Have we as 'twere with a defeated joy,   10
With an auspicious and a dropping eye,
With mirth in funeral and with dirge in marriage,
In equal scale weighing delight and dole,
Taken to wife; nor have we herein barred
Your better wisdoms, which have freely gone   15
With this affair along – for all, our thanks.

Claudius is sending two ambassadors to the present King of Norway, the aged and bedridden uncle of young Fortinbras, asking him to put a stop to his nephew's warlike activities. His reasoning is that the King may not know what is going on, and that it is his subjects who are being formed into an army. Claudius turns to Laertes, son of Polonius, who has a request.

17 **that you know**: what you already know

18 **weak supposal**: poor opinion

20 **disjoint and out of frame**: disrupted and disordered

21 **Colleagued...advantage**: his ally only this impression that he can make gains

23 **Importing**: concerning

24 **bonds of law**: legal agreements

29 **impotent**: powerless

31 **gait**: progress

in that...full proportions: pointing out that the raising of troops, enlisting of men, in quantities necessary for this enterprise

33 **his subject**: his subjects

36 **Giving to you...allow**: the ambassadors are not empowered to negotiate with the King of Norway. The spelling of '*delated*' is an alternative one for 'dilated' – 'fully detailed'.

43 **suit**: request

44 **You cannot...voice**: any reasonable request will be granted by the Danish king

47 **native**: (here) closely allied

48 **instrumental**: of service

> • *What place do Laertes and his father seem to hold in the estimation of Claudius?*

Now follows that you know, young Fortinbras,
Holding a weak supposal of our worth,
Or thinking by our late dear brother's death
Our state to be disjoint and out of frame,   20
Colleagued with this dream of his advantage,
He hath not failed to pester us with message
Importing the surrender of those lands
Lost by his father, with all bonds of law,
To our most valiant brother. So much for him. 25
Now for ourself, and for this time of meeting,
Thus much the business is: we have here writ
To Norway, uncle of young Fortinbras,
Who, impotent and bed-rid, scarcely hears
Of this his nephew's purpose, to suppress   30
His further gait herein, in that the levies,
The lists, and full proportions, are all made
Out of his subject; and we here dispatch
You good Cornelius, and you Valtemand,
For bearers of this greeting to old Norway;   35
Giving to you no further personal power
To business with the King, more than the scope
Of these delated articles allow.
Farewell, and let your haste commend your duty.

CORNELIUS ⎫
           ⎬ In that and all things will we show our duty.   40
VALTEMAND ⎭

KING   We doubt it nothing: heartily farewell.
                      [*Exeunt* VALTEMAND *and* CORNELIUS
And now Laertes what's the news with you?
You told us of some suit; what is't Laertes?
You cannot speak of reason to the Dane,
And lose your voice. What wouldst thou beg,
    Laertes,   45
That shall not be my offer, not thy asking?
The head is not more native to the heart,
The hand more instrumental to the mouth,
Than is the throne of Denmark to thy father.

Laertes asks permission to leave court and return to France. Polonius, though reluctant to see him go, has agreed. Claudius grants his request, and turns to Hamlet. Both Claudius and Hamlet's mother, Gertrude, gently reproach Hamlet for persisting in his grief, asking why, when death is a fate common to all, his father's death should seem unique.

50 dread: revered

58 slow leave: eventual permission

59 laboursome petition: repeated requests

60 Upon...hard consent: consenting to his desire, I gave my grudging agreement

62 Take thy fair hour: choose when you wish to go

63 thy best graces...at thy will: spend your time usefully

65 A little more...kind: Hamlet's first words are an *aside* (see GLOSSARY page 333). Though Claudius and Hamlet are relations – uncle and nephew – (which is more than the vague '*kin*') they are not men of the same kind, and, in a play on words, there is no affection between them.
kind: nature, quality inherited at birth

67 I am too much in the sun: he is too much the centre of attention, and too much 'the son' – which he must resent (see *Pun*, GLOSSARY page 335)

68 nighted colour: sombre clothes and sombre mood

70 vailed lids: lowered eyelids

75 particular with thee: unique to you

- *Are there any differences to be observed in the language used to, and by, Laertes and Hamlet?*
- *Hamlet has recently returned from university for the funeral of his father and his mother's wedding. There he has studied and discussed, words and wit will have been important – 'on the other hand this – on the other that, but then again...' His friends have been young, lively and clever. Start to look at what and who surrounded him at court, and draw your conclusions.*

What wouldst thou have, Laertes?

LAERTES   My dread lord,   50
Your leave and favour to return to France;
From whence though willingly I came to Denmark
To show my duty in your coronation,
Yet now I must confess, that duty done,
My thoughts and wishes bend again toward
        France,   55
And bow them to your gracious leave and
        pardon.

KING   Have you your father's leave? What says Polonius?

POLONIUS   He hath, my lord, wrung from me my slow leave
By laboursome petition, and at last
Upon his will I sealed my hard consent.   60
I do beseech you give him leave to go.

KING   Take thy fair hour Laertes, time be thine,
And thy best graces spend it at thy will.
But now my cousin Hamlet, and my son.

HAMLET   [*Aside*] A little more than kin, and less than kind.   65

KING   How is it that the clouds still hang on you?

HAMLET   Not so, my lord; I am too much in the sun.

QUEEN   Good Hamlet, cast thy nighted colour off,
And let thine eye look like a friend on Denmark.
Do not for ever with thy vailed lids   70
Seek for thy noble father in the dust.
Thou know'st 'tis common, all that lives must
        die,
Passing through nature to eternity.

HAMLET   Ay madam, it is common.

QUEEN   If it be,
Why seems it so particular with thee?   75

HAMLET   Seems madam? Nay it is; I know not 'seems'.
'Tis not alone my inky cloak, good mother,
Nor customary suits of solemn black,

Hamlet's grief is deep and real, not an act put on for show. Claudius briefly commends his mourning then attacks it as excessive. He urges Hamlet to regard him as a father and assures him he is next in line for the throne.

79 **windy...breath**: heavy sighs forced out
80 **fruitful river in the eye**: the eye teeming with tears
81 **the dejected...visage**: sad expression (on the face)
82 **shapes**: outward forms
84 **they are...might play**: these are all outward signs of grief which could be acted. It is worth noting Hamlet's deep interest in the craft of acting, here and elsewhere in the play.
85 **passes show**: is deeper than mere appearance
87 **commendable**: the stress falls on the first syllable
90 **That...lost his**: that dead father's own father had died
91 **filial obligation**: the duty of sons and daughters to parents
92 **obsequious sorrow**: the sorrow proper at a funeral
but to persever...condolement: to insist obstinately on going on grieving ('persever' stress on second syllable)
94 **impious**: lacking in reverence
95 **incorrect**: uncorrected, not submissive
96 **unfortified**: without inner strength
98 **For...heart?**: Why do we take something so to heart which we know has to happen? Why should we obstinately oppose and reject something which is as usual as any of the things commonly observed by our senses?
101 **a fault**: an offence
103 **whose common...fathers**: fathers are dying all the time
105 **the first corse**: an unintentional *irony* (see GLOSSARY page 334) on Claudius's part since the reference is to Abel, killed by his brother Cain
106 **throw to earth**: throw away (in his father's grave)
107 **unprevailing**: pointless
112 **impart toward**: offer this to you

> • *Examine the subject matter of Claudius's reply to Hamlet. Compare the style of Claudius's speech which opens the scene, and this one. What effect do the lists have in this second speech? (lines 87–106).*

Nor windy suspiration of forced breath,
No, nor the fruitful river in the eye,   80
Nor the dejected haviour of the visage,
Together with all forms, moods, shapes of grief,
That can denote me truly. These indeed seem,
For they are actions that a man might play;
But I have that within which passes show –   85
These but the trappings and the suits of woe.

KING   'Tis sweet and commendable in your nature,
            Hamlet,
To give these mourning duties to your father.
But you must know, your father lost a father;
That father lost, lost his; and the survivor
            bound   90
In filial obligation for some term
To do obsequious sorrow; but to persever
In obstinate condolement is a course
Of impious stubbornness, 'tis unmanly grief;
It shows a will most incorrect to heaven,   95
A heart unfortified, a mind impatient,
An understanding simple and unschooled.
For what we know must be, and is as common
As any the most vulgar thing to sense,
Why should we in our peevish opposition   100
Take it to heart? Fie, 'tis a fault to heaven,
A fault against the dead, a fault to nature,
To reason most absurd, whose common theme
Is death of fathers, and who still hath cried,
From the first corse till he that died today,   105
'This must be so'. We pray you throw to earth
This unprevailing woe, and think of us
As of a father, for let the world take note
You are the most immediate to our throne;
And with no less nobility of love   110
Than that which dearest father bears his son,
Do I impart toward you. For your intent
In going back to school in Wittenberg,

Gertrude joins Claudius in asking Hamlet to stay at court and he agrees. Claudius welcomes this decision and expresses his pleasure. He will celebrate by marking each round of drinking with gunfire. Hamlet, left alone, shows that his private mood is very low indeed and talks of suicide. He contrasts his father and Claudius, much to the latter's disfavour, and strongly disapproves of the speedy marriage.

114 **most retrograde...desire**: very much against our wishes
115 **bend you**: submit yourself, consent (to remain)
122 **Be as ourself**: enjoy the same standing as myself
125 **No jocund health...clouds shall tell**: every happy toast drunk today by the King of Denmark shall be announced to the skies by the great cannon
127 **rouse...again**: (cf carouse) round of drinking shall echo from heaven again
129 **solid**: '*sallied*' is the Q2 reading, taken to mean 'sullied' or 'unclean'. The church had long maintained that the body was unclean. '*Solid*' suggests a body that is too stubbornly alive to be disposed of easily.
132 **Or that...self-slaughter**: the sixth commandment 'Thou shalt do no murder' is taken to refer to self-murder also
    canon: set of rules, commandments
133 **How...world**: Hamlet is still grieving, but these are also like the sentiments of someone in a state of depression
136 **rank and gross**: luxuriant and thick
137 **merely**: completely
140 **Hyperion to a satyr**: Hyperion is identified by Shakespeare with the sun god, Apollo, the personification of divine beauty. Satyrs were woodland gods, half man half goat in form, attending on Bacchus. They had a reputation for lechery.
141 **beteem**: allow

> • *What do we learn about Hamlet's mood in this first soliloquy? How far is it possible to say what exactly has caused it?*

It is most retrograde to our desire;
And we beseech you, bend you to remain   115
Here in the cheer and comfort of our eye,
Our chiefest courtier, cousin, and our son.

QUEEN   Let not thy mother lose her prayers Hamlet.
I pray thee stay with us; go not to Wittenberg.

HAMLET   I shall in all my best obey you madam.   120

KING   Why 'tis a loving and a fair reply.
Be as ourself in Denmark. Madam come.
This gentle and unforced accord of Hamlet
Sits smiling to my heart; in grace whereof,
No jocund health that Denmark drinks today,   125
But the great cannon to the clouds shall tell,
And the King's rouse the heavens shall bruit
        again,
Re-speaking earthly thunder. Come away.
                    [*Flourish. Exeunt all but* HAMLET

HAMLET   O that this too too solid flesh would melt,
Thaw and resolve itself into a dew,   130
Or that the Everlasting had not fixed
His canon 'gainst self-slaughter. O God, God,
How weary, stale, flat and unprofitable
Seem to me all the uses of this world!
Fie on 't, ah fie, 'tis an unweeded garden   135
That grows to seed, things rank and gross in
        nature
Possess it merely. That it should come to this –
But two months dead, nay not so much,
        not two –
So excellent a king, that was to this
Hyperion to a satyr, so loving to my mother   140
That he might not beteem the winds of heaven
Visit her face too roughly. Heaven and earth,
Must I remember? Why she would hang on him
As if increase of appetite had grown
By what it fed on, and yet within a month –   145

The suddenness with which his mother's wedding followed the funeral of his father, whom he had plainly both loved and admired, distresses Hamlet. He cannot understand the lack of taste she displayed in choosing Claudius, who, he feels, cannot compare with his father. He is hurt and miserable, and has to keep silent. He greets Horatio and Marcellus.

146 frailty...woman: *personification* of an abstract noun, so that 'frailty' is held to equal 'woman' (see GLOSSARY page 335)

147 or e'er those shoes were old: she had new shoes for the funeral and they were still quite new at the time of her wedding

149 Niobe: according to Greek fable Niobe boasted of her twelve children to the mother of Apollo and Diana. They avenged the insult by killing them all. Niobe wept herself to death and was changed into a stone from which water flowed.

150 wants discourse of reason: lacks the ability to reason

153 I to Hercules: Hercules was the strong and ingenious man of Greek myth, succeeding in accomplishing twelve apparently impossible labours. Hamlet is putting himself at the other end of this scale. By using these classical references Hamlet is pointing to extremes which Shakespeare's audience will readily understand and at the same time ensuring we feel the universal nature of Hamlet's present experience.

154 unrighteous: hypocritical

155 flushing in her galled eyes: redness in her sore eyes

156 post With such dexterity: hurry so smartly

157 incestuous: marriage to one's husband's brother is one of many liaisons expressly forbidden in the *Book of Common Prayer's* 'A Table of Kindred and Affinity'

163 I'll change that name with you: I'll exchange that name – 'good friend' – with you

168 what...Wittenberg?: what does bring you from Wittenberg?

169 a truant disposition: a desire in my nature to play truant, a tendency to laziness

171 Nor...yourself: nor will I allow you to offend my ears by trying to make me believe what you are accusing yourself of

Let me not think on 't – frailty, thy name is
   woman.
A little month or e'er those shoes were old
With which she followed my poor father's body,
Like Niobe all tears, why she, even she –
O God, a beast that wants discourse of reason 150
Would have mourned longer – married with my
   uncle,
My father's brother, but no more like my father
Than I to Hercules; within a month –
Ere yet the salt of most unrighteous tears
Had left the flushing in her galled eyes,   155
She married. O most wicked speed, to post
With such dexterity to incestuous sheets.
It is not, nor it cannot come to good:
But break, my heart, for I must hold my tongue.

Enter HORATIO, MARCELLUS, *and* BARNARDO

HORATIO	Hail to your lordship.
HAMLET	I am glad to see you well 160 Horatio – or I do forget myself.
HORATIO	The same my lord, and your poor servant ever.
HAMLET	Sir, my good friend, I'll change that name with you. And what make you from Wittenberg Horatio? Marcellus. 165
MARCELLUS	My good lord.
HAMLET	I am very glad to see you. Good even sir. But what in faith make you from Wittenberg?
HORATIO	A truant disposition good my lord.
HAMLET	I would not hear your enemy say so, 170 Nor shall you do mine ear that violence To make it truster of your own report Against yourself. I know you are no truant. But what is your affair in Elsinore?

In talking to his friends Hamlet makes plain his attitude to his father's death and his mother's hasty marriage. Hamlet's references to his father lead Horatio into his subject – the visitation by his father's ghost. He goes on to describe what the three of them have seen.

177 I prithee: please, I beg you
179 hard: closely
180 Thrift: economy
   The funeral...tables: the meat pies left over from the funeral feasting were served cold at the marriage feast
182 dearest foe: worst enemy – in the sense of 'the man I most love to hate'. Hamlet would expect this man to be in hell. Compare later (Act 3 scene 3) his reason for not killing Claudius at prayer.
183 Or ever: before
192 Season your admiration: keep your amazement in check
193 With an attent ear: and listen well
198 waste: desolate period. Some suggest a pun heard in waste/waist/middle for the dead period in the middle of the night.
200 at point, exactly, cap-a-pie: correctly in every detail, from head to foot
203 fear-surprised: overcome by fear
204 Within his truncheon's length: as close to them as the length of his baton (indicating his military rank)
   distilled: dissolved

	We'll teach you to drink deep ere you depart. 175
HORATIO	My lord, I came to see your father's funeral.
HAMLET	I prithee do not mock me, fellow-student,
	I think it was to see my mother's wedding.
HORATIO	Indeed my lord it followed hard upon.
HAMLET	Thrift, thrift, Horatio. The funeral baked meats 180
	Did coldly furnish forth the marriage tables.
	Would I had met my dearest foe in heaven
	Or ever I had seen that day Horatio.
	My father – methinks I see my father.
HORATIO	Where my lord?
HAMLET	In my mind's eye Horatio. 185
HORATIO	I saw him once, 'a was a goodly king.
HAMLET	'A was a man, take him for all in all,
	I shall not look upon his like again.
HORATIO	My lord, I think I saw him yesternight.
HAMLET	Saw? Who?
HORATIO	My lord, the King your father. 190
HAMLET	The King my father?
HORATIO	Season your admiration for a while
	With an attent ear, till I may deliver
	Upon the witness of these gentlemen
	This marvel to you.
HAMLET	For God's love let me hear. 195
HORATIO	Two nights together had these gentlemen,
	Marcellus and Barnardo, on their watch,
	In the dead waste and middle of the night,
	Been thus encountered – a figure like your father,
	Armed at point, exactly, cap-a-pie, 200
	Appears before them, and with solemn march
	Goes slow and stately by them; thrice he walked
	By their oppressed and fear-surprised eyes,
	Within his truncheon's length, whilst they
	distilled

Horatio speaks of the fear felt by the men who first saw the
Ghost, and confirms that it is the image of Hamlet's father.
Horatio explains, in answer to Hamlet's question, why he
thinks it did not speak. Hamlet admits he is troubled, learns
that they will keep watch that night and that the Ghost was
in full armour.

205 act: action, effect
207 dreadful: full of dread, awe-struck
209 delivered: reported
216 it: a form of the possessive before 'its'
   address Itself to motion: was about to make a movement
222 writ...duty: part of the duty we owe you – just as if it had
   been some written condition of their service

Almost to jelly with the act of fear,   205
Stand dumb, and speak not to him. This to me
In dreadful secrecy impart they did,
And I with them the third night kept the watch,
Where, as they had delivered, both in time,
Form of the thing, each word made true and
    good,   210
The apparition comes. I knew your father;
These hands are not more like.

HAMLET   But where was this?

MARCELLUS My lord, upon the platform where we watch.

HAMLET   Did you not speak to it?

HORATIO   My lord, I did,
But answer made it none: yet once
    methought   215
It lifted up it head, and did address
Itself to motion like as it would speak;
But even then the morning cock crew loud,
And at the sound it shrunk in haste away,
And vanished from our sight.

HAMLET   'Tis very strange. 220

HORATIO   As I do live, my honoured lord, 'tis true;
And we did think it writ down in our duty
To let you know of it.

HAMLET   Indeed, indeed sirs, but this troubles me.
Hold you the watch tonight?

MARCELLUS ⎫
                                         We do my lord.   225
BARNARDO ⎭

HAMLET   Armed say you?

MARCELLUS ⎫
                                  Armed my lord.
BARNARDO ⎭

HAMLET   From top to toe?

MARCELLUS ⎫
                                  My lord, from head to foot.
BARNARDO ⎭

Hamlet questions the three men closely about the appearance of his father as ghost. He includes what looks like a trick question about the colour of his beard. Hamlet then decides to be present that night with the aim of speaking to the apparition. He asks for their continued silence and arranges the rendezvous.

229 beaver: visor, face-piece of helmet which was hinged and could be raised

235 amazed: bewildered

240 grizzled: grey

242 sable silvered: black flecked with white. The word '*sable*' is still the word for black in heraldry.

243 Perchance: perhaps

I warr'nt: I'm sure, I guarantee

244 assume: take on

245 hell itself should gape: the mouth of hell should open wide

246 bid...peace: these remarks made by Hamlet point up the doubt that always exists when ghosts appear – do they come to bring evil, and possible death and damnation, or are they good spirits? Hamlet is not sure whether (line 244) a spirit has 'taken on' his father's appearance or whether (line 255) it truly is '*My father's spirit*'.

247 If...silence still: if you haven't yet mentioned what you have seen, please continue to keep quiet about it

249 hap: happen

251 requite your loves: repay your affection

HAMLET	Then saw you not his face.	
HORATIO	O yes my lord, he wore his beaver up.	
HAMLET	What, looked he frowningly?	230
HORATIO	A countenance more in sorrow than in anger.	
HAMLET	Pale, or red?	
HORATIO	Nay very pale.	
HAMLET	And fixed his eyes upon you?	
HORATIO	Most constantly.	
HAMLET	I would I had been there.	
HORATIO	It would have much amazed you.	235
HAMLET	Very like, very like – stayed it long?	
HORATIO	While one with moderate haste might tell a hundred.	
MARCELLUS BARNARDO	} Longer, longer.	
HORATIO	Not when I saw't.	
HAMLET	His beard was grizzled – no?	240
HORATIO	It was as I have seen it in his life, A sable silvered.	
HAMLET	I will watch tonight, Perchance 'twill walk again.	
HORATIO	I warr'nt it will.	
HAMLET	If it assume my noble father's person, I'll speak to it though hell itself should gape And bid me hold my peace. I pray you all, If you have hitherto concealed this sight, Let it be tenable in your silence still; And whatsoever else shall hap tonight, Give it an understanding but no tongue. I will requite your loves. So fare you well. Upon the platform 'twixt eleven and twelve I'll visit you.	245

250 |

Having said goodbye to his friends, Hamlet again expresses his unease, and his impatience for the night to come. He anticipates that some crime will be disclosed.

256 doubt: suspect
258 Though...o'erwhelm them: however deeply buried they may be

Laertes, about to leave for France, says goodbye to his sister, Ophelia, and hopes she will write to him. The question of Hamlet's affection for her is raised. Laertes warns it may be short-lived and being a prince he may not be free to marry where he chooses.

 1 **My necessaries are embarked**: my belongings are on the ship
 2 **give benefit...assistant**: are favourable and ships are available
 5 **trifling of his favour**: his pretended affection
 6 **Hold it...primy nature**: think of it as a whim, a bit of nonsense as short-lived as a violet in the springtime of life
 8 **Forward**: precocious, before its proper time
 9 **The perfume...of a minute**: a sweet scent, filling just one moment
10 **No more but so?**: no more than that?
11 **For nature...withal**: growing up is not merely a question of physical size and strength, but as the body grows, so do the mental and spiritual sides, inwardly, at the same time
12 **thews**: muscles
    temple: body
15 **no soil...of his will**: no stain or deceit spoils his honest intentions
17 **His greatness weighed**: when you consider his position

- *What do these exchanges tell us about the relationship between Laertes and Ophelia?*
- *What seems to be Laertes's opinion of Hamlet at this stage?*

ALL	Our duty to your honour.
HAMLET	Your loves, as mine to you. Farewell.

[*Exeunt*

My father's spirit – in arms – all is not well.   255
I doubt some foul play. Would the night
    were come.
Till then sit still my soul. Foul deeds will rise,
Though all the earth o'erwhelm them, to
    men's eyes.   [*Exit*

Scene 3

Enter LAERTES *and* OPHELIA *his sister*

LAERTES   My necessaries are embarked. Farewell.
And sister, as the winds give benefit,
And convoy is assistant, do not sleep,
But let me hear from you.

OPHELIA   Do you doubt that?

LAERTES   For Hamlet, and the trifling of his favour,   5
Hold it a fashion, and a toy in blood;
A violet in the youth of primy nature,
Forward, not permanent, sweet, not lasting,
The perfume and suppliance of a minute,
No more.

OPHELIA   No more but so?

LAERTES   Think it no more.   10
For nature crescent, does not grow alone
In thews and bulk, but as this temple waxes,
The inward service of the mind and soul
Grows wide withal. Perhaps he loves you now,
And now no soil nor cautel doth besmirch   15
The virtue of his will; but you must fear,
His greatness weighed, his will is not his own,
For he himself is subject to his birth.

Laertes says Hamlet may be speaking the truth when he declares his love, but since he might become King his wife will have to be officially approved. Ophelia should not risk her reputation by encouraging him. She agrees to follow his advice if he will live by it too.

20 Carve for himself: serve his own wishes

21 safety: some peope prefer the reading '*sanity*', others '*sanctity*' which adds a spiritual dimension to the concept of the state

22 circumscribed: limited

23 voice...that body: vote and consent of that state

26 in his particular act and place: with his sphere of activities and in his position. F's alternative reading '*his peculiar sect and force*' is glossed as 'the special circumstances of his class and power'.

27 May give his saying deed: may act on what he has been saying

28 main: general

30 credent: trustful

31 or your chaste...importunity: or give in to his demands, which are difficult to resist, and let him sleep with you

34 And keep...desire: a military metaphor. Ophelia's affections are the front-line troops; she should stay safely out of the battle.

36 The chariest maid...enough: the most careful girl is generous enough if she does no more than reveal her beauty to the moon

38 'scapes not...strokes: cannot escape being attacked by slander

39 canker: disease of roses or a pest, the canker-worm. Shakespeare often uses *metaphor* and *simile* (see GLOSSARY pages 335–336) from his knowledge of gardening and the countryside.
the infants of the spring: tender young shoots appearing early in the year

40 buttons be disclosed: buds open

42 Contagious blastments: attacks of blight which spread

44 Youth...near: youth would rebel, even if there were no one around to watch

49 puffed...libertine: boastful and reckless seducer

50 primrose path of dalliance: easy route to flirtation (and worse!)

51 recks not...rede: does not pay attention to his own advice

• *It is easy to think of Ophelia mainly as a victim, but note the spirited reply she gives to her brother here.*

He may not, as unvalued persons do,
Carve for himself, for on his choice depends   20
The safety and health of this whole state,
And therefore must his choice be circumscribed
Unto the voice and yielding of that body
Whereof he is the head. Then if he says he
   loves you,
It fits your wisdom so far to believe it   25
As he in his particular act and place
May give his saying deed, which is no further
Than the main voice of Denmark goes withal.
Then weigh what loss your honour may
   sustain,
If with too credent ear you list his songs,   30
Or lose your heart, or your chaste treasure open
To his unmastered importunity.
Fear it Ophelia, fear it my dear sister,
And keep you in the rear of your affection,
Out of the shot and danger of desire.   35
The chariest maid is prodigal enough,
If she unmask her beauty to the moon;
Virtue itself 'scapes not calumnious strokes.
The canker galls the infants of the spring
Too oft before their buttons be disclosed,   40
And in the morn and liquid dew of youth
Contagious blastments are most imminent.
Be wary then, best safety lies in fear.
Youth to itself rebels, though none else near.

OPHELIA   I shall the effect of this good lesson keep   45
As watchman to my heart. But good my brother,
Do not as some ungracious pastors do,
Show me the steep and thorny way to heaven,
Whiles like a puffed and reckless libertine
Himself the primrose path of dalliance treads,   50
And recks not his own rede.

LAERTES   O fear me not.
I stay too long – but here my father comes.

Polonius comes upon his son and daughter and is surprised that Laertes has not yet left. However, he now takes the opportunity to deliver a lecture to Laertes, composed of wise sayings about friends, clothes, quarrelling, expressing opinions, buying clothes, borrowing or lending money and integrity. Laertes says goodbye to his father again.

54 Occasion smiles...leave: it is good fortune to have a second chance to say goodbye

56 The wind...for: the wind is filling your sails and the others are waiting for you

58 precepts: instructions

58 these few...character: (stress on second syllable) set down or memorize these few instructions

59 Give...act: do not express your thoughts and do not act on any unruly thought

61 Be thou...familiar: be friendly, but not with everyone

62 their adoption tried: when their friendship has been tried and tested

63 Grapple them: hold them

64 But do...courage: Polonius tells him not to be too eager to give his hand to any untried person he's only just met
courage: some people prefer the reading 'comrade'. The word '*courage*' meant both 'heart' and 'spirit', and 'person'.

67 Bear't that: manage things so that

69 censure: judgement

70 habit: clothing

72 For...chief in that: people are often judged by their dress and Frenchmen of rank and position or of superior degree or nobility are the most gifted at choosing the right clothes. (Laertes, of course, is returning to France.)

77 borrowing...husbandry: borrowing damages the whole business of managing your money

81 my blessing...thee: may my blessing make this advice bear fruit

83 The time invites you: it is time you were on your way

- *What does Polonius reveal about himself in this homily to his son, his first speech of any length in the play?*

Enter POLONIUS

> A double blessing is a double grace;
> Occasion smiles upon a second leave.

POLONIUS   Yet here Laertes? Aboard, aboard, for shame;   55
The wind sits in the shoulder of your sail,
And you are stayed for. There – my blessing
    with thee.
And these few precepts in thy memory
Look thou character. Give thy thoughts no tongue,
Nor any unproportioned thought his act.   60
Be thou familiar, but by no means vulgar.
Those friends thou hast, and their adoption tried,
Grapple them unto thy soul with hoops of steel;
But do not dull thy palm with entertainment
Of each new-hatched, unfledged courage.
    Beware   65
Of entrance to a quarrel, but being in,
Bear't that th' opposed may beware of thee.
Give every man thy ear, but few thy voice;
Take each man's censure, but reserve thy
    judgement.
Costly thy habit as thy purse can buy,   70
But not expressed in fancy; rich, not gaudy,
For the apparel oft proclaims the man;
And they in France of the best rank and station
Or of a most select and generous, chief in that.
Neither a borrower nor a lender be,   75
For loan oft loses both itself and friend,
And borrowing dulleth edge of husbandry.
This above all, to thine own self be true,
And it must follow, as the night the day,
Thou canst not then be false to any man.   80
Farewell, my blessing season this in thee.

LAERTES   Most humbly do I take my leave my lord.

POLONIUS   The time invites you; go, your servants tend.

LAERTES   Farewell Ophelia, and remember well

Laertes, before leaving, reminds Ophelia to remember what he has said to her. Polonius asks what this was, and she mentions Hamlet. This triggers an interrogation on the part of Polonius who has already heard that Hamlet has been visiting her. Ophelia clearly thinks Hamlet's expressions of love are genuine. Polonius warns her of her youth and inexperience.

89 **touching**: concerning
90 **Marry well bethought**: to be sure, well remembered
93 **bounteous**: generous
95 **caution**: warning
97 **behoves**: befits
99 **tenders**: offers, declarations
101 **green girl Unsifted**: inexperienced and untried girl
106 **ta'en**: taken
   tenders: (here) offers of money
107 **sterling**: genuine. Originally a pound sterling was a pound weight of silver pennies, whereas some currencies already used base metals for their coinage, as we do today.
   Tender yourself: take more care of yourself with the double meaning of: Offer yourself at a higher rate (see *Pun*, GLOSSARY page 335).
108 **not to...thus**: a metaphor taken from horsemanship. A horse ridden long and fast to a state of exhaustion would not be able to breathe properly.
109 **tender me a fool**: present me as a fool, make me look a fool
110 **importuned...love**: (stress on second syllable) expressed his love
111 **fashion**: his way of behaving, just a whim
112 **go to**: go on! (ie how can she believe this?)
113 **hath...to his speech**: has backed up what he has said

> • *What is your intuitive reaction to where the truth lies when you read this whole conversation?*

What I have said to you.

OPHELIA   'Tis in my memory locked,   85
And you yourself shall keep the key of it.

LAERTES   Farewell.   [*Exit Laertes*

POLONIUS   What is't Ophelia he hath said to you?

OPHELIA   So please you, something touching the Lord
                    Hamlet.

POLONIUS   Marry well bethought.   90
'Tis told me he hath very oft of late
Given private time to you, and you yourself
Have of your audience been most free and
                    bounteous.
If it be so, as so 'tis put on me,
And that in way of caution, I must tell you,   95
You do not understand yourself so clearly
As it behoves my daughter, and your honour.
What is between you? Give me up the truth.

OPHELIA   He hath my lord of late made many tenders
Of his affection to me.   100

POLONIUS   Affection? Pooh, you speak like a green girl
Unsifted in such perilous circumstance.
Do you believe his tenders as you call them?

OPHELIA   I do not know my lord what I should think.

POLONIUS   Marry I'll teach you; think yourself a baby,   105
That you have ta'en these tenders for true pay
Which are not sterling. Tender yourself more
                    dearly;
Or – not to crack the wind of the poor phrase
Running it thus – you'll tender me a fool.

OPHELIA   My lord he hath importuned me with love   110
In honourable fashion.

POLONIUS   Ay, fashion you may call it; go to, go to.

OPHELIA   And hath given countenance to his speech, my
                    lord,
With almost all the holy vows of heaven.

Polonius insists that Hamlet's words are fired with his present feelings of love for her, but Ophelia must not believe him. He is young, and his position allows him more scope than she can permit herself. He may want her, but not to marry her. She is not to speak to him again. Ophelia promises to obey her father.

115 **springes...woodcocks**: snares to catch woodcocks (a game-bird, something like a snipe and considered rather stupid.)
116 **prodigal**: generously, lavishly
118 **extinct in both**: with both light and heat extinguished
121 **Be somewhat scanter**: limit
122 **Set...parley**: set more store on your negotiating position than to accept his demand to discuss terms for surrender. The *metaphor* (see GLOSSARY page 335) is that of a castle – her virginity – under siege.
125 **larger tether**: a longer tethering rope. Hamlet is allowed more licence than Ophelia.
126 **In few**: in short
127 **for they are brokers...beguile**: for they are marriage-brokers, go-betweens, who are not offering what they say they are, but making you listen to dishonourable entreaties, promising blessed and holy marriage, all the better to charm you. There are punning references: broker is marriage broker, shady financier, dealer in secondhand clothes; investments are financial dealings, clothes; bonds are both financial and marriage bonds.
133 **slander any moment leisure**: debase any free moment

> • *Assess Polonius's attitude to relationships.*

Hamlet, Horatio and Marcellus are on the castle battlements just after midnight. It is very cold.

1 **shrewdly**: keenly
2 **eager**: sharp
3 **lacks of twelve**: not yet midnight

POLONIUS   Ay, springes to catch woodcocks. I do know,   115
When the blood burns, how prodigal the soul
Lends the tongue vows. These blazes daughter,
Giving more light than heat, extinct in both,
Even in their promise, as it is a-making,
You must not take for fire. From this time   120
Be somewhat scanter of your maiden presence.
Set your entreatments at a higher rate
Than a command to parley. For Lord Hamlet,
Believe so much in him that he is young,
And with a larger tether may he walk   125
Than may be given you. In few Ophelia,
Do not believe his vows, for they are brokers,
Not of that dye which their investments show,
But mere implorators of unholy suits,
Breathing like sanctified and pious bonds   130
The better to beguile. This is for all:
I would not in plain terms from this time forth
Have you so slander any moment leisure
As to give words or talk with the Lord
    Hamlet.
Look to 't I charge you; come your ways.   135

OPHELIA   I shall obey, my lord.   [*Exeunt*

Scene 4

Enter HAMLET, HORATIO, *and* MARCELLUS

HAMLET   The air bites shrewdly, it is very cold.

HORATIO   It is a nipping and an eager air.

HAMLET   What hour now?

HORATIO   I think it lacks of twelve.

MARCELLUS   No, it is struck.

HORATIO   Indeed? I heard it not; it then draws near the
    season   5

From inside the three hear trumpets and cannon-fire when a toast is drunk. Hamlet dislikes this practice and resents the impression it gives to other nations. He sees how one defect in a man can seem to colour the whole personality and affect others' opinion of him.

6 **held his wont**: was accustomed
8 **doth wake...reels**: holding his celebrations tonight, with toasts, drinking and wild dances
10 **Rhenish**: wine from the Rhine
12 **triumph**: celebration of his toast
15 **it is a custom...observance**: a custom much better left out
17 **east and west**: in all directions, the world over
18 **traduced and taxed**: slandered and accused
19 **clepe**: call
    with swinish...addition: put a stain on any distinction we may have by calling us pigs
22 **pith and marrow...attribute**: the essential, innermost nature of our qualities
24 **mole of nature**: some birthmark
27 **By the...complexion**: some excess in their physical make-up. (A person's constitution was thought to be composed of the four humours: blood, phlegm, choler and melancholy which needed to be kept in proper balance. From this belief we have the descriptions of people as being 'sanguine', 'phlegmatic', 'choleric' or 'melancholy', depending on which humour was seen to predominate.)
28 **pales**: fences
29 **o'er-leavens...manners**: just as too much yeast will cause dough to be sour, or not rise properly, so will some habit, carried to excess, ruin otherwise acceptable manners
32 **nature's livery**: a uniform showing that nature is your master
    fortune's star: a mark made by chance
33 **his virtues...fault**: however pure, however varied a man's merits may be, he will be subject to blame for that one fault

- *Note any indications of what Hamlet might have been like as king.*

Wherein the spirit held his wont to walk.
>   [*A flourish of trumpets, and cannon fire within*
What does this mean my lord?

HAMLET   The King doth wake tonight and takes his rouse,
Keeps wassail, and the swaggering up-spring
>   reels;
And as he drains his draughts of Rhenish down,   10
The kettle-drum and trumpet thus bray out
The triumph of his pledge.

HORATIO   Is it a custom?

HAMLET   Ay marry is't,
But to my mind, though I am native here,
And to the manner born, it is a custom   15
More honoured in the breach than the
>   observance.
This heavy-headed revel east and west
Makes us traduced and taxed of other nations.
They clepe us drunkards, and with swinish phrase
Soil our addition; and indeed it takes   20
From our achievements, though performed at
>   height,
The pith and marrow of our attribute.
So, oft it chances in particular men,
That for some vicious mole of nature in them,
As in their birth, wherein they are not guilty –   25
Since nature cannot choose his origin –
By the o'ergrowth of some complexion,
Oft breaking down the pales and forts of reason,
Or by some habit, that too much o'er-leavens
The form of plausive manners – that these men,   30
Carrying, I say, the stamp of one defect,
Being nature's livery, or fortune's star,
His virtues else be they as pure as grace,
As infinite as man may undergo,
Shall in the general censure take corruption   35

The Ghost appears. Hamlet immediately addresses it, still doubting whether it is a good or evil spirit, but giving it all the names his father would have had. He then specifically asks why this spirit has had to leave his tomb and revisit the earth. The Ghost beckons him away as though it wants to speak to him alone. Hamlet's friends warn him not to go.

36 **The dram of eale...scandal**: it is not possible to know the correct reading of this line, but the sense appears to be that the smallest drop of evil poisons the whole, the least doubt brings the whole noble enterprise into question
39 **ministers of grace**: messengers of God
40 **spirit of health...damned**: a good spirit or an evil demon
41 **airs**: gentle breezes
43 **questionable shape**: shape that I must put questions to
47 **canonized**: buried in accordance with the rites of the church
   hearsed: coffined
48 **cerements**: burial clothes, waxed cloth to wrap a dead body in (modern French *cire* means wax)
   sepulchre: tomb
52 **in complete steel**: (stress on first syllable of '*complete*' in full armour
53 **glimpses**: fitful gleams
54 **hideous**: terrifying
   fools of nature: ignorant human beings
55 **horridly...disposition**: shaking ourselves so violently
59 **As if it...desire**: as if there were something it wanted to communicate
61 **more removed ground**: somewhere further off

- *Can you find any clues about whether the Ghost is a 'spirit of health' or 'goblin damned'?*

From that particular fault. The dram of eale
Doth all the noble substance of a doubt
To his own scandal.

Enter GHOST

HORATIO	Look my lord, it comes.
HAMLET	Angels and ministers of grace defend us.

Be thou a spirit of health or goblin damned,   40
Bring with thee airs from heaven, or blasts
     from hell,
Be thy intents wicked, or charitable,
Thou com'st in such a questionable shape,
That I will speak to thee. I'll call thee Hamlet,
King, father, royal Dane. O answer me.   45
Let me not burst in ignorance, but tell
Why thy canonized bones, hearsed in death,
Have burst their cerements; why the sepulchre,
Wherein we saw thee quietly interred,
Hath oped his ponderous and marble jaws,   50
To cast thee up again. What may this mean,
That thou, dead corse, again in complete steel
Revisits thus the glimpses of the moon,
Making night hideous, and we fools of nature
So horridly to shake our disposition   55
With thoughts beyond the reaches of our souls?
Say, why is this? Wherefore? What should we do?
                              [GHOST *beckons*

HORATIO   It beckons you to go away with it,
As if it some impartment did desire
To you alone.

MARCELLUS   Look with what courteous action 60
It waves you to a more removed ground.
But do not go with it.

HORATIO   No, by no means.

HAMLET   It will not speak; then I will follow it.

HORATIO   Do not my lord.

Hamlet dismisses his friends' fear for him, saying he does not value his life, and that his soul, being immortal like the Ghost, cannot be corrupted. Horatio is concerned that the spirit may draw Hamlet to his death in the sea at the foot of the cliff. Hamlet is desperate to follow the Ghost and forces them to let him go. Horatio and Marcellus decide to follow, at a distance.

65 set…pin's fee: value my life at the cost of a pin

69 the flood: the sea

71 beetles: overhangs (like beetle brows – scowling eyebrows)

73 deprive…reason: deprive you of the rule of reason

75 toys of desperation: desperate fancies

78 It waves me still: it is still beckoning me on

81 fate: destiny, future

83 Nemean lion's nerve: the first of the twelve labours of Hercules was to kill the Nemean lion, which had been terrifying people. Its skin was so tough that his club made no impression, so he squeezed it to death and ever after wore its skin. It is interesting to compare Hamlet's reference here to the Hercules story, to his reference in Act 1 scene 2 line 153. **nerve**: sinew

85 lets: hinders, prevents

87 waxes: grows

89 Have after: let's go after him

> • *There are further pointers here to Horatio's personality and his role in the play.*

HAMLET	Why, what should be the fear?
	I do not set my life at a pin's fee, 65
	And for my soul, what can it do to that
	Being a thing immortal as itself?
	It waves me forth again. I'll follow it.
HORATIO	What if it tempt you toward the flood my lord,
	Or to the dreadful summit of the cliff 70
	That beetles o'er his base into the sea,
	And there assume some other horrible form,
	Which might deprive your sovereignty of reason
	And draw you into madness? Think of it.
	The very place puts toys of desperation, 75
	Without more motive, into every brain
	That looks so many fathoms to the sea,
	And hears it roar beneath.
HAMLET	It waves me still.
	Go on, I'll follow thee.
MARCELLUS	You shall not go my lord.
HAMLET	Hold off your hands. 80
HORATIO	Be ruled, you shall not go.
HAMLET	My fate cries out,
	And makes each petty artery in this body
	As hardy as the Nemean lion's nerve.
	Still am I called. Unhand me gentlemen.
	By heaven I'll make a ghost of him that
	lets me. 85
	I say, away! Go on, I'll follow thee.

[*Exeunt* GHOST *and* HAMLET

HORATIO	He waxes desperate with imagination.
MARCELLUS	Let's follow, 'tis not fit thus to obey him.
HORATIO	Have after. To what issue will this come?
MARCELLUS	Something is rotten in the state of Denmark. 90
HORATIO	Heaven will direct it.
MARCELLUS	Nay, let's follow him.

[*Exeunt*

When Hamlet asks the Ghost to speak, saying he will not follow him any further, the Ghost says Hamlet will feel bound to seek revenge, when he hears his story. He confirms that he is his father's spirit, and that he will be in Purgatory until the sins he was unable to confess have been purged away. He is not allowed to tell the terrible secrets of Purgatory.

6 **bound**: obliged
11 **fast in fires**: he is in Purgatory. The Church held that souls which were destined for Heaven had nevertheless to be purged of their sins until they were fit to meet God.
13 **But that**: except for the fact that
16 **harrow up**: tear apart
17 **Make...spheres**: make both your eyes burst out from your head, like stars leaving their proper course
18 **knotted and combined**: tangled and wound together
19 **particular**: individual
   an end: on end; 'an' is an obsolete form
20 **fretful porpentine**: bad-tempered porcupine
21 **eternal blazon**: proclamation of what goes on in the immortal world

> • *Hamlet, and the audience, are given the confirmation that Purgatory has unspeakable horrors in store. This adds weight to all the later emphasis on confession and absolution as a prelude to a good death.*

Scene ⑤ ────────────

Enter GHOST *and* HAMLET

HAMLET	Where wilt thou lead me? Speak, I'll go no further.
GHOST	Mark me.
HAMLET	I will.
GHOST	My hour is almost come

    When I to sulphurous and tormenting flames
    Must render up myself.

HAMLET	Alas poor ghost!
GHOST	Pity me not, but lend thy serious hearing 5

    To what I shall unfold.

HAMLET	Speak, I am bound to hear.
GHOST	So art thou to revenge, when thou shalt hear.
HAMLET	What?
GHOST	I am thy father's spirit,

    Doomed for a certain term to walk the night,   10
    And for the day confined to fast in fires,
    Till the foul crimes done in my days of nature
    Are burnt and purged away. But that I am forbid
    To tell the secrets of my prison-house,
    I could a tale unfold whose lightest word   15
    Would harrow up thy soul, freeze thy young
        blood,
    Make thy two eyes like stars start from their
        spheres,
    Thy knotted and combined locks to part,
    And each particular hair to stand an end,
    Like quills upon the fretful porpentine.   20
    But this eternal blazon must not be
    To ears of flesh and blood. List, list, o list!
    If thou didst ever thy dear father love –

HAMLET	O God!

The Ghost reveals that he was murdered by his brother, Claudius, not bitten by a snake. He also alleges, with disgust, that Gertrude whom he loved and honoured in accordance with his marriage vows, had already been seduced before his death by his brother. Lust had led her astray.

25 unnatural: monstrous

27 as in the best it is: as it is even in the most extenuating circumstances

28 strange and unnatural: it was fratricide – murder of a brother. This crime, like other murders of blood relations, is considered more '*unnatural*' than other forms of killing. Also this was a murder of envy, for gain.

31 apt: ready to respond

32 fat...ease: gross weed that grows so luxuriantly

33 Lethe: the river of forgetfulness which, according to Greek myth, flowed through Hades. The souls, waiting to cross, drank from it and so forgot their existence on earth.

37 forged process: invented description

38 Rankly abused: massively deceived

40 prophetic soul: Hamlet has felt all along that things are wrong, but he is not claiming to have suspected this crime

43 wits: mental powers

44 wit: intellect

46 will: desire

49 even with the vow: with that very vow

53 moved: affected

54 lewdness...heaven: lust pays court to it in angelic form

56 sate...bed: become glutted in a heavenly bed

- *Notice the context of the first mention of words such as* '*unnatural*' *and* '*incestuous*'.

GHOST	Revenge his foul and most unnatural murder. 25
HAMLET	Murder?
GHOST	Murder most foul, as in the best it is, But this most foul, strange and unnatural.
HAMLET	Haste me to know 't, that I with wings as swift As meditation or the thoughts of love, 30 May sweep to my revenge.
GHOST	I find thee apt, And duller shouldst thou be than the fat weed That roots itself in ease on Lethe wharf, Wouldst thou not stir in this. Now Hamlet, hear. 'Tis given out that, sleeping in my orchard, 35 A serpent stung me; so the whole ear of Denmark Is by a forged process of my death Rankly abused. But know, thou noble youth, The serpent that did sting thy father's life Now wears his crown.
HAMLET	O my prophetic soul! 40 My uncle?
GHOST	Ay, that incestuous, that adulterate beast, With witchcraft of his wits, with traitorous gifts – O wicked wit and gifts that have the power So to seduce – won to his shameful lust 45 The will of my most seeming-virtuous Queen. O Hamlet, what a falling-off was there, From me whose love was of that dignity That it went hand in hand even with the vow I made to her in marriage, and to decline 50 Upon a wretch whose natural gifts were poor To those of mine. But virtue, as it never will be moved, Though lewdness court it in a shape of heaven; So lust, though to a radiant angel linked, 55 Will sate itself in a celestial bed, And prey on garbage. But soft, methinks I scent the morning air;

Hamlet's father claims that while he was resting in his garden, Claudius crept up and poured poison in his ears. It took instant effect, clotting his blood and producing scaly sores all over his body. He was sent unprepared to his death and now suffers the torments of Purgatory. Although asking Hamlet for vengeance, he tells him to leave his mother to God. He senses morning is near, and leaves. Hamlet is devastated by the news.

59 orchard: orchard or garden

61 secure: (stress on first syllable) when he felt relaxed and safe

62 hebona: a poisonous tree or plant – possibly ebony or henbane

64 leperous distilment: the liquid obtained from the poisonous plant, causing a scaly outbreak on the skin

66 quicksilver: mercury

67 gates and alleys: veins and pathways

68 sudden vigour...milk: suddenly taking effect, it clots and curdles, like acid dropped into milk (eager is French 'aigre' – 'sour', wine vinegar is 'vinaigre' in French – wine that has gone sour)

71 tetter barked...loathsome crust: skin eruption crusted over like leprosy, with horrid and revolting sores

75 dispatched: deprived by murder

76 blossoms of my sin: my sins full-blown

77 Unhouseled...unaneled: without the sacrament, without preparation for death, without extreme unction (anointing the head of a dying person with holy oil)

85 Taint not thy mind: do not let it affect your mind
contrive: plot

89 matin: morning (cf modern French)

90 'gins to pale...fire: the glow-worm's light seems to become fainter as daylight grows

93 shall I couple hell?: shall I add hell (to these exclamations)

• *What is the Ghost actually asking of his son?*

Brief let me be. Sleeping within my orchard,
My custom always of the afternoon,   60
Upon my secure hour thy uncle stole,
With juice of cursed hebona in a vial,
And in the porches of my ears did pour
The leperous distilment, whose effect
Holds such an enmity with blood of man,   65
That swift as quicksilver it courses through
The natural gates and alleys of the body,
And with a sudden vigour it doth posset
And curd, like eager droppings into milk,
The thin and wholesome blood; so did it mine,   70
And a most instant tetter barked about,
Most lazar-like, with vile and loathsome crust
All my smooth body.
Thus was I sleeping, by a brother's hand
Of life, of crown, of queen, at once dispatched;   75
Cut off even in the blossoms of my sin,
Unhouseled, disappointed, unaneled,
Not reckoning made, but sent to my account
With all my imperfections on my head –
O horrible! O horrible, most horrible!   80
If thou hast nature in thee, bear it not,
Let not the royal bed of Denmark be
A couch for luxury and damned incest.
But howsoever thou pursuest this act,
Taint not thy mind, nor let thy soul contrive   85
Against thy mother aught; leave her to heaven,
And to those thorns that in her bosom lodge
To prick and sting her. Fare thee well at once.
The glow-worm shows the matin to be near,
And 'gins to pale his uneffectual fire.   90
Adieu, adieu, adieu. Remember me.   [*Exit*

HAMLET   O all you host of heaven! O earth! What else?
           And shall I couple hell? O fie! Hold, hold,
               my heart,
           And you my sinews, grow not instant old,

Hamlet vows to follow the spirit's injunction to 'remember him', and to do so will dispose of everything he has ever learnt which is irrelevant to this overriding concern. He curses his mother and Claudius. When Horatio and the others appear, anxious for his safety, he will not tell them what has happened.

95 bear me stiffly up: keep me upright
96 holds a seat...globe: has a place in this disordered world, with a possible punning reference to the confusion in his head (*Pun*, see GLOSSARY page 335)
98 table: writing tablet, notebook
99 fond: foolish
100 saws: maxims, sayings
  forms: shapes, images
  pressures: impressions
101 observation: duty
110 my word: he has not yet made any formal vow to the ghost
111 'Adieu...me': the Ghost's words will serve to remind Hamlet constantly, throughout the play, what is required of him
118 Come bird, come: Hamlet answers with a falconer's call

But bear me stiffly up. Remember thee?   95
Ay thou poor ghost, whiles memory holds a seat
In this distracted globe. Remember thee?
Yea, from the table of my memory
I'll wipe away all trivial fond records,
All saws of books, all forms, all pressures past   100
That youth and observation copied there,
And thy commandment all alone shall live
Within the book and volume of my brain,
Unmixed with baser matter – yes, by heaven!
O most pernicious woman!   105
O villain, villain, smiling, damned villain!
My tables – meet it is I set it down,
That one may smile, and smile, and be a villain;
At least I am sure it may be so in Denmark:
                                    [*Writes*
So uncle, there you are. Now to my word;   110
It is 'Adieu, adieu, remember me'.
I have sworn't.

Enter HORATIO *and* MARCELLUS

MARCELLUS ⎫ HORATIO ⎭	My lord, my lord!
MARCELLUS	Lord Hamlet!
HORATIO	Heaven secure him. 115
HAMLET	So be it.
HORATIO	Hillo, ho, ho, my lord!
HAMLET	Hillo, ho, ho, boy! Come bird, come.
MARCELLUS	How is 't my noble lord?
HORATIO	What news my lord? 120
HAMLET	O wonderful!
HORATIO	Good my lord tell it.
HAMLET	No, you will reveal it.
HORATIO	Not I my lord, by heaven.

Having asked his friends to be discreet, Hamlet then speaks in generalities, and says they should part. Horatio senses that Hamlet is not talking sense, but at the mention of the word '*offence*' Hamlet's mind again turns to what he has been told and he informs his friends quite brusquely that he will not tell them, but swears them to secrecy about what they do know.

128 arrant knave: complete villain

131 circumstance: words

140 by Saint Patrick: the patron saint of Purgatory, but also known for ridding Ireland of snakes. Perhaps Hamlet is thinking not only of Purgatory, where his father's spirit is in torment, but also of '*The serpent that did sting thy father's life...*' (Act 1 scene 5 line 39).

143 For: as for

144 O'ermaster: overcome

> • *How would you describe Hamlet's state of mind and mode of speech when the Ghost has gone?*

MARCELLUS	Nor I my lord.
HAMLET	How say you then, would heart of man once think it 125 But you'll be secret?
HORATIO MARCELLUS }	Ay by heaven my lord.
HAMLET	There's never a villain dwelling in all Denmark But he's an arrant knave.
HORATIO	There needs no ghost, my lord, come from the grave To tell us this.
HAMLET	Why right, you are in the right, 130 And so without more circumstance at all I hold it fit that we shake hands and part; You as your business and desire shall point you, For every man has business and desire, Such as it is, and for mine own poor part 135 I will go pray.
HORATIO	These are but wild and whirling words my lord.
HAMLET	I am sorry they offend you, heartily, Yes faith, heartily.
HORATIO	There's no offence my lord.
HAMLET	Yes by Saint Patrick but there is, Horatio, 140 And much offence too. Touching this vision here – It is an honest ghost, that let me tell you – For your desire to know what is between us O'ermaster 't as you may. And now good friends, As you are friends, scholars, and soldiers, 145 Give me one poor request.
HORATIO	What is 't my lord? We will.
HAMLET	Never make known what you have seen tonight.

Hamlet now makes Horatio and Marcellus swear, upon his sword, that they will never speak of what they have seen. The Ghost, back in his own place, repeats the word 'swear', and every time they hear him, they move on. They are struck by the strangeness of the events. Hamlet warns them that he may appear to act strangely.

152 **Upon my sword**: the hilt and blade of the sword form a cross. Oaths were commonly sworn on the Bible or on a cross.
156 **truepenny**: honest fellow
157 **in the cellarage**: down below
162 **hic et ubique**: (Latin) here and everywhere
169 **pioneer**: digger, miner or member of military pioneer or engineer corps for tunnelling or excavating
     remove: move off
171 **And...welcome**: the law of hospitality must make a stranger welcome
173 **in your philosophy**: in philosophy or science (not in Horatio's own philosophy)

HORATIO	} My lord we will not.
MARCELLUS	

HAMLET   Nay but swear 't.

HORATIO   In faith my lord not I.   150

MARCELLUS   Nor I my lord in faith.

HAMLET   Upon my sword.

MARCELLUS   We have sworn my lord already.

HAMLET   Indeed, upon my sword, indeed.

GHOST   [*Beneath*] Swear.   155

HAMLET   Ha, ha, boy, say'st thou so? Art thou there, true-
                  penny?
              Come on – you hear this fellow in the cellarage –
              Consent to swear.

HORATIO   Propose the oath, my lord.

HAMLET   Never to speak of this that you have seen,
              Swear by my sword.   160

GHOST   [*Beneath*] Swear.

HAMLET   Hic et ubique? Then we'll shift our ground.
              Come hither gentlemen,
              And lay your hands again upon my sword,
              Swear by my sword   165
              Never to speak of this that you have heard.

GHOST   [*Beneath*] Swear by his sword.

HAMLET   Well said old mole, canst work i' th' earth so fast?
              A worthy pioneer. Once more remove, good
                  friends.

HORATIO   O day and night, but this is wondrous strange.   170

HAMLET   And therefore as a stranger give it welcome.
              There are more things in heaven and earth,
                  Horatio,
              Than are dreamt of in your philosophy.
              But come –
              Here as before, never, so help you mercy,   175

Hamlet insists Horatio and Marcellus are never to hint that they know what is the matter with him, or what may have caused any strangeness in him. The Ghost again reinforces this and they swear. Hamlet expresses his gratitude to, and affection for, them and curses the burden that has been placed on him.

176 **How...myself**: however oddly I may seem to behave
177 **As I perchance...on**: as I may later on think it fit to assume strange moods
180 **encumbered**: folded
183 **'If...speak' or 'There be...might'**: 'if we cared to speak' or 'there are those, who if they were allowed'
184 **giving out**: hinting
188 **perturbed**: disturbed
189 **commend me**: entrust myself, a leave-taking phrase
194 **The time...joint**: the world has become corrupted
    O cursed spite...set it right: that fortune should bear me such malice that I was ever born to put things right

How strange or odd some'er I bear myself –
As I perchance hereafter shall think meet
To put an antic disposition on –
That you at such times seeing me never shall,
With arms encumbered thus, or this
    head-shake,   180
Or by pronouncing of some doubtful phrase,
As 'Well, well, we know', or 'We could, an if we
    would',
Or 'If we list to speak', or 'There be, an if they
    might',
Or such ambiguous giving out, to note
That you know aught of me – this do swear   185
So grace and mercy at your most need help you.

GHOST   [*Beneath*] Swear.

HAMLET   Rest, rest, perturbed spirit. [*They swear*] So
    gentlemen,
With all my love I do commend me to you;
And what so poor a man as Hamlet is   190
May do, t' express his love and friending to you,
God willing, shall not lack. Let us go in together,
And still your fingers on your lips I pray.
The time is out of joint. O cursed spite,
That ever I was born to set it right.   195
Nay come, let's go together.   [*Exeunt*

CTIVITIES

Keeping track

Scene 1

1 What mood and atmosphere are created in the first scene, and how does Shakespeare achieve this effect?
2 How do Horatio and the sentries react to the Ghost? What is their understanding of its nature and intentions?
3 What does Horatio's speech (lines 79–107) reveal about the background to events on stage?
4 What do the references to '*the King*' after line 41 tell you about the attitude of Horatio and the two guards towards Hamlet's father?

Scene 2

1 What is Claudius trying to do in his first speech (lines 1–16)?
2 How does he try to do it and is he successful in his intention?
3 In lines 17–39 Claudius explains what he is doing to deal with the military and political crisis which threatens Denmark. What do you think of the way he handles this crisis?
4 How does Claudius behave towards Laertes and Polonius when he deals with Laertes' request to return to France (lines 42–62)? What political skills does he show in this exchange?
5 What arguments do Claudius and Gertrude use to try to persuade Hamlet that he is behaving unreasonably?
6 Hamlet reacts violently to his mother's use of the word '*seems*' and he launches into a verbal attack on her. Why does this word (line 76) have such significance for him and what does the strength of Hamlet's attack reveal?
7 Hamlet's first soliloquy reveals a mood of suicidal despair. Why exactly does he feel like this? Is this mood justified by what has happened and what he knows?

Scene 3

1 Laertes and Polonius both offer Ophelia 'good advice'. What does this scene reveal about their attitudes to people and life?
2 What do Polonius and Laertes think of Hamlet?

Scenes 4 and 5

1 In these scenes Hamlet learns the 'truth' about his father's murder and his mother's betrayal. What is Hamlet's initial reaction to the Ghost (Scene 4 lines 39–57)?

2 How does the Ghost persuade Hamlet to take action (Scene 5)? (Look closely at what he says and how he says it.) Why does he succeed so easily?

3 How does Hamlet react to the Ghost's revelations?

4 What exactly has the Ghost persuaded Hamlet to do?

5 What do you think Hamlet should do now? What do you want him to do? What are the alternatives?

6 Does the fact that the 'truth' has been revealed by a ghost make any difference?

7 What do you understand from lines 195–196:
> 'O cursed spite,
> That ever I was born to set it right'?

Is Hamlet having doubts already?

Drama

1 Imagine you are the set designers for a theatre production of *Hamlet*. Produce drawings and designs for the opening scene, which capture or evoke the appropriate atmosphere. You have a free hand to be as inventive as you like. The conventional approach would probably include grey stone battlements, soldiers in long cloaks and a smoke machine. What would it be like, set in a penthouse suite with state of the art security systems or in a police state with Nazi style uniforms or . . .? You decide.

2 Now think about the problem of portraying the Ghost. How would you do this on stage to make it convincing and frightening – remembering that a modern audience would be used to the sophistication of horror movie effects?
   • What are the pros and cons of having an actor or a voice over?
   • Some small companies would double up the Ghost with another character, some might even openly use the same actor to play the Ghost and Claudius. What would be the advantages and disadvantages of this approach?

Discuss your ideas and try out the best in action.

3 Use FORUM THEATRE (see page 297) to explore the moment when Hamlet says '*But I have that within which passes show –*' (Act 1 scene 2 line 85).

Look at the soliloquy (Act 1 scene 2 lines 129–159) for ideas. Start with Hamlet and gradually include all the members of the court to find all the nuances of tension and subtext.

4 Improvise modern versions of the exchanges between Ophelia, Polonius and Laertes. The two men both give her advice – does she heed them?

If status relationships were measured on a scale of 10 to 1, from the most powerful to the lowest status, the conventional reading might place Polonius on 8, Laertes at 5 and Ophelia at 2. Play about with these status rankings, altering the balance and see what difference it makes to the portrayals. Find and alter the subtexts.

5 • The actor playing the part of the Ghost is having trouble making the allusion to hell a convincing speech (Act 1 scene 5 lines 9–23). What advice could you give to help him imagine the horrors to which he refers? Elizabethans had a very vivid picture of hell: ours may be different. In groups, encourage your actor to imagine the horrors which will make him shiver with fear.

   • Look at the Ghost's speech (Act 1 scene 5 lines 42–88). Divide it into sections of about five lines each, using the punctuation as a guideline. Either in groups, or as a whole class, choose different people to deliver the lines, as though the Ghost's voice was coming from a variety of directions, while one student becomes the cowering Hamlet receiving the story as a series of blows.

The key elements

In each Act of the play there are key scenes, speeches or developments which you will need to think about and study in detail. In Act 1 these are:
• the major characters
• the first court scene
• the first soliloquy
• the Ghost and its revelations.

Key scene

Hamlet's first soliloquy: Act 1 scene 2

Keying it in

1 This speech comes after we have seen Claudius and Gertrude attempting to persuade Hamlet to '*look like a friend on Denmark*'. Look at Act I scene 2 lines 76–86.
   • What is Hamlet's mood?
   • What unspoken accusations does he make?

2 Look again at lines 65–120.
- What evidence is there so far of Hamlet's attitude to Claudius?
- Why does he want to leave Denmark?
- Why does Claudius try so hard to make him stay?

The speech itself

3 Look at lines 129–137.
When Hamlet is left alone on stage, his first lines give us an insight into his emotional state. He is experiencing a mood of suicidal despair.
- How do the language and imagery of the lines convey Hamlet's feelings?
- Do you think Hamlet's grief goes beyond 'normal' mourning for a loved one?

4 Look at lines 138–146.
This section reveals Hamlet's view of the relationship between his mother and his father.
- how had he seen the relationship?
- how does Hamlet make the contrast between his father and Claudius?
- why do you think he says '*Must I remember?*' (line 143)
Hamlet concludes that, '*frailty, thy name is woman.*'
- is this fair on Gertrude?
- is this fair on '*woman*' in general?
- what are the implications for Hamlet's feelings for Ophelia?

5 Look at lines 147–159.
This section of the soliloquy reveals even more about Hamlet's attitude to his mother and her recent marriage.
- What does he object to:
    the fact that she remarried at all
    that she married this particular man
    the timing of the marriage?
- What evidence, if any, can you find to support these possible explanations?
- How far do you 'understand' his feelings and sympathize with him?

Overview

In this soliloquy the keynote is the mood of profound disillusion. Hamlet expresses a sense of disgust with his mother, with women and with life in general. His revulsion is so powerful and intense that he wishes he were dead.
1 List the reasons for his feelings of disgust.
2 How do the language and structure of the speech convey the intensity of his feelings?

Close study

Scene 5 lines 92–112 ('*O all you host of heaven!*')
The soliloquy comes immediately after the Ghost's revelations.
1 How does the language of the opening two lines convey Hamlet's feelings?
2 What is meant by '*And shall I couple hell?*'
3 What are Hamlet's fears about his '*heart*' and '*sinews*'?
4 What does Hamlet mean when he says '*whiles memory holds a seat In this distracted globe*'?
5 How does he show his determination to fulfil his duty to revenge?
6 What are the '*trivial fond records*' he refers to in line 99?
7 What does he mean by '*baser matter*' in line 104?
8 How does his language in lines 104–105 reveal his attitude to Gertrude and Claudius?
9 Do you think it is significant that he mentions Gertrude first?
10 How do the language and structure of this speech as a whole suggest Hamlet's mood?

Hamlet and revenge

Act 1 also sets in motion the theme of revenge which is central to our response to the play. The Ghost places the responsibility of revenge on Hamlet by appealing to his sense of filial duty and by playing on his feelings of outrage at murder and disgust at sexual betrayal.

Hamlet reacts passionately and violently to the Ghost's revelations and he accepts the burden of revenge instantly and willingly. His first thoughts are to '*sweep to my revenge*' and he dedicates himself to the task, promising to erase from his mind '*all trivial fond records*'.
• Do you find his reaction 'normal' and 'natural'?
• What would you think of Hamlet if he did not respond with this surge of 'blood' and violent passion?

It is also worth noting that in this initial mood of violent passion Hamlet expresses complete confidence in the Ghost. He says to Horatio '*It is an honest ghost*' (Act 1 scene 5 line 142).

However, there are some hints even at this stage that Hamlet may not find revenge an entirely straightforward business. When he says, '*And shall I couple hell?*' (Act 1 scene 5 line 93) perhaps Hamlet is aware of the enormity of the task and of the awesome implications of involvement with evil. When he says, '*O cursed spite That ever I was born to set it right*', he seems to be experiencing unease and even a sense of reluctance. He appears to be questioning his adequacy as a revenger.

There remains the issue of the '*antic disposition*'. Hamlet tells Horatio and the others that he may assume an appearance of madness and swears them to secrecy. He gives no explanation for this decision and it is often taken to be an obviously sensible part of his strategy to achieve revenge.

However:

- why does he suddenly decide to pretend to be mad
- what is his purpose
- what can he gain by this?

By the end of Act 1, Hamlet has accepted that he has a duty to revenge his father's murder and betrayal, but it is possible to detect some unease in him and his plan of action is not entirely clear.

Assignments

1 In Act 1 we are introduced to six major characters. They are:

Hamlet   Claudius   Gertrude
Ophelia   Laertes   Polonius

In note form, record your first impressions of each of them.

Identify key quotations to use as evidence to support your views.

Essays

2 Imagine you are an ambassador from England, newly arrived in Denmark. You have to write a report to the English king informing him of recent developments and the political situation in Denmark. Write your report.

3 Look closely at Hamlet's first encounter with the Ghost in Act 1. How does the Ghost persuade Hamlet to accept the role of revenger?

Polonius is employing Reynaldo to deliver money and letters to Laertes in France. Reynaldo is also being asked by Polonius to find Danish acquaintances of his son. He is to claim some small knowledge of Laertes, and to suggest to people who might know Laertes that the young man is leading a rather wild existence.

1 **notes**: letters
7 **Danskers**: Danes
8 **what means...keep**: what means they have and where they lodge
10 **encompassment...question**: by this roundabout means and general drift of enquiry
11 **come you...touch it**: you will come nearer the point of your questions than by any direct approach
13 **Take you...him**: pretend to be slightly acquainted with him
20 **forgeries**: inventions
rank: offensive
22 **wanton**: wilful
24 **gaming**: gambling

> • *What further revelations are there here about Polonius's character? How does he perceive his role as father?*

Act two

Scene 1

Enter POLONIUS *and* REYNALDO

POLONIUS   Give him this money, and these notes, Reynaldo.

REYNALDO   I will my lord.

POLONIUS   You shall do marvellous wisely, good Reynaldo,
Before you visit him, to make inquire
Of his behaviour.

REYNALDO   My lord, I did intend it.   5

POLONIUS   Marry well said, very well said. Look you sir,
Inquire me first what Danskers are in Paris,
And how, and who, what means, and where
     they keep,
What company, at what expense; and finding
By this encompassment and drift of question,   10
That they do know my son, come you more
     nearer
Than your particular demands will touch it.
Take you as 'twere some distant knowledge of him,
As thus, 'I know his father and his friends,
And in part him' – do you mark this Reynaldo?   15

REYNALDO   Ay, very well my lord.

POLONIUS   'And in part him – but', you may say, 'not well:
But, if't be he I mean, he's very wild;
Addicted so and so'; and there put on him
What forgeries you please, marry none so rank   20
As may dishonour him, take heed of that;
But sir, such wanton, wild, and usual slips
As are companions noted and most known
To youth and liberty.

REYNALDO   As gaming my lord?

Reynaldo is taken aback at some of the suggestions he is expected to make about Laertes. He says that to suggest he goes with prostitutes would dishonour him. Without saying so explicitly, Polonius makes it clear that Reynaldo's task is to spy on his son and to find out what kind of life he is leading far from home, in a foreign country. Polonius forgets what he was saying.

26 **Drabbing**: associating with prostitutes
30 **That...incontinency**: not that he is promiscuous
31 **breathe...quaintly**: hint at his faults so ingeniously
32 **taints of liberty**: flaws resulting from his freedom
33 **flash and outbreak of a fiery mind**: sudden spontaneous outburst of a passionate mind
34 **A savageness...assault**: a wildness of untamed passion which can attack any young man
38 **fetch of warrant**: approved trick
39 **sullies**: blemishes
40 **a little...working**: as though Laertes has been just a little tarnished by his experiences
41 **party in converse**: the person you are talking to
42 **prenominate**: aforementioned
44 **He closes...consequence**: he agrees with you along these lines
48 **does 'a this...marry**: Polonius loses track of what he was saying and Reynaldo has to prompt him

POLONIUS	Ay, or drinking, fencing, swearing, quarrelling, 25
	Drabbing – you may go so far.
REYNALDO	My lord, that would dishonour him.
POLONIUS	Faith no, as you may season it in the charge.
	You must not put another scandal on him,
	That he is open to incontinency; 30
	That's not my meaning. But breathe his faults so
	quaintly,
	That they may seem the taints of liberty,
	The flash and outbreak of a fiery mind,
	A savageness in unreclaimed blood,
	Of general assault.
REYNALDO	But my good lord – 35
POLONIUS	Wherefore should you do this?
REYNALDO	Ay my lord,
	I would know that.
POLONIUS	Marry sir, here's my drift,
	And I believe it is a fetch of warrant.
	You laying these slight sullies on my son
	As 'twere a thing a little soiled i' th' working, 40
	Mark you, your party in converse, him you would
	sound,
	Having ever seen in the prenominate crimes
	The youth you breathe of guilty, be assured
	He closes with you in this consequence;
	'Good sir', or so, or 'friend', or 'gentleman', 45
	According to the phrase or the addition
	Of man and country.
REYNALDO	Very good my lord.
POLONIUS	And then, sir, does 'a this – he does – what was I
	about to say? By the mass I was about to say
	something. Where did I leave? 50
REYNALDO	At 'closes in the consequence', at 'friend or so',
	and, 'gentleman'.
POLONIUS	At 'closes in the consequence', ay marry.

Polonius demonstrates to Reynaldo how lies will help to discover the truth. He also tells him to observe Laertes on his own account. Reynaldo leaves and Ophelia, very agitated, comes to find her father. Hamlet has visited her in a very dishevelled state and with a terrible expression.

57 o'ertook in 's rouse: found drunk
60 Videlicet: (Latin) that is to say
62 takes: catches
63 And thus...reach: and in this way, we who are both wise and have a good grasp of affairs
64 With...bias: outflanking, and by indirect attempts
   windlasses: crafty devices
   assays: tests, trials
   of bias: oblique
65 By indirections...out: find out the truth by indirect means
68 God buy ye: goodbye
70 in yourself: personally
72 And...music: and make sure he is carrying on with his music
78 closet: private room
79 unbraced: unfastened
80 fouled: dirty
81 down-gyved: fallen down (so that they looked like 'gyves' – chains round his ankles)
83 in purport: in its significance

> • *What is it in Hamlet's conduct that has frightened Ophelia?*

He closes thus: 'I know the gentleman;
I saw him yesterday, or th' other day,   55
Or then, or then; with such, or such; and as you
  say,
There was 'a gaming, there o'ertook in 's rouse,
There falling out at tennis', or perchance,
'I saw him enter such a house of sale',
Videlicet a brothel, or so forth.   60
See you now;
Your bait of falsehood takes this carp of truth.
And thus do we of wisdom, and of reach,
With windlasses, and with assays of bias,
By indirections find directions out;   65
So by my former lecture and advice
Shall you my son. You have me, have you not?

REYNALDO   My lord, I have.

POLONIUS   God buy ye, fare you well.

REYNALDO   Good my lord.

POLONIUS   Observe his inclination in yourself.   70

REYNALDO   I shall my lord.

POLONIUS   And let him ply his music.

REYNALDO   Well, my lord.

POLONIUS   Farewell.   [*Exit Reynaldo*

Enter OPHELIA

How now Ophelia, what's the matter?   75

OPHELIA   O my lord, my lord, I have been so affrighted.

POLONIUS   With what, i' th' name of God?

OPHELIA   My lord, as I was sewing in my closet,
Lord Hamlet with his doublet all unbraced,
No hat upon his head, his stockings fouled,   80
Ungartered, and down-gyved to his ankle,
Pale as his shirt, his knees knocking each other,
And with a look so piteous in purport
As if he had been loosed out of hell
To speak of horrors – he comes before me.   85

Ophelia reports how Hamlet acted in her presence, holding her by the wrist, gazing at her and sighing, and then keeping his eyes fixed on her as he left the room. When he hears this, Polonius concludes that Hamlet's love is genuine, after all, and that Ophelia's obedience in rejecting his advances has driven him mad. Polonius says they must go to the King.

91 perusal: study
92 As 'a: as if he
96 bulk: body, frame
101 bended their light on me: gazed at me
104 Whose...itself: the violent nature of which leads to self-destruction
113 quoted: observed
114 wreck: ruin
  beshrew my jealousy: curse my suspicious nature!
115 it is as proper...discretion: it is as common for old people to see too much in what goes on, as for the young ones to lack sound judgement in such matters

> • *Why do you think Hamlet (1) said nothing and (2) acted as he did in Ophelia's presence? From the evidence is it likely that Polonius has got it right?*

POLONIUS   Mad for thy love?

OPHELIA   My lord I do not know,
But truly I do fear it.

POLONIUS   What said he?

OPHELIA   He took me by the wrist, and held me hard;
Then goes he to the length of all his arm,
And with his other hand thus o'er his brow,   90
He falls to such perusal of my face
As 'a would draw it. Long stayed he so;
At last, a little shaking of mine arm,
And thrice his head thus waving up and down,
He raised a sigh so piteous and profound   95
As it did seem to shatter all his bulk,
And end his being; that done, he lets me go,
And with his head over his shoulder turned,
He seemed to find his way without his eyes,
For out a-doors he went without their helps,   100
And to the last bended their light on me.

POLONIUS   Come, go with me, I will go seek the King.
This is the very ecstasy of love,
Whose violent property fordoes itself,
And leads the will to desperate undertakings   105
As oft as any passion under heaven
That does afflict our natures. I am sorry.
What, have you given him any hard words of late?

OPHELIA   No my good lord, but as you did command,
I did repel his letters, and denied   110
His access to me.

POLONIUS   That hath made him mad.
I am sorry that with better heed and judgement
I had not quoted him. I feared he did but trifle,
And meant to wreck thee, but beshrew my jealousy.
By heaven it is as proper to our age   115
To cast beyond ourselves in our opinions,
As it is common for the younger sort
To lack discretion. Come, go we to the King.

Polonius believes that it would be more dangerous to conceal what he sees now as Hamlet's true feelings than to reveal what he knows to the King and Queen.

119 **close**: secret
   which...love: this must be made known which, if it was concealed, might cause more grief

Claudius, with his Queen, is receiving Rosencrantz and Guildenstern, for whom he has sent. They have known Hamlet from his earliest years, Claudius says, and he hopes that if they keep company with Hamlet they may find out what is causing his present disturbed behaviour. The Queen supports him in this, and promises their gratitude.

2 **Moreover that**: in addition to the fact that
6 **Sith...that it was**: since neither his outward appearance nor his personality is as it was before
7 **that it was**: what it used to be
8 **put him...of himself**: so parted him from his right mind
12 **sith...haviour**: since that time you have been so close to his youthful interests
13 **vouchsafe your rest**: agree to stay
15 **to gather...remedy**: Claudius asks the two, as they keep Hamlet company, to take every opportunity to pick up any pointers to what is troubling Hamlet. Once this is discovered, Claudius says, perhaps he can help Hamlet.
21 **adheres**: feels himself close
22 **gentry**: courtesy
24 **supply and profit of our hope**: assistance and advancement of what we hope for
26 **remembrance**: recognition

• *Look for truth and lies and diplomatic utterances cloaking villainy.*

This must be known, which, being kept close might move
More grief to hide than hate to utter love.   [*Exeunt* 120

Scene 2

Flourish. Enter KING, QUEEN, ROSENCRANTZ,
GUILDENSTERN, *and Attendants*

KING   Welcome dear Rosencrantz and Guildenstern.
Moreover that we much did long to see you,
The need we have to use you did provoke
Our hasty sending. Something have you heard
Of Hamlet's transformation; so call it,   5
Sith nor th' exterior nor the inward man
Resembles that it was. What it should be,
More than his father's death, that thus hath put
    him
So much from th' understanding of himself,
I cannot dream of. I entreat you both,   10
That being of so young days brought up with him,
And sith so neighboured to his youth and haviour,
That you vouchsafe your rest here in our court
Some little time, so by your companies
To draw him on to pleasures, and to gather,   15
So much as from occasion you may glean,
Whether aught to us unknown afflicts him thus
That opened lies within our remedy.

QUEEN   Good gentlemen, he hath much talked of you,
And sure I am, two men there are not living   20
To whom he more adheres. If it will please you
To show us so much gentry and good will,
As to expend your time with us awhile,
For the supply and profit of our hope,
Your visitation shall receive such thanks   25
As fits a King's remembrance.

Rosencrantz and Guildenstern accept their mission, pointing out that they could have been ordered, not merely requested, to carry out this task. They are led away to Hamlet. Polonius comes to announce the return of ambassadors who had been sent to Norway. He also suggests that he has found the cause of Hamlet's madness, as he calls it.

27 by the sovereign power: ie because they are their king and queen

28 dread pleasures: *'dread'* was usually used in addressing royalty – as 'my dread lord'. A different phrase is created here, to sound excessive, and slightly silly.

30 bent: extent (as in a bow fully bent)

42 still: always

44 hold: maintain. My duty and my soul are God's and the King's to command.

47 Hunts...used to do: is not as hot on the trail of matters of state as it once was

52 fruit: fruit as dessert

53 grace: honour

ROSENCRANTZ   Both your majesties
           Might by the sovereign power you have of us,
           Put your dread pleasures more into command
           Than to entreaty.

GUILDENSTERN   But we both obey,
           And here give up ourselves, in the full bent,   30
           To lay our service freely at your feet
           To be commanded.

KING   Thanks Rosencrantz and gentle Guildenstern.

QUEEN   Thanks Guildenstern and gentle Rosencrantz.
           And I beseech you instantly to visit   35
           My too much changed son. Go some of you,
           And bring these gentlemen where Hamlet is.

GUILDENSTERN Heavens make our presence and our practices
           Pleasant and helpful to him.

QUEEN   Ay, amen.

      [*Exeunt* ROSENCRANTZ, GUILDENSTERN, *and some* ATTENDANTS

           Enter POLONIUS

POLONIUS   Th' ambassadors from Norway, my good lord,   40
           Are joyfully returned.

KING   Thou still hast been the father of good news.

POLONIUS   Have I my lord? I assure my good liege,
           I hold my duty as I hold my soul,
           Both to my God, and to my gracious King.   45
           And I do think – or else this brain of mine
           Hunts not the trail of policy so sure
           As it hath used to do – that I have found
           The very cause of Hamlet's lunacy.

KING   O speak of that, that do I long to hear.   50

POLONIUS   Give first admittance to th' ambassadors;
           My news shall be the fruit to that great feast.

KING   Thyself do grace to them, and bring them in.

                                    [*Exit* POLONIUS

Valtemand and Cornelius have been on a successful mission to Norway. The king, uncle of young Fortinbras, discovered that the army raised by his nephew was to march against Denmark. He put a stop to this, made the young man promise not to threaten Denmark again and asked for safe passage for the army through Denmark when it was sent against the Poles instead.

55 **head**: origin
   distemper: affliction, sickness
58 **sift him**: examine him closely
61 **Upon our first**: on the first expression of our views
66 **impotence**: helplessness
67 **falsely borne in hand**: taken advantage of
   Was/sends: note the change in style of the report here. So far, Valtemand has reported on the facts of the success of their mission in the past tense. From here on, the present tense and the omission of the subject of the sentence, when it is 'understood' makes for a more immediate and dramatic report – almost like a modern sports commentary. Claudius is meant to gain the impression that the ambassadors have been clever and efficient. Note, too, the diplomatic and face-saving elements in the gift of money to young Fortinbras, the discovery of a more satisfactory enemy, and the request for safe passage through Denmark.
69 **in fine**: in conclusion
71 **assay**: trial (of strength) – never again to take up arms
81 **our more considered time**: when we have more time for consideration

- *Note the second instalment of the Fortinbras story.*

He tells me, my dear Gertrude, he hath found
The head and source of all your son's distemper.   55

QUEEN   I doubt it is no other but the main,
His father's death, and our o'erhasty marriage.

KING   Well, we shall sift him.

Enter POLONIUS, *with* VALTEMAND *and* CORNELIUS

Welcome, my good friends.
Say Valtemand, what from our brother Norway?

VALTEMAND   Most fair return of greetings and desires.   60
Upon our first, he sent out to suppress
His nephew's levies, which to him appeared
To be a preparation 'gainst the Polack;
But better looked into, he truly found
It was against your highness; whereat grieved   65
That so his sickness, age, and impotence
Was falsely borne in hand, sends out arrests
On Fortinbras; which he in brief obeys,
Receives rebuke from Norway, and in fine,
Makes vow before his uncle never more   70
To give th' assay of arms against your majesty.
Whereon old Norway, overcome with joy,
Gives him three score thousand crowns in
    annual fee,
And his commission to employ those soldiers,
So levied, as before, against the Polack,   75
With an entreaty, herein further shown,
                            [*Giving a paper*
That it might please you to give quiet pass
Through your dominions for this enterprise,
On such regards of safety and allowance
As therein are set down.

KING   It likes us well;   80
And at our more considered time, we'll read,
Answer, and think upon this business.
Meantime, we thank you for your well-took labour.
Go to your rest, at night we'll feast together.

When Valtemand and Cornelius have left, Polonius indulges in a lengthy introduction to what he has discovered about Hamlet's sickness. He gets tied up in his own wordiness and then comes to the point and starts to read one of Hamlet's letters to Ophelia, which is in a very exaggerated style.

86 expostulate: set out one's views, discuss
90 wit: mental powers, intellect
91 tediousness: long-windedness
  flourishes: ornaments, embellishments, decoration
93 Mad...let that go: Polonius has found himself trapped in a circular argument of his own making – '*to define true madness* ' is to be '*mad*' – and hastily abandons it
95 More matter with less art: the Queen demands more substance with less ornamentation
98 figure: ie figure of speech
99 farewell it: say farewell to it
103 For this...by cause: this unfortunate madness we have observed does have a cause
105 Perpend: consider
108 gather and surmise: draw your conclusions
113 &c: (et cetera) the continuation of the greeting at the beginning of the letter, a recognized formula
115 faithful: true to you

- *Look at – or rather listen to – Polonius's way with words. Observe too, throughout the play, the fun Shakespeare has with language. In addition to Polonius, the list will include Rosencrantz and Guildenstern; the language of love letters; some 'dramatic' language; Osric; the grave-digger. Notice how we are often led to understand the nonsense effect by people's reaction to what is said.*

                       Most welcome home.

                            [*Exeunt* VALTEMAND *and* CORNELIUS

POLONIUS   This business is well ended. 85
My liege, and madam, to expostulate
What majesty should be, what duty is,
Why day is day, night night, and time is time,
Were nothing but to waste night, day, and time.
Therefore since brevity is the soul of wit,   90
And tediousness the limbs and outward flourishes,
I will be brief: your noble son is mad.
Mad call I it, for to define true madness,
What is 't but to be nothing else but mad?
But let that go.

QUEEN   More matter with less art.   95

POLONIUS Madam, I swear I use no art at all.
That he's mad 'tis true, 'tis true 'tis pity,
And pity 'tis 'tis true – a foolish figure,
But farewell it, for I will use no art.
Mad let us grant him then, and now remains   100
That we find out the cause of this effect,
Or rather say, the cause of this defect,
For this effect defective comes by cause.
Thus it remains, and the remainder thus.
Perpend;   105
I have a daughter – have while she is mine –
Who in her duty and obedience, mark,
Hath given me this. Now gather and surmise.

                                [*Reads*

'To the celestial and my soul's idol, the most
beautified Ophelia' – That's an ill phrase,   110
a vile phrase; 'beautified' is a vile phrase, but you
shall hear. Thus: 'In her excellent white bosom,
these, &c.'

QUEEN Came this from Hamlet to her?

POLONIUS Good madam stay awhile; I will be faithful.   115
     'Doubt thou the stars are fire;

Polonius finishes reading Hamlet's love-letter and Claudius
asks how Ophelia has received these declarations of love.
Polonius protests that he is faithful to the King and Queen
and that he told Ophelia not to see or speak to Hamlet.
When Hamlet was rejected, Polonius continues, he became
melancholy.

120 ill at these numbers: no good at writing verse
124 machine is to him: he still has this body
126 And more above...to mine ear: furthermore she has told
  me about all his approaches to her, as and when they
  happened, how they were communicated and where
131 fain: gladly
136 played the desk, or table-book: ie registered what was
  happening and let it continue
137 given...and dumb: flattered my feelings by turning a
  blind eye and saying nothing
138 Or...idle sight: gazed idly at this love without realizing
  what was going on
139 round: openly
141 out of thy star: above your position in life, out of your
  orbit
142 prescripts: instructions
143 resort: visit
144 tokens: little presents
145 took the fruits: reaped the benefit
146 he repelled: when he had been rejected, he...
148 Thence to a watch: from that to staying awake all night
149 lightness: lightheartedness
  declension: downward slope

> • *We have further insights into Polonius's character and
> the way he regards his responsibilities.*

> Doubt that the sun doth move;
> Doubt truth to be a liar;
> But never doubt I love.
>
> O dear Ophelia, I am ill at these numbers, I have 120
> not art to reckon my groans; but that I love thee
> best, O most best, believe it. Adieu.
>
> Thine evermore most dear lady, whilst this
> machine is to him, HAMLET.'
>
> This in obedience hath my daughter shown me, 125
> And more above, hath his solicitings,
> As they fell out by time, by means, and place,
> All given to mine ear.

KING   But how hath she
Received his love?

POLONIUS   What do you think of me?

KING   As of a man faithful and honourable.   130

POLONIUS   I would fain prove so. But what might you think,
When I had seen this hot love on the wing,
As I perceived it, I must tell you that,
Before my daughter told me, what might you,
Or my dear Majesty your Queen here think,   135
If I had played the desk, or table-book,
Or given my heart a winking, mute and dumb,
Or looked upon this love with idle sight;
What might you think? No, I went round to
    work,
And my young mistress thus I did bespeak: 140
'Lord Hamlet is a prince out of thy star;
This must not be'. And then I prescripts gave her
That she should lock herself from his resort,
Admit no messengers, receive no tokens.
Which done, she took the fruits of my advice;   145
And he repelled, a short tale to make,
Fell into a sadness, then into a fast,
Thence to a watch, thence into a weakness,
Thence to a lightness, and, by this declension,

Polonius finishes his explanation of Hamlet's decline into
madness. He suggests that to check on his theory they
secretly observe a meeting between Ophelia and Hamlet,
which Polonius will contrive.

159 centre: centre of the earth, the most inaccessible place
   try: test
161 lobby: ante-room
162 loose: let loose. This suggests that Polonius looks on
   Ophelia as being in his keeping, more like a dog than a
   daughter. There is the added suggestion of 'loosing' an
   animal for breeding purposes.
163 arras: wall-hanging
165 be...thereon: has not lost his reason as a result
166 Let me...carters: if Polonius is wrong he will claim he is
   no longer fit to be a counsellor, but he'll run a farm and
   men who drive carts
170 board: speak to

	Into the madness wherein now he raves,	150
	And all we mourn for.	
KING	Do you think 'tis this?	
QUEEN	It may be, very like.	
POLONIUS	Hath there been such a time – I would fain know that –	
	That I have positively said ''Tis so',	
	When it proved otherwise?	
KING	Not that I know.	155
POLONIUS	[*Points to his head and shoulder*] Take this, from this, if this be otherwise.	
	If circumstances lead me, I will find	
	Where truth is hid, though it were hid indeed	
	Within the centre.	
KING	How may we try it further?	
POLONIUS	You know sometimes he walks four hours together	160
	Here in the lobby.	
QUEEN	So he does indeed.	
POLONIUS	At such a time, I'll loose my daughter to him.	
	Be you and I behind an arras then;	
	Mark the encounter; if he love her not,	
	And be not from his reason fall'n thereon,	165
	Let me be no assistant for a state,	
	But keep a farm and carters.	
KING	We will try it.	

Enter HAMLET

QUEEN	But look where sadly the poor wretch comes reading.	
POLONIUS	Away, I do beseech you both, away.	
	I'll board him presently.	

[*Exeunt* KING, QUEEN, *and* ATTENDANTS

O give me leave   170

Hamlet's replies when Polonius speaks to him seem to bear out the counsellor's opinion. The conversation sounds inconsequential and it soon turns on Ophelia. Hamlet's punning references and the quickness of his mind compared with his opponent's, make it easy for Polonius to draw the conclusions he wishes.

174 fishmonger: some see this merely as Hamlet's joke – to call the pompous, high-sounding counsellor a fishmonger. Others add the secondary meaning of 'pimp', since Polonius is about to send Ophelia to Hamlet.

181 For...carrion: it was thought that the action of the sun bred maggots in dead flesh – but maggots, of course, hatch from flies' eggs laid in the warm flesh. The carrion is sun-kissed and breeds maggots. If the son (the same punning reference was used in Act 1 scene 2) kisses the daughter, she may breed.

185 not...conceive: her child would be illegitimate

187 harping on: going on about

194 matter: the subject of the book (Hamlet is reading) *or* the quarrel. Hamlet chooses the meaning that Polonius does not intend.

197 satirical rogue: writer of the book. These contents enable Hamlet to be rude about Polonius indirectly, since it is 'in the book'.

199 purging thick amber: producing a yellowish discharge
plum-tree gum: a clear amber-coloured resin which is not only produced from the damaged tree bark, but also from the stone-end of the plum itself. It is very sticky.

200 wit: understanding

201 weak hams: weak muscles at the back of the thighs and in the buttocks

> • *Investigate the signs indicating real or assumed madness in Hamlet.*

	How does my good Lord Hamlet?	
HAMLET	Well, God-a-mercy.	
POLONIUS	Do you know me my lord?	
HAMLET	Excellent well, you are a fishmonger.	
POLONIUS	Not I my lord.	175
HAMLET	Then I would you were so honest a man.	
POLONIUS	Honest, my lord?	
HAMLET	Ay sir, to be honest as this world goes, is to be one man picked out of ten thousand.	
POLONIUS	That's very true my lord.	180
HAMLET	For if the sun breed maggots in a dead dog, being a good kissing carrion – have you a daughter?	
POLONIUS	I have my lord.	
HAMLET	Let her not walk i' th' sun. Conception is a blessing, but not as your daughter may conceive – friend look to 't.	185
POLONIUS	[*Aside*] How say you by that? Still harping on my daughter. Yet he knew me not at first; 'a said I was a fishmonger: 'a is far gone, far gone, and truly in my youth I suffered much extremity for love, very near this. I'll speak to him again. What do you read my lord?	190
HAMLET	Words, words, words.	
POLONIUS	What is the matter my lord?	
HAMLET	Between who?	195
POLONIUS	I mean the matter that you read, my lord.	
HAMLET	Slanders sir, for the satirical rogue says here that old men have grey beards, that their faces are wrinkled, their eyes purging thick amber and plum-tree gum, and that they have a plentiful lack of wit, together with most weak hams; all which sir, though I most powerfully and potently believe, yet	200

Hamlet continues to talk intelligent nonsense or nonsensical intelligence – Polonius in asides recognizes method in his madness. Polonius intends to proceed with the Ophelia plan and takes his leave. Rosencrantz and Guildenstern find Hamlet and the three exchange greetings, with Hamlet still in a rather provocative vein.

209 **out of the air**: this could be assumed to mean 'the open air' but they are in the ante-room. It could mean 'out of the draught' as he is considered to be sick, or similarly, out of an airy room into a darkened sickroom.

210 **pregnant**: quick-witted, full of meaning
happiness: aptness, appropriateness

212 **delivered of**: this picks up the 'pregnant' metaphor

218 **withal – except my life**: with – and again the suggestion of suicide

229 **As...earth**: neither well nor badly, like most human beings

231 **not the very button...shoe?**: neither right at the top nor at the very bottom

> • *Examine the double act of Rosencrantz and Guildenstern. Their names mean 'wreath' (or garland) of roses' and 'golden star' – do you think these names might have any special significance?*

	I hold it not honesty to have it thus set down; for yourself sir should be old as I am, if like a crab you could go backward.
	205
POLONIUS	[*Aside*] Though this be madness, yet there is method in't. Will you walk out of the air my lord?
HAMLET	Into my grave.
POLONIUS	Indeed that's out of the air. [*Aside*] How pregnant sometimes his replies are; a happiness 210 that often madness hits on, which reason and sanity could not so prosperously be delivered of. I will leave him, and suddenly contrive the means of meeting between him and my daughter – my honourable lord, I will most humbly take my 215 leave of you.
HAMLET	You cannot sir take from me any thing that I will more willingly part withal – except my life, except my life, except my life.
POLONIUS	Fare you well my lord. 220
HAMLET	These tedious old fools.

Enter ROSENCRANTZ *and* GUILDENSTERN

POLONIUS	You go to seek the Lord Hamlet, there he is.
ROSENCRANTZ	[*To Polonius*] God save you sir. [*Exit* POLONIUS
GUILDENSTERN	My honoured lord
ROSENCRANTZ	My most dear lord 225
HAMLET	My excellent good friends. How dost thou Guildenstern? Ah Rosencrantz. Good lads how do ye both?
ROSENCRANTZ	As the indifferent children of the earth.
GUILDENSTERN	Happy, in that we are not over-happy; 230 On Fortune's cap we are not the very button.
HAMLET	Nor the soles of her shoe?
ROSENCRANTZ	Neither my lord.

Hamlet talks to Rosencrantz and Guildenstern in much the
same style as he did with Polonius. He calls Denmark a
prison and admits to bad dreams but he does not take these
old acquaintances into his confidence.

234 the middle of her favours: Fortune's favours, with the
   suggestion of sexual favours
236 her privates we: we are her private parts *or* ordinary
   subjects *or*, rather against the sense so far, intimate
237 secret parts: private parts
238 strumpet: whore. The goddess Fortune is commonly
   accused of distributing her favours at random.
241 Then is doomsday near: the end of the world must be
   approaching because honesty and the world cannot exist
   together
248 confines, wards, and dungeons: places of imprisonment
252 nothing...thinking makes it so: it's all a question of
   mental attitude. A common theme in literature of the
   period.
260 Which dreams...dream: the dreams are themselves
   ambition, for the dream of the ambition comes first and
   the achievement copies, is the shadow of, the original
   dream.
266 Then are...shadows: Hamlet, in debating style, takes this
   clever argument to its conclusion. Beggars have no
   ambition, so they must be bodies and not shadows. Kings
   and heroes, presumably ambitious, must supply shadows
   for the beggars. The word *'outstretched'* is suitable for
   heroes who have reached out to grasp their ambition, or
   for long shadows.

> • *Can you distinguish any differences in the form
> Hamlet's madness takes, depending on the company he
> is in?*

HAMLET	Then you live about her waist, or in the middle
	or her favours? 235
GUILDENSTERN	Faith her privates we.
HAMLET	In the secret parts of Fortune? O most true, she is a
	strumpet. What news?
ROSENCRANTZ	None my lord, but that the world's grown
	honest. 240
HAMLET	Then is doomsday near – but your news is not true.
	Let me question more in particular. What have you,
	my good friends, deserved at the hands of Fortune,
	that she sends you to prison hither?
GUILDENSTERN	Prison my lord? 245
HAMLET	Denmark's a prison.
ROSENCRANTZ	Then is the world one.
HAMLET	A goodly one, in which there are many confines,
	wards, and dungeons, Denmark being one o'
	th' worst. 250
ROSENCRANTZ	We think not so my lord.
HAMLET	Why then 'tis none to you; for there is nothing
	either good or bad but thinking makes it so. To me
	it is a prison.
ROSENCRANTZ	Why then your ambition makes it one; 'tis too 255
	narrow for your mind.
HAMLET	O God, I could be bounded in a nutshell, and
	count myself a king of infinite space, were it not
	that I have bad dreams.
GUILDENSTERN	Which dreams indeed are ambition, for the 260
	very substance of the ambitious is merely the
	shadow of a dream.
HAMLET	A dream itself is but a shadow.
ROSENCRANTZ	Truly, and I hold ambition of so airy and light
	a quality, that it is but a shadow's shadow. 265
HAMLET	Then are our beggars bodies, and our monarchs

Hamlet asks why they have come to Elsinore. He suggests they were sent for and gets them to admit it. He starts to tell them why, so that they need not break any promise of secrecy to the King and Queen.

268 fay: faith
270 sort you: class you, include you
272 I am...attended: I have useless servants, possibly also a reference to being 'attended' by bad dreams
273 beaten way: beaten track
276 Beggar that I am: he refers to their earlier conversation, claiming he is without ambition
277 too dear a halfpenny: not worth much at all
278 Is it...visitation?: is it your own idea, have you come to visit of your own free will?
282 Why...purpose: Hamlet is reminding them ironically that they are not supposed to tell him the truth
284 modesties: sense of shame
craft: cunning
288 conjure you: make a solemn appeal to you
289 by the consonancy of our youth: by the way we got on together in our youth
291 by what...withal: by whatever is more dear, which a better proposer of oaths might think up, to charge you with
292 be even...with me: level with me
295 of: on
298 my anticipation prevent your discovery: my telling you first will prevent your having to tell me

> • *Is it possible to make any useful distinction between Rosencrantz and Guildenstern?*

and outstretched heroes the beggars' shadows.
Shall we to th' court, for by my fay I cannot reason?

ROSENCRANTZ } We'll wait upon you.
GUILDENSTERN }

HAMLET   No such matter. I will not sort you with the   270
              rest of my servants; for to speak to you like an
              honest man, I am most dreadfully attended. But,
              in the beaten way of friendship, what make you at
              Elsinore?

ROSENCRANTZ To visit you my lord, no other occasion.   275

HAMLET   Beggar that I am, I am even poor in thanks, but I
              thank you; and sure, dear friends, my thanks are too
              dear a halfpenny. Were you not sent for? Is it your
              own inclining? Is it a free visitation? Come, come,
              deal justly with me. Come, come – nay, speak.   280

GUILDENSTERN What should we say my lord?

HAMLET   Why, any thing but to th' purpose. You were sent
              for, and there is a kind of confession in your looks,
              which your modesties have not craft enough to
              colour. I know the good King and Queen have 285
              sent for you.

ROSENCRANTZ To what end my lord?

HAMLET   That you must teach me. But let me conjure you,
              by the rights of our fellowship, by the consonancy
              of our youth, by the obligation of our ever-   290
              preserved love, and by what more dear a better
              proposer can charge you withal, be even and direct
              with me, whether you were sent for or no?

ROSENCRANTZ [*Aside to* GUILDENSTERN] What say you?

HAMLET   [*Aside*] Nay then I have an eye of you. If you 295
              love me, hold not off.

GUILDENSTERN My lord, we were sent for.

HAMLET   I will tell you why; so shall my anticipation prevent

Hamlet explains his present mood without giving much
away. He builds up the conventional view of the earth and of
man, only to destroy the illusion of beauty and excellence. A
company of actors is on its way to the castle.

300 moult no feather: remain whole, keep its integrity
301 forgone...exercises: done without all my usual sporting
activities
302 it goes...disposition: I am in such low spirits
303 that...promontory: that this splendid structure, the
earth, seems to me a barren headland
305 brave o'erhanging firmament: fine sky hanging over us
306 fretted with golden fire: patterned with stars. These are
references also to the theatre building.
308 pestilent...vapours: poisonous mass of foggy air
310 faculties: his abilities
form and moving: shape and movement
311 express: appropriate
312 apprehension: understanding
313 paragon: most perfect example
314 quintessence: the most essential element; in medieval
philosophy the substance of which the stars and planets
were made, and present in all things
321 lenten: entertainment in Lent, a time of fasting, would
not be very lavish
322 coted: overtook
325 tribute on me: his dues from me – hospitality and
payment
326 foil and target: sword and shield
327 gratis: (Latin) for nothing, in vain
the humorous man: a stock character; humour in the
Elizabethan sense (see note Act 1 scene 4 line 27). This
was an eccentric character who would quarrel and fall into
rages.
329 tickle a th' sere: easily set off. The sere is the catch which
keeps the hammer of a gun at full or half cock.
331 halt for 't: sound lame and stumbling as a result
333 tragedians: troupe of actors
334 Their residence...both ways: they were doubly better off
when they stayed put

your discovery, and your secrecy to the King and
Queen moult no feather. I have of late, but   300
wherefore I know not, lost all my mirth, forgone all
custom of exercises; and indeed it goes so heavily
with my disposition, that this goodly frame the
earth, seems to me a sterile promontory, this most
excellent canopy the air, look you, this brave   305
o'erhanging firmament, this majestical roof fretted
with golden fire, why, it appears no other thing to
me but a foul and pestilent congregation of
vapours. What a piece of work is a man, how noble
in reason, how infinite in faculties, in form and   310
moving, how express and admirable in action, how
like an angel in apprehension, how like a god: the
beauty of the world, the paragon of animals. And
yet to me, what is this quintessence of dust? Man
delights not me; no, nor woman neither,   315
though by your smiling you seem to say so.

ROSENCRANTZ My lord, there was no such stuff in my thoughts.

HAMLET Why did ye laugh then, when I said 'man delights
not me'?

ROSENCRANTZ To think, my lord, if you delight not in man,   320
what lenten entertainment the players shall receive
from you. We coted them on the way, and hither
are they coming to offer you service.

HAMLET He that plays the king shall be welcome – his
majesty shall have tribute on me; the   325
adventurous knight shall use his foil and target, the
lover shall not sigh gratis, the humorous man shall
end his part in peace, the clown shall make those
laugh whose lungs are tickle a th' sere, and the lady
shall say her mind freely – or the blank verse   330
shall halt for 't. What players are they?

ROSENCRANTZ Even those you were wont to take such delight
in, the tragedians of the city.

HAMLET How chances it they travel? Their residence both in

The talk is of the current disputes in the London theatre.
Newly-formed troupes of child actors are all the rage.
Playwrights criticize and satirize established adult actors.

336 I think...innovation: I think they have been forbidden to
   play in the city because of the recent upheavals. This could
   mean the King's death, his widow's remarriage and the
   preparations for war. Some believe it also refers to the new
   children's acting companies, which had recently become
   popular, and the rebellion by the Earl of Essex in 1601.

338 Do...followed?: are they still as well thought of as when I
   was in the city? Do they still have such a following?

342 endeavour: efforts

343 aery of children, little eyases: brood of children, young
   hawks. The reference is to the young choristers of the
   Chapel Royal and St. Paul's, who acted plays.

344 cry out on the top of question: in their high voices they
   carry on the argument (the dispute about child actors)

345 tyrannically: unjustly

346 berattle the common stages: fill the public playhouses
   with the row they make

347 that many...thither: many young men wearing swords
   are afraid of (what may have been written by) goose quills
   and hardly dare show themselves at the theatre

349 How...sing?: How are they looked after financially? Will
   they only follow their profession until their voices break?

353 common players: professional actors
   if their...better: if they find no better means of making a
   living

354 their...succession: their writers are damaging the children's
   future. They will be adult actors themselves one day.

357 to do: unruliness

358 tarre them: incite them, drive them on

359 no money...question: only plays where writers of children's
   plays and adult actors attacked each other made money

364 carry it away?: win

365 Hercules and his load too: Hercules' load is the world
   which he was often depicted as carrying on his back. This
   is also supposed to have been the symbol for the Globe
   Theatre.

368 make mouths at him: make faces at him (behind his back)

| | reputation and profit was better both ways. | 335 |

ROSENCRANTZ I think their inhibition comes by the means of
the late innovation.

HAMLET Do they hold the same estimation they did when I
was in the city? Are they so followed?

ROSENCRANTZ No indeed are they not.   340

HAMLET How comes it? Do they grow rusty?

ROSENCRANTZ Nay, their endeavour keeps in the wonted
pace; but there is sir, an aery of children, little
eyases, that cry out on the top of question, and are
most tyrannically clapped for 't; these are now   345
the fashion, and so berattle the common stages – so
they call them – that many wearing rapiers are
afraid of goose-quills, and dare scarce come thither.

HAMLET What, are they children? Who maintains 'em? How
are they escoted? Will they pursue the quality   350
no longer than they can sing? Will they not say
afterwards, if they should grow themselves to
common players – as it is most like, if their
means are no better – their writers do them wrong,
to make them exclaim against their own   355
succession?

ROSENCRANTZ Faith there has been much to do on both sides;
and the nation holds it no sin to tarre them to
controversy. There was for a while no money bid
for argument, unless the poet and the player   360
went to cuffs in the question.

HAMLET Is't possible?

GUILDENSTERN O there has been much throwing about of brains.

HAMLET Do the boys carry it away?

ROSENCRANTZ Ay, that they do my lord, Hercules and his   365
load too.

HAMLET It is not very strange, for mine uncle is King of
Denmark, and those that would make mouths at

Hamlet talks about his madness, knowing that word will get
back to the King and Queen. He mocks Polonius, out of
earshot, and hears from him of the actors' arrival.

370 ducats: gold or silver coins
   in little: in miniature
371 'S blood: God's blood! – an exclamation
372 philosophy: science
374 Your hands: the formal welcome after the earlier
   exchange of greetings
375 appurtenance: accompaniment
376 fashion and ceremony: greeting proper to the time and
   the circumstances
   comply...garb: do what is right in this area
377 lest my extent...yours: in case the welcome I extend to
   the players, which I tell you must be made obvious,
   should seem to be better than the one I give you
383 I am but mad...southerly: a reference to the supposed
   influence of the weather on madness, and an insistence to
   Rosencrantz and Guildenstern that he is not mad all the
   time. Hamlet knows they will be reporting back and
   anything which might confuse them must be good for him.
384 a hawk from a handsaw: some commentators insist that
   Hamlet is saying he can tell one bird from another, or one
   tool from another. In this case *'handsaw'* becomes
   'hernshaw' (heron) or *'hawk'* becomes the small board
   which plasterers use. Others want to make his madness
   seem more extreme by his claiming to distinguish bird
   from tool. Another possibility is *'hawk'* meaning 'hack' (a
   garden tool, like a hoe), but Hamlet may well have
   wanted to show Rosencrantz and Guildenstern that he
   regards them as birds of prey.
388 swaddling-clouts: clothes in which a baby was wrapped
   tightly
389 Happily: perhaps
390 twice a child: in his second childhood
392 you say right sir...indeed: Hamlet pretends there is a
   conversation going on which has not mentioned Polonius
395 When Roscius...Rome: a great and gifted Roman actor
398 Buz, buz!: a stock response to a rumour that is not
   believed

him while my father lived, give twenty, forty, fifty, a
hundred ducats apiece for his picture in little.   370
'S blood, there is something in this more than
natural, if philosophy could find it out.

[*Flourish of trumpets within*

GUILDENSTERN There are the players.

HAMLET   Gentlemen, you are welcome to Elsinore. Your
              hands. Come then, th' appurtenance of   375
              welcome is fashion and ceremony; let me comply
              with you in this garb, lest my extent to the players,
              which I tell you must show fairly outwards, should
              more appear like entertainment than yours. You are
              welcome; but my uncle-father and aunt-mother 380
              are deceived.

GUILDENSTERN In what my dear lord?

HAMLET   I am but mad north-north-west; when the wind is
              southerly I know a hawk from a handsaw.

              Enter POLONIUS

POLONIUS   Well be with you, gentlemen.   385

HAMLET   Hark you Guildenstern, and you too, at each ear
              a hearer – that great baby you see there is not yet
              out of his swaddling-clouts.

ROSENCRANTZ Happily he's the second time come to them,
              for they say an old man is twice a child.   390

HAMLET   I will prophesy, he comes to tell me of the players,
              mark it – you say right sir, a Monday morning,
              'twas then indeed.

POLONIUS   My lord, I have news to tell you.

HAMLET   My lord, I have news to tell you. When Roscius 395
              was an actor in Rome –

POLONIUS   The actors are come hither my lord.

HAMLET   Buz, buz!

POLONIUS   Upon mine honour –

Polonius continues to talk of the theatre, whereas Hamlet immediately returns to talk of daughters. The troupe of players arrives and Hamlet greets them like old friends.

400 on his ass: Hamlet may be using the repeat of upon/on to mock Polonius's honour, with a *punning* reference to 'arse'. (see GLOSSARY page 335)

401 tragedy...historical-pastoral: Polonius rattles through the categories of plays, but much drama could not even then sensibly be categorized like this, as Shakespeare is telling us.

404 scene individable...unlimited: in the first, the action takes place in one spot, whereas in *'poem unlimited'* there could be many scenes. Goethe, the eighteenth century German playwright, used Shakespeare's innovative work in this area as a pattern for the writing of short scenes which allowed dramatic changes of place and pace.

405 Seneca: Roman tragic dramatist

406 Plautus: Roman comic dramatist. Both would have been well known to Elizabethan audiences.
the law of writ and the liberty: Polonius claims they wrote plays that kept to the rules and sometimes remained free of them

408 Jephthah: Jephthah (*Judges 11 30–40*) vowed that if God gave him victory over the Ammonites, he would sacrifice the first living creature to come out of his house on his return. This was his only child, his daughter, and he had to sacrifice her. She begged for time to go into the hills to mourn the fact that she would die a virgin. Ophelia too will die a virgin.

421 As by lot...was: Hamlet quotes from a popular ballad called *Jephthah, Judge of Israel*

424 the first row...comes: the first line of the pious ballad will have to lead you in to the rest – for my recitation of it is cut short here (by the entrance of the actors)

428 valanced: fringed – he has grown a beard, hence the pun in *'beard me'* – confront me

431 nearer to heaven: taller

432 altitude of a chopine: height of a shoe with a thick cork sole

HAMLET   Then came each actor on his ass –   400

POLONIUS   The best actors in the world, either for tragedy,
            comedy, history, pastoral, pastoral-comical,
            historical-pastoral, tragical-historical, tragical-
            comical-historical-pastoral, scene individable, or
            poem unlimited. Seneca cannot be too heavy,   405
            nor Plautus too light for the law of writ and the
            liberty. These are the only men.

HAMLET   O Jephthah, judge of Israel, what a treasure hadst
            thou!

POLONIUS   What a treasure had he my lord?   410

HAMLET   Why
                 'One fair daughter, and no more,
                      The which he loved passing well'.

POLONIUS   [*Aside*] Still on my daughter.

HAMLET   Am I not i' th' right old Jephthah?   415

POLONIUS   If you call me Jephthah my lord, I have a daughter
            that I love passing well.

HAMLET   Nay that follows not.

POLONIUS   What follows then my lord?

HAMLET   Why   420
                 'As by lot, God wot',
            and then you know
                 'It came to pass, as most like it was' –
            the first row of the pious chanson will show you
            more, for look where my abridgment comes.   425

            Enter PLAYERS

            You are welcome masters, welcome all, I am
            glad to see thee well. Welcome good friends. O my
            old friend, why thy face is valanced since I saw thee
            last; com'st thou to beard me in Denmark? What,
            my young lady and mistress; by 'r lady, your   430
            ladyship is nearer to heaven than when I saw
            you last by the altitude of a chopine. Pray God your

Hamlet remembers a speech from a play the actors once
performed and he quotes some of it. Its subject was the
revenge killing for the death of a father.

433 piece of...the ring: if a crack spread from the edge of a
coin to the ring containing the monarch's head it was no
longer 'good'. 'Cracked' may also refer to loss of virginity
or to the breaking of the boy's voice, spoiling his talent
for female roles.

434 We'll e'en to 't...we see: falcons were trained to bring
down one particular prey – but not in France. Hamlet
intends to attack Claudius through the actors.

437 quality: professional skills

442 caviare to the general: an acquired taste, not for people
in general

443 cried in the top of mine: were more valid than mine

444 well-digested in the scenes: the scenes well arranged

445 as much modesty as cunning: as much restraint as skill

447 sallets: salads – cold spicy dishes of a mix of vegetables
sometimes with egg, meat or fish. Here 'no variety or spice'.

448 indict...affection: accuse the author of pretence

449 as wholesome...than fine: as sound as it was pleasing,
owing more to a natural attractiveness than to a contrived
magnificence

456 Pyrrhus: when Troy was under siege by the Greeks
Pyrrhus went to avenge the death of Achilles, his father
Hyrcanian beast: tiger

458 rugged: rough

460 couched: hidden
ominous horse: the Greeks tricked the Trojans into
accepting an enormous wooden horse into their city. It
was full of fighting men. At night they killed the guards
and let in the Greek army.

461 complexion: appearance

462 heraldry: used here for 'colour'. After the killing he is
covered in blood; 'gules' is the heraldic word for red.

463 tricked: as in 'tricked out', decorated with

465 Baked...streets: baked on by the heat of the streets until
it forms a crust

466 tyrannous: harsh

voice like a piece of uncurrent gold be not cracked
within the ring. Masters, you are all welcome. We'll
e'en to 't like French falconers, fly at any thing   435
we see. We'll have a speech straight; come give us a
taste of your quality; come, a passionate speech.

FIRST PLAYER What speech my lord?

HAMLET I heard thee speak me a speech once, but it was
never acted, or if it was, not above once, for   440
the play I remember pleased not the million, 'twas
caviare to the general; but it was, as I received it,
and others, whose judgments in such matters cried
in the top of mine, an excellent play, well digested in
the scenes, set down with as much modesty as   445
cunning. I remember one said there were no
sallets in the lines to make the matter savoury, nor
no matter in the phrase that might indict the author
of affection, but called it an honest method, as
wholesome as sweet, and by very much more   450
handsome than fine. One speech in it I chiefly
loved, 'twas Æneas' tale to Dido, and thereabout of
it especially where he speaks of Priam's slaughter. If
it live in your memory, begin at this line – let me
see, let me see –   455
'The rugged Pyrrhus; like th' Hyrcanian beast' –
'tis not so, it begins with Pyrrhus –
  'The rugged Pyrrhus, he whose sable arms,
  Black as his purpose, did the night resemble
  When he lay couched in th' ominous horse,   460
  Hath now this dread and black complexion
    smeared
  With heraldry more dismal; head to foot
  Now is he total gules, horridly tricked
  With blood of fathers, mothers, daughters, sons,
  Baked and impasted with the parching
    streets,   465
  That lend a tyrannous and a damned light
  To their lord's murder. Roasted in wrath

The first player takes over the speech from Hamlet, describing the death of Priam in lurid terms.

468 **o'er-sized with coagulate gore**: coated with sticky clotted blood. 'Size' is a liquid glue.

469 **carbuncles**: precious stones, large and bulging and supposed to dart rays of light

473 **discretion**: judgement

Anon he finds him: he soon finds Priam

474 **antique**: ancient

475 **Rebellious to**: refusing to obey

476 **Repugnant to**: resisting

478 **with the whiff...sword**: struck by the draught of this dread sword. Shakespeare is here writing a *pastiche* (see GLOSSARY page 335) of the heroic drama of his day.

479 **unnerved**: weakened, grown old and feeble

senseless Ilium: Troy, insensible

481 **Stoops to his base**: falls to the ground

482 **Takes prisoner...to stick**: Pyrrhus was distracted as he heard the tremendous crash of the falling tower. His sword, which was slicing down on old Priam's white head, seemed to halt, held in mid-air.

485 **painted tyrant**: tyrant in a painting

486 **like a neutral...matter**: like someone who has not taken sides, Pyrrhus stood unable to take action

488 **against some storm**: when a storm is near

489 **the rack**: the massed clouds

490 **the orb below**: the earth

492 **Doth rend the region**: tears the sky apart

494 **Cyclops**: giants with one eye in the middle of their forehead. It was their job to forge iron for Vulcan, the gods' blacksmith, on Mount Aetna.

495 **Mars's armour**: the god of war's armour

proof eterne: everlasting resistance

498 **strumpet Fortune**: Fortune, the whore – *personification* of an abstract idea (see GLOSSARY page 335)

499 **synod**: assembly

500 **fellies**: wooden pieces forming the rim of a wheel

501 **nave**: hub of a wheel, navel, with a pun on 'knave' meaning 'rogue'

         and fire,
         And thus o'er-sized with coagulate gore,
         With eyes like carbuncles, the hellish Pyrrhus
         Old grandsire Priam seeks'.   470
         So proceed you.

POLONIUS   'Fore God my lord, well spoken, with good accent
         and good discretion.

FIRST PLAYER   'Anon he finds him
         Striking too short at Greeks; his antique sword,
         Rebellious to his arm, lies where it falls,   475
         Repugnant to command; unequal matched,
         Pyrrhus at Priam drives, in rage strikes wide,
         But with the whiff and wind of his fell sword
         Th' unnerved father falls. Then senseless Ilium,
         Seeming to feel this blow, with flaming top   480
         Stoops to his base; and with a hideous crash
         Takes prisoner Pyrrhus' ear; for lo, his sword
         Which was declining on the milky head
         Of reverend Priam, seemed i' th' air to stick;
         So as a painted tyrant Pyrrhus stood,   485
         And like a neutral to his will and matter,
         Did nothing.
         But as we often see against some storm
         A silence in the heavens, the rack stand still,
         The bold winds speechless, and the orb below   490
         As hush as death, anon the dreadful thunder
         Doth rend the region; so after Pyrrhus' pause,
         Aroused vengeance sets him new a-work;
         And never did the Cyclops' hammers fall
         On Mars's armour forged for proof eterne   495
         With less remorse than Pyrrhus' bleeding sword
         Now falls on Priam.
         Out, out, thou strumpet Fortune! All you gods,
         In general synod take away her power,
         Break all the spokes and fellies from her wheel, 500
         And bowl the round nave down the hill of
            heaven,

The first player continues his lines, as requested, with the speech about Hecuba, Priam's wife, and her reaction to his death. The actor is moved by his own acting, and Polonius calls a halt to it. Hamlet tells him to make sure the players are well looked after.

502 fiends: devils
505 jig or tale of bawdry: song and dance (with which a play often ended) or lewd tale
506 Hecuba: Priam's second wife, alleged to have borne him nineteen children
507 mobled: with her face muffled, covered up
511 bisson rheum: tears half-blinding her
a clout...diadem: a cloth wrapped around the head which recently wore a crown
513 About...loins: round about her shrunken loins, exhausted with child-bearing
515 Who this had seen...pronounced: anyone who had seen this would, with a poisonous tongue, have declared treason against the state ruled by Fortune
517 did see: had seen
520 instant burst of clamour: sudden scream
522 Would have made milch...gods': would have made the burning stars weep tears of milk and created passion in the gods' eyes
524 Look, whe'r: (whether) see if
528 bestowed: lodged
529 abstract...of the time: summing-up and a brief contemporary history

As low as to the fiends.'

POLONIUS   This is too long.

HAMLET   It shall to the barber's with your beard. Prithee, say
             on – he's for a jig or a tale of bawdry, or he   505
             sleeps – say on, come to Hecuba.

FIRST PLAYER 'But who, ah woe, had seen the mobled queen –'

HAMLET   'The mobled queen'?

POLONIUS   That's good, 'mobled queen' is good.

FIRST PLAYER 'Run barefoot up and down, threat'ning the
                  flames   510
             With bisson rheum, a clout upon that head
             Where late the diadem stood, and for a robe,
             About her lank and all o'er-teemed loins,
             A blanket in the alarm of fear caught up –
             Who this had seen, with tongue in venom
                  steeped,   515
             'Gainst Fortune's state would treason have
                  pronounced;
             But if the gods themselves did see her then,
             When she saw Pyrrhus make malicious sport
             In mincing with his sword her husband's limbs,
             The instant burst of clamour that she made,   520
             Unless things mortal move them not at all,
             Would have made milch the burning eyes of
                  heaven,
             And passion in the gods'.

POLONIUS   Look, whe'r he has not turned his colour, and has
             tears in 's eyes – prithee no more.   525

HAMLET   'Tis well, I'll have thee speak out the rest of
             this soon. Good my lord, will you see the players
             well bestowed? Do you hear, let them be well used,
             for they are the abstract and brief chronicles of the
             time; after your death you were better have a   530
             bad epitaph than their ill report while you live.

POLONIUS   My lord, I will use them according to their desert.

As Polonius leads the players away, Hamlet detains the first
player and asks for a particular play – *The Murder of Gonzago*
– the following evening. He also asks if the player could learn
an extra speech and insert it in the play. The actor agrees.
Hamlet, when he is alone, comments on the way the actor
seemed moved by his lines, whereas he, with a very real cause
for grief, can say nothing.

533 God's bodkin: an oath, replacing 'God's bodykins' –
God's little body
534 'scape whipping: escape being whipped – the legal
punishment for unlicensed actors, who were considered to
be vagabonds
536 bounty: generosity
548 look you mock him not: Hamlet may be concerned that
the players have noticed his attitude to Polonius and be
tempted to imitate it
554 peasant slave: low rascal
557 conceit: imagination
558 his visage wanned: his face grew pale
559 distraction in his aspect: madness in his looks
560 whole function...conceit: his every action, every gesture,
suiting his imagined mood

> • *What is Hamlet's mood in his second soliloquy and
> what has contributed to this?*

HAMLET	God's bodkin man, much better. Use every man after his desert, and who shall 'scape whipping? Use them after your own honour and dignity: 535 the less they deserve, the more merit is in your bounty. Take them in.
POLONIUS	Come sirs.
HAMLET	Follow him friends, we'll hear a play tomorrow. [*Exit* POLONIUS *with all the* PLAYERS *but the* FIRST.] Dost thou hear me old friend, can you play the 540 Murder of Gonzago?
FIRST PLAYER	Ay my lord.
HAMLET	We'll ha 't tomorrow night. You could for a need study a speech of some dozen or sixteen lines, which I would set down and insert in 't, 545 could you not?
FIRST PLAYER	Ay my lord.
HAMLET	Very well. Follow that lord, and look you mock him not. [*Exit* FIRST PLAYER] My good friends, I'll leave you till night. You are welcome to 550 Elsinore.
ROSENCRANTZ	Good my lord.

HAMLET	Ay, so God buy to you [*Exeunt* ROSENCRANTZ *and*
	                                GUILDENSTERN]
	                  Now I am alone.
	O what a rogue and peasant slave am I!
	Is it not monstrous that this player here, 555
	But in a fiction, in a dream of passion,
	Could force his soul so to his own conceit,
	That from her working all his visage wanned;
	Tears in his eyes, distraction in his aspect,
	A broken voice, and his whole function suiting 560
	With forms to his conceit – and all for nothing?
	For Hecuba!
	What's Hecuba to him, or he to Hecuba,
	That he should weep for her? What would he do,

Hamlet blames himself for not yet having taken revenge for his father's murder. He calls himself a coward for making use of words, not deeds. He has had the idea that, when presented with a play telling the story of what they have done, murderers have confessed their crimes. He will arrange for the players to act such a play before his uncle, and he will watch him carefully.

567 **cleave the general ear**: split the audience's ears
   horrid: causing horror, dreadful
568 **the free**: those free of guilt
569 **Confound**: confuse, perplex
   amaze: bewilder
572 **muddy-mettled**: dull of spirit (mettle) and mud-coloured, tarnished metal
   peak: droop around the place (cf modern English 'peaky')
573 **John-a-dreams**: the name for a stupid, dreamy fellow
   unpregnant of: unmoved by
575 **property**: the man he was, his whole personality
576 **defeat**: destruction
577 **pate**: head
579 **gives me the lie i' the throat...lungs**: accuses me of lying (cf modern English 'he's lying in his teeth'). Lying 'As deep as to the lungs' must mean a very serious lie indeed.
582 **'Swounds**: God's wounds, an oath
583 **pigeon-livered and lack gall**: the pigeon, seen as a mild bird was thought to have no gall, the alleged source of bitterness
585 **the region kites**: the kites of the air (birds of prey and also scavengers)
587 **kindless**: unnatural
592 **unpack my heart**: unburden, relieve my heart
593 **drab**: whore, slatternly woman
594 **stallion**: male whore *or* 'scullion', kitchen maid, used as term of abuse – a loud, low woman
595 **About**: set about your task

Had he the motive and the cue for passion   565
That I have? He would drown the stage with
      tears,
And cleave the general ear with horrid speech,
Make mad the guilty, and appal the free,
Confound the ignorant, and amaze indeed
The very faculties of eyes and ears.   570
Yet I,
A dull and muddy-mettled rascal, peak,
Like John-a-dreams, unpregnant of my cause,
And can say nothing; no, not for a King,
Upon whose property and most dear life   575
A damned defeat was made. Am I a coward?
Who calls me villain, breaks my pate across,
Plucks off my beard, and blows it in my face,
Tweaks me by the nose, gives me the lie i' the
      throat,
As deep as to the lungs – who does me this?   580
Ha!
'Swounds, I should take it; for it cannot be
But I am pigeon-livered and lack gall
To make oppression bitter, or ere this
I should ha' fatted all the region kites   585
With this slave's offal. Bloody, bawdy villain,
Remorseless, treacherous, lecherous, kindless
      villain!
O vengeance!
Why, what an ass am I. This is most brave,
That I, the son of a dear father murdered,   590
Prompted to my revenge by heaven and hell,
Must, like a whore, unpack my heart with words,
And fall a-cursing like a very drab,
A stallion!
Fie upon 't, foh! About, my brains; hum, I have
      heard   595
That guilty creatures sitting at a play
Have by the very cunning of the scene

Hamlet is not prepared to act against Claudius until he can be sure that the ghost is telling him the truth. He is conscious that in his melancholy state he is particularly liable to be deceived in this way. He will use the play to get some form of proof.

598 presently: instantly, straightaway
599 malefactions: misdeeds, crimes
601 organ: although murder hasn't the power of speech, it will find some way of expressing itself
604 tent: probe
blench: flinch
609 potent: skilful in his use of, powerfully effective with
610 Abuses me: deceives, deludes me
grounds More relative than this: more substantial reasons

- *Why does Hamlet need to be satisfied on the question of Claudius's guilt?*

Been struck so to the soul, that presently
They have proclaimed their malefactions.
For murder, though it have no tongue, will
    speak   600
With most miraculous organ. I'll have these
    players
Play something like the murder of my father
Before mine uncle; I'll observe his looks,
I'll tent him to the quick; if 'a do blench,
I know my course. The spirit that I have seen   605
May be a devil, and the devil hath power
T' assume a pleasing shape; yea, and perhaps,
Out of my weakness and my melancholy,
As he is very potent with such spirits,
Abuses me to damn me. I'll have grounds   610
More relative than this – the play's the thing
Wherein I'll catch the conscience of the King. [*Exit*

CTIVITIES

Keeping track

Scene 1

1 The scene begins with Polonius sending one of his servants to Paris to spy on Laertes. How exactly is Reynaldo to discover what Laertes is doing?
2 How does this short section confirm or extend your first impressions of Polonius?
3 When Ophelia enters the scene she describes an encounter with Hamlet which has taken place off-stage. What exactly did Hamlet do in this meeting with Ophelia?
4 How does Polonius explain Hamlet's behaviour, and what evidence does he have to support this theory?
5 Why do you think he decides to tell the king?
6 There has obviously been some lapse of time between Act 1 and the opening of Act 2. Does this report of Hamlet's appearance and behaviour surprise you?

Scene 2

1 Why have Rosencrantz and Guildenstern appeared in Elsinore, and how do Claudius and Gertrude persuade them to co-operate with their plans?
2 Why do you think Rosencrantz and Guildenstern co-operate so willingly?
3 The return of the ambassadors brings news of a diplomatic success for Claudius. What are the terms of the treaty which has been negotiated?
4 What is Polonius's explanation of Hamlet's behaviour?
5 How does Polonius propose to test his theory?
6 How does Hamlet behave towards Polonius when he enters the scene?
7 Is there 'method' in Hamlet's madness?
8 As Polonius leaves the stage, Rosencrantz and Guildenstern enter. What possible explanation does Rosencrantz suggest for Hamlet's 'loss of mirth'?
9 How does Hamlet react to their probing?
10 The arrival of the Players prompts Hamlet to ask for a performance of a particular speech, describing the killing of Priam by Pyrrhus (lines 456–502). What impression do you get of Pyrrhus, and how

does the language of the speech create this impression?
11 The focus of the speech changes to Hecuba's reaction to the cold –
blooded slaughter of her husband (lines 507–523). How does
Hecuba react to the killing of Priam, and how does the Player react
to the speech he is performing?
12 Why do you think Hamlet asked for this particular speech: in what
ways is Pyrrhus of interest to him? Are there any parallels between
Hecuba and Gertrude?

Drama

1 Ophelia
   • The actress playing Ophelia feels that she does not want to portray
     her as a weakling. How can she achieve this? Look at her lines in
     Scene 1. In small groups, help one actress find ways of making the
     lines strong.
   • Hotseat Ophelia before and after she sees the mad Hamlet.
   • Young women in Elizabethan times had less power than teenage
     girls today. How do you think you would take the idea of your
     father reading your love letters to his boss's son out loud in public?
     Imagine the scene immediately after this, when Ophelia comes face
     to face with her father.
2 Look at the exchange between Hamlet and Polonius (Act 2 scene 2
   lines 169–219).
   Work in threes and practise these lines.
   • Perform them very fast.
   • Imagine Reynaldo is there to receive Polonius's asides.
   • Repeat them to find out Polonius's non-verbal responses to
     Hamlet's baffling twists and turns.
   • How mad is Hamlet at this point?
   • How can the actor show the variations in madness or antic
     disposition?
3 Rosencrantz and Guildenstern
   • Look at the exchanges between Hamlet, Rosencrantz and
     Guildenstern in Scene 2. There are some clever word plays. In
     threes, work on any sequence of ten or so lines. Sort out the
     wordplays and deliver them in a snappy manner. Work out the
     subtext, working out the interplay of Hamlet's suspicion and their
     subterfuge. When Guildenstern is speaking to Hamlet, what is
     Rosencrantz doing?
     Following these exchanges, Rosencrantz and Guildenstern report
     back to Claudius, but they don't tell the whole story. In pairs,
     imagine the two men planning what they will say to Claudius and
     what suspicions they will leave unsaid. Remember they are in a
     difficult position and must be careful what they say.

Key elements

In Act 2 these are:
- the major characters (mainly Hamlet, Ophelia and Polonius)
- Ophelia's description of the '*antic disposition*'
- Hamlet's exchange with Rosencrantz and Guildenstern
- the Player's speech
- Hamlet's second soliloquy.

The key scene

Hamlet's second soliloquy: scene 2 lines 553–612

Keying it in

1 This speech comes after the Player's demonstration of visible emotion as he describes the death of Priam and Hecuba's grief.
- What has Hamlet actually been doing since he vowed to avenge his father?
- What state of mind is he in during this part of the play?
- Does he seem to have a clear focus on revenge?
- Does he have any clear plan at this stage of the action?

The speech itself

2 Look at lines 553–562.
   It is conceivable that the Player's speech could have affected Hamlet in several ways. For example, it is possible that he could have been inspired into bloody action by the description of Pyrrhus.
- How does he react to the Player's speech?
- How do the language and structure of these lines convey the strength of Hamlet's feelings?
- Why does the Player provoke such an intense response from Hamlet?

3 Look at lines 563–589.
   In these lines Hamlet compares his own behaviour with the emotion shown by the Player. He concludes that his failure to act has two possible explanations.
- What are they?
- How does Hamlet feel about himself?
- Do you agree with him?
   Towards the end of this section of the speech his mood changes as his passion turns outside himself and he launches into a violent tirade against Claudius.

- How does the language convey his feelings here?
- What is revealed by the stress on both 'bloody' and 'bawdy' in his abuse of his uncle?

4 Look at lines 590–594.

    The tone of the speech changes again in these lines.
- How would you describe the tone of these lines?
- How does Hamlet feel about the way he has just spoken about Claudius?
- How does language convey his feelings?

5 Look at lines 595–612.

    Hamlet now begins to construct a plan of action.
- What exactly is he proposing to do?
- What reasons does he give for this course of action?
- How would you describe his mood by the end of the speech?

Overview

If the keynote of the first soliloquy is the mood of profound disillusion then, here, it is the overwhelming sense of self-disgust which leads to his plan to stage the inner play, in an attempt to prove whether or not Claudius is guilty of murder.
- Why is Hamlet so disgusted with himself?
- Choose two quotations which illustrate his self-disgust.

The speech contains several twists and turns and also some dramatic changes of mood.
- Look closely at the argumentative structure of the speech. How does Hamlet get from 'O what a rogue and peasant slave am I!' to 'the play's the thing'?
- What emotions does he experience during this speech?

Close study

Act 2 scene 2 lines 298–316
1 What view of the world does Hamlet express here?
2 What view of human beings does he express here?
3 How does the language of the speech convey Hamlet's feelings?
4 For what purposes does the speech use sharp contrasts?
5 Is Hamlet telling the 'truth' to Rosencrantz and Guildenstern in this speech?
6 How far do you think this is a genuine statement of Hamlet's feelings?
7 Do you think it is simply an evasive tactic?
8 Where else in the play so far has Hamlet expressed similar views?

Hamlet and revenge

1 After the initial surge of 'blood' when the Ghost reveals the 'truth' about Claudius, Hamlet could have pursued his target in one of two ways. He could have confronted Claudius in a mood of passionate fury or he could have engaged in devious, calculated scheming designed to achieve his revenge. He does neither. He does not act against Claudius either immediately or decisively. It is in this space between the end of Act 1 and the end of Act 2 that Hamlet hesitates.

Look at what he says and does during this time.
- Does he have a single focus on revenge?
- What are his other preoccupations?
- Do they distract him from his purpose?
- Do you share his sense of disgust at his failure to act?

2 The Player's speech is chosen by Hamlet and you may see in it a dramatization of the active, implacable revenger in the figure of Pyrrhus. This is perhaps what Hamlet wants to be, or may have to become.
- Do you think he is capable of acting like Pyrrhus?
- Do you want him to be like Pyrrhus?

3 The speech also stresses Hecuba's grief and in a way it is an indictment of Gertrude's failure to mourn, and her lack of loyalty to her husband.
- Can you find any other examples of Hamlet being distracted from revenge by his feelings about women and sex?

4 The second soliloquy explores the possibilities that his failure to take action is evidence either of a lack of real feeling for his father or straightforward cowardice. Hamlet admits that he has done nothing, is disgusted with himself and frustrated by his own aimlessness.

He then argues that he needs firm proof before he can safely proceed against Claudius.
- Are his doubts genuine?
- How do you make sense of '*It is an honest ghost*' and '*the spirit that I have seen may be a devil*'?
- Are his doubts simply a rationalization of his failure to take action?

5 By the end of Act 2, Hamlet has improvised a plan which may unmask Claudius. However, he has plunged into confusion and uncertainty and he is experiencing violent swings of mood.

Assignments

1 Hamlet's '*antic disposition*' is a matter of concern for several characters. Make a list of the various explanations given in this Act for Hamlet's apparent madness.

Essay

2 How does the arrival of the Players in Elsinore influence Hamlet and his actions?

Claudius asks Rosencrantz and Guildenstern what they have learnt about Hamlet's madness. They tell him that they were well received and that Hamlet spoke to them quite freely. He seemed pleased, they say, to hear about the arrival of the troupe of actors.

1 **drift of conference**: leading of the conversation
2 **puts on this confusion**: pretends to be mentally disturbed
3 **Grating**: jarring on
7 **forward**: inclined
8 **crafty madness**: a pretended madness
12 **forcing of his disposition**: a self–imposed politeness which he did not really feel
13 **Niggard of question**: asking few questions
14 **assay him To**: suggest to him
17 **o'er-raught**: overtook

> • *How effective have Rosencrantz and Guildenstern been at carrying out the first part of their task?*

Act three

Scene 1

Enter KING, QUEEN, POLONIUS, OPHELIA,
ROSENCRANTZ *and* GUILDENSTERN

KING   And can you, by no drift of conference,
               Get from him why he puts on this confusion,
               Grating so harshly all his days of quiet
               With turbulent and dangerous lunacy?

ROSENCRANTZ   He does confess he feels himself distracted   5
               But from what cause 'a will by no means speak.

GUILDENSTERN   Nor do we find him forward to be sounded,
               But with a crafty madness keeps aloof,
               When we would bring him on to some confession
               Of his true state.

QUEEN   Did he receive you well?   10

ROSENCRANTZ   Most like a gentleman.

GUILDENSTERN   But with much forcing of his disposition.

ROSENCRANTZ   Niggard of question, but of our demands
               Most free in his reply.

QUEEN   Did you assay him
               To any pastime?   15

ROSENCRANTZ   Madam, it so fell out that certain players
               We o'er-raught on the way; of these we told him,
               And there did seem in him a kind of joy
               To hear of it. They are about the court,
               And as I think, they have already order   20
               This night to play before him.

POLONIUS   'Tis most true.
               And he beseeched me to entreat your majesties
               To hear and see the matter.

Claudius asks Rosencrantz and Guildenstern to encourage
Hamlet's interest in the players. He asks Gertrude to leave as
he and Polonius intend to arrange a 'chance' meeting
between Hamlet and Ophelia in order to spy on them.
Polonius hopes to prove that Hamlet is in love with her.

26 give him...edge: stimulate his interest even more
27 drive his purpose: encourage him
29 closely: secretly
31 Affront Ophelia: come face to face with Ophelia
32 lawful espials: legitimate spies
33 bestow: position
35 as he is behaved: according to his behaviour
41 wonted: usual, accustomed
43 Gracious: (your) gracious (majesty) – to the king
45 colour Your loneliness: explain away the fact that you are
    alone
47 devotion's visage...himself: we often put on a holy face
    and appear to be doing pious deeds to hide the devil's work
50 How...conscience: how that whiplash stings my conscience
51 The harlot's...it: the cheek of a loose woman, made
    beautiful with make-up thickly applied, is not more ugly
    compared to the cosmetics, than is my deed to the falsely
    painted words I'm covering it up with. Claudius in this
    aside (see GLOSSARY page 333) is acknowledging his guilt to
    us before the test Hamlet is planning for him.

> • *The parents are solemnly arranging to spy on what*
> *may be an intimate conversation between their adult*
> *son and daughter. Is there really any serious*
> *justification for this, or is it just another symptom of*
> *the moral sickness that has invaded the castle? Which is*
> *the phrase in which Claudius feels he has to justify*
> *himself and Polonius?*

KING   With all my heart, and it doth much content me
     To hear him so inclined.   25
     Good gentlemen, give him a further edge,
     And drive his purpose into these delights.

ROSENCRANTZ We shall my lord.

              [*Exeunt* ROSENCRANTZ *and* GUILDENSTERN

KING   Sweet Gertrude leave us too,
     For we have closely sent for Hamlet hither,
     That he, as 'twere by accident, may here   30
     Affront Ophelia.
     Her father and myself, lawful espials,
     Will so bestow ourselves that, seeing unseen,
     We may of their encounter frankly judge,
     And gather by him, as he is behaved,   35
     If 't be th' affliction of his love or no
     That thus he suffers for.

QUEEN   I shall obey you.
     And for your part Ophelia, I do wish
     That your good beauties be the happy cause
     Of Hamlet's wildness; so shall I hope your virtues 40
     Will bring him to his wonted way again,
     To both your honours.

OPHELIA   Madam, I wish it may.

                    [*Exit* QUEEN

POLONIUS Ophelia, walk you here. Gracious, so please you,
     We will bestow ourselves. – Read on this book,
     That show of such an exercise may colour   45
     Your loneliness. – We are oft to blame in this;
     'Tis too much proved, that with devotion's visage
     And pious action we do sugar o'er
     The devil himself.

KING   [*Aside*]   O 'tis too true.
     How smart a lash that speech doth give my
         conscience.   50
     The harlot's cheek, beautied with plast'ring art,
     Is not more ugly to the thing that helps it

Hamlet comes in debating whether death is simply the end of life, the absence of everything and so of all problems; or possibly, and frighteningly, the beginning of something that we cannot know or even guess at.

56 To be, or not to be: to go on existing, or to cease to exist. Hamlet is mentally testing the continuation of his life, against its absence.

58 slings: some suspect a misprint for 'stings', but slings were used from earliest times to hurl missiles at the enemy

60 To die...no more: in literature as in life, sleep is often welcome. But sleep can be disturbed by nightmares and in line 65 Hamlet realizes this.

61 by a sleep...heir to: just by being human we are subject to 'shocks'. 'Shock' is the term for the blow of sword on sword in battle. Hamlet here is still occupied with the hope that death equals sleep equals an end.

63 consummation: satisfactory conclusion, perfect fulfilment

65 rub: difficulty, hindrance. A metaphor from the game of bowls – any impediment to the course of the bowl.

67 shuffled off...coil: got rid of this business of being alive – 'shuffle off' contains a sense of shiftiness, of being evasive

68 there's...long life: that's the consideration that makes calamity so long-lived (with the echo 'long life itself is a calamity')

70 of time: that merely living through time brings

71 contumely: scorn

73 the spurns...takes: the disdain which someone who deserves better has to put up with from unworthy people

75 quietus: death – a legal term for full payment of a debt, but also carrying the suggestion of rest and quiet

76 a bare bodkin: just a dagger
fardels: burdens

79 bourn: boundary

83 conscience: (1) inward knowledge or consciousness. Here, the ability to work things out, to understand that things may not be as we first thought or as we might like them to be. (2) conscience in the sense of the knowledge of right and wrong.

84 native hue of resolution...thought: resolution, being a bold and positive product of the sanguine humour would be red. Converted into indecisiveness it turns pale.

Than is my deed to my most painted word.
O heavy burthen!

POLONIUS   I hear him coming, let's withdraw my lord.   55
                            [*Exeunt* KING *and* POLONIUS
              Enter HAMLET

HAMLET   To be, or not to be, that is the question:
              Whether 'tis nobler in the mind to suffer
              The slings and arrows of outrageous fortune,
              Or to take arms against a sea of troubles,
              And by opposing end them? To die, to sleep –   60
              No more; and by a sleep to say we end
              The heart-ache, and the thousand natural shocks
              That flesh is heir to; 'tis a consummation
              Devoutly to be wished. To die, to sleep –
              To sleep, perchance to dream, ay there's the rub, 65
              For in that sleep of death what dreams may come
              When we have shuffled off this mortal coil,
              Must give us pause; there's the respect
              That makes calamity of so long life.
              For who would bear the whips and scorns of
                    time,   70
              Th' oppressor's wrong, the proud man's
                    contumely,
              The pangs of despised love, the law's delay,
              The insolence of office, and the spurns
              That patient merit of th' unworthy takes
              When he himself might his quietus make   75
              With a bare bodkin? Who would fardels bear,
              To grunt and sweat under a weary life,
              But that the dread of something after death,
              The undiscovered country from whose bourn
              No traveller returns, puzzles the will,   80
              And makes us rather bear those ills we have,
              Than fly to others that we know not of?
              Thus conscience does make cowards of us all,
              And thus the native hue of resolution

This fear of the unknown, Hamlet suggests, numbs us into inaction. He becomes aware that Ophelia is there. She offers to return his gifts, which Hamlet denies sending her. He speaks abruptly to her, making similar connections between chastity, beauty and immorality as her father and brother have already done.

86 pitch and moment: scope and importance
87 With this regard: on this account
    their currents turn awry: change their intended direction
88 Soft you now: hush, be silent
89 Nymph: beautiful girl, maiden
    orisons: prayers
93 remembrances: gifts
96 aught: anything
98 with them...composed: accompanied by such charming words
99 their perfume lost: since the affection with which they were given no longer exists
101 wax: grow, become
103 honest: chaste
108 admit no discourse: not hold any conversation, ie chastity and beauty are a dangerous combination
109 commerce: dealings
111 the power...a bawd: it is easier for the power of beauty to turn chastity to prostitution
113 his: its
114 paradox: something which cannot be accounted for by using reason

> • *How can we account for Hamlet's behaviour towards Ophelia? Do you find any comparisons with her father's and brother's lectures to her?*

Is sicklied o'er with the pale cast of thought,   85
And enterprises of great pitch and moment
With this regard their currents turn awry,
And lose the name of action. Soft you now,
The fair Ophelia. – Nymph, in thy orisons
Be all my sins remembered.

OPHELIA   Good my lord,   90
How does your honour for this many a day?

HAMLET   I humbly thank you, well, well, well.

OPHELIA   My lord, I have remembrances of yours
That I have longed long to re-deliver.
I pray you now receive them.

HAMLET   No, not I,   95
I never gave you aught.

OPHELIA   My honoured lord, you know right well you did,
And with them words of so sweet breath composed
As made these things more rich. Their perfume
        lost,
Take these again, for to the noble mind   100
Rich gifts wax poor when givers prove unkind.
There my lord.

HAMLET   Ha, ha, are you honest?

OPHELIA   My lord?

HAMLET   Are you fair?   105

OPHELIA   What means your lordship?

HAMLET   That if you be honest and fair, your honesty should
admit no discourse to your beauty.

OPHELIA   Could beauty, my lord, have better commerce than
with honesty?   110

HAMLET   Ay truly, for the power of beauty will sooner
transform honesty from what it is to a bawd, than
the force of honesty can translate beauty into his
likeness. This was sometime a paradox, but now the
time gives it proof. I did love you once.   115

Hamlet continues to reject Ophelia, to her considerable distress. His insistence that she should go to a nunnery, with his ranting speech and violent sentiments, convince her he is mentally unbalanced.

117 for virtue...relish of it: *'inoculate'* and *'stock'* are technical terms borrowed from horticulture. A graft (containing a bud or 'eye' – Latin 'oculus') is taken from a rose bush or fruit tree and inserted into the stem of a stock of the same species. The graft is usually attractive while the stock is vigorous. The resulting plant should share the best qualities of both. Hamlet is saying that the characteristics of the old stock will persist.

118 relish: trace, taste, tinge

121 Get thee to a nunnery: a place where Ophelia can remain chaste and not continue the procreation of wicked sinful creatures. Even the most ordinary men are full of sins: Hamlet enumerates his.

122 indifferent honest: fairly virtuous

126 at my beck: waiting to be called on

129 arrant knaves: notorious rogues, out and out villains

130 Go...nunnery: perhaps speaking as a father might to an errant daughter reminds Hamlet of Polonius. There is no indication in the text that he knows he is being spied on – he might have had more verbal fun with it if he had known.

137 be thou: even if you are

138 calumny: slander

141 monsters: a husband, deceived by his wife, was said to be a 'cuckold' and to grow horns, thus to look like a monster

144 paintings: using cosmetics

146 you jig, you amble: dance steps. The word *'jig'* suggests a rapid, jerky action, *'amble'* an easy more gliding motion. The word *'jig'* can also refer to singing or playing a tune in this style.

you lisp, you nickname: you speak affectedly and childishly, you give made-up names. Hamlet is commenting unfavourably on the flirtatious tricks women get up to, to attract men.

149 on't: of it

OPHELIA   Indeed my lord you made me believe so.

HAMLET   You should not have believed me, for virtue cannot
            so inoculate our old stock, but we shall relish of it. I
            loved you not.

OPHELIA   I was the more deceived.   120

HAMLET   Get thee to a nunnery, why wouldst thou be a
            breeder of sinners? I am myself indifferent honest,
            but yet I could accuse me of such things, that it
            were better my mother had not borne me. I am
            very proud, revengeful, ambitious, with more   125
            offences at my beck, than I have thoughts to put
            them in, imagination to give them shape, or time to
            act them in. What should such fellows as I do
            crawling between earth and heaven? We are arrant
            knaves all, believe none of us. Go thy ways to a   130
            nunnery. Where's your father?

OPHELIA   At home my lord.

HAMLET   Let the doors be shut upon him, that he may play
            the fool no where but in 's own house. Farewell.

OPHELIA   O help him, you sweet heavens!   135

HAMLET   If thou dost marry, I'll give thee this plague for thy
            dowry – be thou as chaste as ice, as pure as snow,
            thou shalt not escape calumny. Get thee to a
            nunnery, go farewell. Or if thou wilt needs marry,
            marry a fool for wise men know well enough   140
            what monsters you make of them. To a nunnery
            go, and quickly too. Farewell.

OPHELIA   O heavenly powers, restore him!

HAMLET   I have heard of your paintings too, well enough;
            God has given you one face, and you make   145
            yourselves another; you jig, you amble, and you
            lisp, you nickname God's creatures, and make your
            wantonness your ignorance. Go to, I'll no more
            on 't; it hath made me mad. I say we will have no
            more marriage. Those that are married already,   150

When Hamlet leaves Ophelia, she expresses her grief at his state of mind and we glimpse what hopes she – and others – had of him. Claudius cannot see love in what he has observed and has plans to send Hamlet away for a change of scene. Polonius still puts Hamlet's derangement down to neglected love.

151 shall live: shall remain (married)
  keep as they are: remain single
155 Th' expectancy and rose: the great hope, the incomparable prince
156 The glass of fashion and the mould of form: a pattern for others to follow, a model of behaviour
157 observed: honoured by, looked up to by
159 musicked vows: his vows sounded like music to her
162 blown youth: youth in full bloom (like a rose)
163 ecstasy: madness
168 sits on brood: like a bird on a clutch of eggs
169 doubt: fear
  disclose: bringing out
172 set it down: decided, determined
173 neglected tribute: money, called Danegeld, paid annually by Anglo-Saxons in the eleventh century to buy off attacks by the Danes
176 This...heart: to settle (here) is to sink to the bottom like dregs or sediment in wine. What it is that has '*something -settled*' in Hamlet's heart should be unclear to the observers, but Claudius has taken fright.
178 fashion of himself: behaviour normal to him

- *In Ophelia's sad reaction, we have the chance to see Hamlet as he was observed by her before the dramatic changes brought about by his father's murder. Be aware of similar suggestions elsewhere in the play.*
- *What impressions does Claudius have now of Hamlet's madness?*

all but one, shall live, the rest shall keep as they are.
To a nunnery go.   [*Exit*

OPHELIA   O what a noble mind is here o'erthrown!
               The courtier's, soldier's, scholar's, eye, tongue,
                   sword,
               Th' expectancy and rose of the fair state,   155
               The glass of fashion, and the mould of form,
               Th' observed of all observers, quite, quite down,
               And I of ladies most deject and wretched,
               That sucked the honey of his musicked vows,
               Now see that noble and most sovereign reason,   160
               Like sweet bells jangled, out of time and harsh;
               That unmatched form and feature of blown youth
               Blasted with ecstasy. O woe is me,
               T' have seen what I have seen, see what I see.

               Enter KING *and* POLONIUS

KING   Love? His affections do not that way tend;   165
               Nor what he spake, though it lacked form a little,
               Was not like madness. There's something in his soul
               O'er which his melancholy sits on brood,
               And I do doubt the hatch and the disclose
               Will be some danger; which for to prevent,   170
               I have in quick determination
               Thus set it down: he shall with speed to England,
               For the demand of our neglected tribute.
               Haply the seas and countries different,
               With variable objects, shall expel   175
               This something-settled matter in his heart,
               Whereon his brains still beating puts him thus
               From fashion of himself. What think you on 't?

POLONIUS   It shall do well. But yet do I believe
               The origin and commencement of his grief   180
               Sprung from neglected love. How now Ophelia?
               You need not tell us what Lord Hamlet said;
               We heard it all. My lord, do as you please,
               But if you hold it fit, after the play

Polonius sets up a tête-à-tête between Hamlet and Gertrude, his mother, in the hope that she can find out the truth.

186 **round**: direct, plain-spoken
187 **in the ear...conference**: where I can hear everything that is being said
188 **If she finds him not**: if she cannot discover what is at the bottom of this

Hamlet instructs the actors in the performance of the speech he has given them to introduce into the play. At the same time he criticizes acting which is overdone and also ignorant elements in the audience.

3 **I had as lief**: I would just as soon
7 **acquire...a temperance**: get for yourselves and then produce in your acting a moderation
9 **robustious**: boisterous
10 **periwig-pated**: wearing a wig
11 **groundlings**: the section of the audience which stood in front of and around the stage in the cheapest part of the theatre
12 **are capable of nothing but**: respond only to
13 **inexplicable dumb shows**: mime, where the meaning is not always clear
14 **o'erdoing Termagant**: overdoing Termagant – an imaginary god supposed by Christians to be worshipped by Muslims and represented in mystery plays as a violent character
15 **Herod**: also portrayed as a violent man in the mystery plays and, of course, traditionally the murderer of innocent children killed on his orders
20 **modesty**: self-control, restraint
21 **from**: a long way from
22 **end**: intention

- *Do you detect any indirect comment on Hamlet's own predicament in his instructions to the players?*

Let his queen mother all alone entreat him   185
To show his grief; let her be round with him,
And I'll be placed, so please you, in the ear
Of all their conference. If she finds him not,
To England send him; or confine him where
Your wisdom best shall think.

KING   It shall be so.   190
Madness in great ones must not unwatched go.
                                                        [*Exeunt*

Scene 2

Enter HAMLET *and three of the Players*

HAMLET   Speak the speech I pray you as I pronounced it to
you, trippingly on the tongue; but if you mouth it
as many of our players do, I had as lief the town-
crier spoke my lines. Nor do not saw the air too
much with your hand thus, but use all gently; for 5
in the very torrent, tempest, and as I may say, the
whirlwind of your passion, you must acquire and
beget a temperance that may give it smoothness.
O it offends me to the soul, to hear a robustious
periwig-pated fellow tear a passion to tatters, to 10
very rags, to split the ears of the groundlings, who
for the most part are capable of nothing but
inexplicable dumb shows and noise. I would have
such a fellow whipped for o'erdoing Termagant; it
outherods Herod, pray you avoid it.   15

FIRST PLAYER I warrant your honour.

HAMLET   Be not too tame neither, but let your own
discretion be your tutor. Suit the action to the
word, the word to the action, with this special
observance, that you o'erstep not the modesty   20
of nature. For any thing so o'erdone is from the
purpose of playing, whose end both at the first, and

Hamlet continues to set down what he considers the true purpose of theatre and to castigate bad actors and clowns who extemporize too freely. Polonius assures him that both the King and Queen will see the play.

25 the very age...and pressure: a true reflection of the period – pinpointing the shape it takes and the influences on it

26 Now this...theatre of others: when something is overacted or done badly, although it may make foolish spectators laugh, it must make sensible people feel sad; the judgement of one of these sensible people must, you will agree, be of more significance than that of a theatre full of the foolish ones

overdone...tardy off: overacted or done badly

27 unskilful: ignorant

28 the censure of the which one: the judgment of one of whom

32 profanely: irreverently

35 nature's journeymen: apprentices of Nature, still learning the craft of making people

38 indifferently: reasonably well

41 no more...for them: clowns in plays traditionally improvized, rather like some stand-up comics today.

43 barren spectators: members of the audience who are not responding

44 in the mean time...considered: by doing this some important element of the plot may need to be put across

49 piece of work: artistic composition

51 presently: immediately

now, was and is, to hold as 'twere the mirror up to
nature; to show virtue her own feature, scorn her
own image, and the very age and body of the   25
time his form and pressure. Now this overdone, or
come tardy off, though it makes the unskilful laugh,
cannot but make the judicious grieve; the censure
of the which one must in your allowance o'erweigh
a whole theatre of others. O there be players that 30
I have seen play, and heard others praise, and that
highly – not to speak it profanely – that neither
having th' accent of Christians, nor the gait of
Christian, pagan, nor man, have so strutted and
bellowed, that I have thought some of nature's   35
journeymen had made men, and not made them
well, they imitated humanity so abominably.

FIRST PLAYER I hope we have reformed that indifferently with us
sir.

HAMLET O reform it altogether; and let those that play   40
your clowns speak no more than is set down for
them, for there be of them that will themselves
laugh, to set on some quantity of barren spectators
to laugh too, though in the mean time some
necessary question of the play be then to be   45
considered; that's villainous, and shows a most
pitiful ambition in the fool that uses it. Go make
you ready.   [*Exeunt* PLAYERS

Enter POLONIUS, ROSENCRANTZ, *and* GUILDENSTERN

How now my lord, will the King hear this piece of
work?   50

POLONIUS And the Queen too, and that presently.

HAMLET Bid the players make haste. [*Exit* POLONIUS] Will
you two help to hasten them?

ROSENCRANTZ ⎫
                      ⎬ Ay my lord.
GUILDENSTERN ⎭

[*Exeunt* ROSENCRANTZ *and* GUILDENSTERN

Hamlet calls on Horatio to observe the King, during the progress of the play, so that they may compare notes afterwards on his reactions and make a judgement about whether he is guilty of the murder of Hamlet's father. But first he tells Horatio how much he values him.

57 **just**: honourable
58 **my conversation coped withal**: as I have ever met with in all my dealings
60 **advancement**: promotion, favours
63 **candied tongue**: sugared tongue
64 **crook the pregnant hinges**: bend the eager joints – kneel
65 **thrift**: gain, rewards
67 **of men distinguish**: discriminate between people
   election: choice
72 **blood and judgment...co-meddled**: passion and reason are so well balanced
73 **a pipe for Fortune's finger**: an instrument on which Fortune can play her tunes. Hamlet is praising people like Horatio who are more likely to make things happen than to be victims of chance.
79 **circumstance**: details
81 **afoot**: being played out
82 **Even with...mine uncle**: watch my uncle as closely as though your soul itself were expected to comment on the result.
83 **occulted**: hidden, secret
84 **unkennel**: used in fox-hunting of driving a fox from its lair. Here 'disclose' or 'bring to light'.

- *Hamlet gives Horatio an assessment of what true friendship is. Is it possible for a man in his position to have a friend with whom he can be completely open? Is he completely open with Horatio?*

HAMLET	What ho, Horatio! 55

Enter HORATIO

HORATIO	Here sweet lord, at your service.
HAMLET	Horatio, thou art e'en as just a man
	As e'er my conversation coped withal.
HORATIO	O my dear lord –
HAMLET	Nay, do not think I flatter,

For what advancement may I hope from thee   60
That no revenue hast but thy good spirits
To feed and clothe thee? Why should the poor be
     flattered?
No, let the candied tongue lick absurd pomp,
And crook the pregnant hinges of the knee
Where thrift may follow fawning. Dost thou
     hear?   65
Since my dear soul was mistress of her choice,
And could of men distinguish, her election
Hath sealed thee for herself, for thou hast been
As one in suffering all that suffers nothing,
A man that Fortune's buffets and rewards   70
Hast ta'en with equal thanks; and blest are those
Whose blood and judgment are so well
     co-meddled,
That they are not a pipe for Fortune's finger
To sound what stop she please. Give me that man
That is not passion's slave, and I will wear him   75
In my heart's core, ay in my heart of heart,
As I do thee – something too much of this –
There is a play tonight before the King;
One scene of it comes near the circumstance
Which I have told thee of my father's death.   80
I prithee when thou seest that act afoot,
Even with the very comment of thy soul
Observe mine uncle. If his occulted guilt
Do not itself unkennel in one speech,

Horatio agrees to Hamlet's plan for observing the King. At the entry of the King and Queen, Polonius, Ophelia and other members of the court, Hamlet's apparently inconsequential, punning and challenging style of speech returns.

85 **a damned ghost**: a ghost from Hell, telling lies and trying to damn Hamlet's soul

87 **Vulcan's stithy**: Vulcan's forge. Vulcan was the gods' blacksmith, the forge was on the volcanic Mount Aetna. One of his jobs was to make thunderbolts for Jove.

90 **In censure of his seeming**: and form our opinion from the way he looks and acts

93 **I must be idle**: Hamlet is concerned that he must not be seen to be busily and intelligently occupied in conversation with Horatio, which might arouse his uncle's suspicions. The word *'idle'* also means 'crazy'. He must put on his madness again.

95 **How fares...Hamlet?**: how is ...getting on? The word *'cousin'* is any close relation. Hamlet chooses to answer another meaning of *'fare'* – 'to live on', 'to eat'.

96 **the chameleon's dish**: the chameleon, a tropical lizard-like creature which can adapt its colouring to its surroundings, was commonly supposed to live on air

97 **capons**: cockerels, castrated to keep them plump and tender, fattened up for roasting

107 **calf**: a stupid or meek and harmless person

111 **metal more attractive**: a more magnetic metal, with a play on the word 'mettle' meaning 'spirit', 'temperament' or 'disposition' (see *pun*, GLOSSARY page 335)

	It is a damned ghost that we have seen,	85
	And my imaginations are as foul	
	As Vulcan's stithy. Give him heedful note,	
	For I mine eyes will rivet to his face,	
	And after we will both our judgments join	
	In censure of his seeming.	
HORATIO	Well my lord;	90
	If 'a steal aught the whilst this play is playing,	
	And 'scape detecting, I will pay the theft.	
HAMLET	They are coming to the play; I must be idle.	
	Get you a place.	

Danish march. A flourish. Enter KING, QUEEN, POLONIUS, OPHELIA, ROSENCRANTZ, GUILDENSTERN, *and others*

KING	How fares our cousin Hamlet?	95
HAMLET	Excellent i' faith, of the chameleon's dish; I eat the air, promise-crammed, you cannot feed capons so.	
KING	I have nothing with this answer, Hamlet; these words are not mine.	
HAMLET	No, nor mine now. [*To* POLONIUS] My lord, you played once i' th' university, you say?	100
POLONIUS	That did I my lord, and was accounted a good actor.	
HAMLET	What did you enact?	
POLONIUS	I did enact Julius Caesar, I was killed i' th' Capitol; Brutus killed me.	105
HAMLET	It was a brute part of him to kill so capital a calf there. Be the players ready?	
ROSENCRANTZ	Ay my lord, they stay upon your patience.	
QUEEN	Come hither my dear Hamlet, sit by me.	110
HAMLET	No, good mother, here's metal more attractive.	
POLONIUS	[*To the* KING] O ho, do you mark that?	
HAMLET	Lady, shall I lie in your lap?	

Hamlet disconcerts Ophelia with thinly-veiled sexual backchat. He refers again to his father's recent death and his mother's cheerfulness. The mime element of the actors' play begins with an affectionate king and queen. The queen leaves the king asleep in the garden whereupon a man comes in, removes the crown, kisses it and pours poison in the king's ears.

117 **country matters**: the rather more basic and direct approach to sex, supposed to be common among unsophisticated rural people, but also the sexual pun intended in the first syllable of *'country'*

121 **Nothing**: 'thing' is also used for the male or female sexual organ

125 **your only jig-maker**: your one and only entertainer

131 **sables**: rich, lustrous dark furs, and the heraldic word for black, which is used in mourning

135 **not thinking on**: being forgotten
     the hobby-horse: one of the characters in the traditional Morris dance. The hobby-horse too represents a lustful person.

136 **For O, for...forgot**: a line of a ballad popular at the time

> • *Hamlet's conversation with Ophelia consists of very broad sexual innuendo. What do you think is the point of this?*

OPHELIA	No my lord.
HAMLET	I mean, my head upon your lap. 115
OPHELIA	Ay my lord.
HAMLET	Do you think I meant country matters?
OPHELIA	I think nothing, my lord.
HAMLET	That's a fair thought to lie between maid's legs.
OPHELIA	What is, my lord? 120
HAMLET	Nothing.
OPHELIA	You are merry my lord.
HAMLET	Who, I?
OPHELIA	Ay my lord.
HAMLET	O God, your only jig-maker. What should a 125 man do but be merry, for look you how cheerfully my mother looks, and my father died within these two hours.
OPHELIA	Nay, 'tis twice two months, my lord.
HAMLET	So long? Nay then let the devil wear black, for 130 I'll have a suit of sables. O heavens, die two months ago, and not forgotten yet? Then there's hope a great man's memory may outlive his life half a year, but by 'r lady he must build churches then, or else shall 'a suffer not thinking on, with the hobby- 135 horse, whose epitaph is 'For O, for O, the hobby-horse is forgot'.

Trumpets sound. The Dumb Show enters

Enter a KING *and a* QUEEN *very lovingly; the* QUEEN *embracing him, and he her. She kneels, and makes show of protestation unto him. He takes her up, and declines his head upon her neck: lays him down upon a bank of flowers: she, seeing him asleep, leaves him. Anon comes in a fellow, takes off his crown, kisses it, and pours poison in the* KING'S *ears, and exits. The* QUEEN *returns; finds the* KING *dead, and makes*

The mime continues with the poisoner appearing to mourn the dead king. He then courts the queen who, after hesitation, accepts him. Ophelia has difficulty understanding the Dumb Show. There is a very brief spoken prologue and the play proper begins with the Player King and Queen commenting on thirty years of marriage.

139 miching mallecho: form, origin and meaning are uncertain, but the best sense is taken to be 'skulking mischief'

140 Belike...play: perhaps this dumb show is to tell us what the play is about

142 The players...tell all: the actors cannot keep a secret, they'll let it all spill out

145 Ay or any show...show him: Hamlet continues the sexual innuendo with a play on words meaning 'exposure'

148 naught: Ophelia takes the point and calls him 'bad', 'offensive'

150 clemency: indulgence

152 posy of a ring: a necessarily short message or verse inscribed in a ring given as a present or token of love (cf *The Merchant of Venice* where the message in a ring is *'love me and leave me not'*)

155 Phoebus' cart: the chariot of the sun. The idea was that the sun god's progress through the skies lit the world from dawn to dusk.

156 Neptune's salt-wash...orbed ground: the sea and the earth

159 Since love...bands: since we were married. A six-line speech conveys the information that they have been married for thirty years.
Hymen: god of marriage, a sort of overgrown Cupid. He is symbolized by the bridal-torch and veil he carries.

passionate action. The POISONER, *with some two or three* MUTES, *comes in again, seeming to lament with her. The dead body is carried away. The* POISONER *woos the* QUEEN *with gifts: she seems harsh awhile, but in the end accepts his love.*   [*Exeunt*

OPHELIA   What means this, my lord?

HAMLET   Marry, this is miching mallecho; it means mischief.

OPHELIA   Belike this show imports the argument of the   140
              play.

              Enter PROLOGUE

HAMLET   We shall know by this fellow. The players cannot
              keep counsel, they'll tell all.

OPHELIA   Will a' tell us what the show meant?

HAMLET   Ay or any show that you will show him. Be not   145
              ashamed to show, he'll not shame to tell you
              what it means.

OPHELIA   You are naught, you are naught. I'll mark the play.

PROLOGUE   For us, and for our tragedy,
              Here stooping to your clemency,   150
              We beg your hearing patiently.   [*Exit*

HAMLET   Is this a prologue, or the posy of a ring?

OPHELIA   'Tis brief, my lord.

HAMLET   As woman's love.

              Enter two PLAYERS, KING *and* QUEEN

PLAYER KING Full thirty times hath Phœbus' cart gone round 155
              Neptune's salt-wash, and Tellus' orbed ground,
              And thirty dozen moons with borrowed sheen
              About the world have times twelve thirties been,
              Since love our hearts, and Hymen did our hands
              Unite commutual in most sacred bands.   160

PLAYER QUEEN So many journeys may the sun and moon
              Make us again count o'er ere love be done.

The stage king and queen now speak of the king's poor health and the queen vehemently denies that she would ever marry again if he were to die. She says that to marry another husband when the first has died would be like causing his death for a second time. He says that circumstances change what were our firm intentions.

165 **distrust you**: am concerned (about your health)
167 **women's fear and love...in extremity**: fear and love in a woman go together – either all or nothing
169 **proof**: testing, experience of it
174 **operant...to do**: my active powers stop working
180 **None wed...the first**: Hamlet has not been told by the ghost that Gertrude connived at her husband's murder, but in marrying Claudius she appears guilty by association
181 **wormwood**: the plant *Artemisia Absintium*, known for its bitter taste and used as a *metaphor* (see GLOSSARY page 335) for bitterness, unpleasantness
182 **instances...move**: causes that motivate a second marriage
183 **respects of thrift**: concern for advantage
186 **think**: believe
188 **slave to memory**: entirely subservient to memory
189 **of violent birth**: powerful when it first comes to life
    poor validity: not very robust
192 **Most necessary 'tis**: inevitable
196 **The violence...destroy**: the strength of grief or joy prevents either being translated into action

> • *Look for comparisons and contrasts between the Player Queen and Gertrude.*

But woe is me, you are so sick of late,
So far from cheer, and from your former state,
That I distrust you. Yet though I distrust,   165
Discomfort you my lord it nothing must.
For women's fear and love hold quantity;
In neither aught, or in extremity.
Now, what my love is, proof hath made you know,
And as my love is sized, my fear is so.   170
Where love is great, the littlest doubts are fear;
Where little fears grow great, great love grows
          there.

PLAYER KING   Faith I must leave thee love, and shortly too,
My operant powers their functions leave to do,
And thou shalt live in this fair world behind,   175
Honoured, beloved, and haply one as kind
For husband shalt thou –

PLAYER QUEEN   O confound the rest,
Such love must needs be treason in my breast.
In second husband let me be accurst;
None wed the second but who killed the first.   180

HAMLET   [*Aside*] That's wormwood, wormwood.

PLAYER QUEEN The instances that second marriage move
Are base respects of thrift, but none of love.
A second time I kill my husband dead,
When second husband kisses me in bed.   185

PLAYER KING   I do believe you think what now you speak,
But what we do determine, oft we break.
Purpose is but the slave to memory,
Of violent birth, but poor validity,
Which now like fruit unripe sticks on the tree,   190
But fall unshaken when they mellow be,
Most necessary 'tis that we forget
To pay ourselves what to ourselves is debt.
What to ourselves in passion we propose,
The passion ending, doth the purpose lose.   195
The violence of either grief or joy

The stage king declares that human life is full of uncertainty. Although we may make plans, circumstances are bound to change. His queen protests she would not remarry after his death. She leaves him to rest. Hamlet asks Gertrude's opinion of the play.

198 Where joy...accident: people who experience strong emotions will feel grief or joy with equal intensity and one emotion can easily swing to the opposite extreme

200 for aye: for ever

202 prove: put to the test

204 The great man...flies: if a great man is brought down, you will see the man who was his favourite run for cover

205 The poor advanced: poor man given promotion

206 hitherto: up to this point

208 who...doth try: someone who in need turns to a friend who does not help him

209 seasons him: turns him into

212 devices: plans
    still: continually

219 An anchor's cheer: such food and drink as a hermit (an anchorite) might have
    scope: limit, extent

220 Each opposite...and it destroy: let each contrary force that is able to make joy turn pale, oppose what I hope will turn out well and destroy it

222 here and hence: in the present life and in the next world

224 If she...now!: supposing she were to break her word now!

226 fain I would beguile: I'd like to while away

228 mischance: bad luck, ill fortune

230 doth protest too much: makes too many vows

- *In lines 216–223 the Player Queen has sworn an oath depriving herself of practically everything that makes day-to-day human life pleasant, or at least tolerable, if she were to marry again after becoming a widow. What effect would you expect this speech to have on Gertrude?*

Their own enactures with themselves destroy.
Where joy most revels, grief doth most lament;
Grief joys, joy grieves, on slender accident.
This world is not for aye, nor 'tis not strange   200
That even our loves should with our fortunes
    change;
For 'tis a question left us yet to prove,
Whether love lead fortune, or else fortune love.
The great man down, you mark his favourite flies,
The poor advanced makes friends of enemies.   205
And hitherto doth love on fortune tend;
For who not needs shall never lack a friend,
And who in want a hollow friend doth try,
Directly seasons him his enemy.
But orderly to end where I begun,   210
Our wills and fates do so contrary run
That our devices still are overthrown;
Our thoughts are ours, their ends none of our own.
So think thou wilt no second husband wed,
But die thy thoughts when thy first lord is dead.   215

PLAYER QUEEN Nor earth to me give food, nor heaven light,
Sport and repose lock from me day and night,
To desperation turn my trust and hope,
An anchor's cheer in prison be my scope,
Each opposite that blanks the face of joy   220
Meet what I would have well, and it destroy.
Both here and hence pursue me lasting strife,
If once a widow, ever I be wife.

HAMLET   If she should break it now!

PLAYER KING 'Tis deeply sworn. Sweet, leave me here awhile;   225
My spirits grow dull, and fain I would beguile
The tedious day with sleep.   [*Sleeps*

PLAYER QUEEN   Sleep rock thy brain,
And never come mischance between us twain. [*Exit*

HAMLET   Madam, how like you this play?

QUEEN   The lady doth protest too much, methinks.   230

Claudius asks anxiously about any offensive material there
might be in the play. Hamlet reassures him ambiguously,
continues his conversation, still full of sexual innuendo, with
Ophelia, but is eager for the play to proceed.

232 **argument**: plot (of the play)
   offence: anything to cause offence
237 **Tropically**: figuratively and possibly also a play on the
   word 'trap', which is the use Hamlet is making of the
   play. 'Trope' is a figure of speech where a word or phrase
   is used in a sense different from the one proper to it.
242 **galled jade**: a worn-out horse with saddle sores
243 **withers**: the highest part of a horse's back, between the
   shoulder blades
   unwrung: not chafed
245 **chorus**: in classical Greek plays the chorus would explain
   the action of the play or tell what happened off stage
247 **puppets dallying**: the flirtation of the characters in a
   puppet play. In line with Hamlet's recent remarks to
   Ophelia some sexual reference is suspected, but is unclear.
248 **keen**: sharp
249 **It would...mine edge**: you would be forced to groan if
   you, a virgin, were to relieve my need for sex (take the
   keen edge off my sexual appetite)
250 **Still better and worse**: ever more clever and more
   offensive
251 **mis-take**: take wrongly or falsely
252 **pox...faces**: curse it, stop pulling your damned faces – ie
   leave off the dumb show
253 **'the croaking raven...revenge'**: a quotation from two
   lines of an anonymous play about Richard III
254 **apt**: ready
255 **Confederate season**: time conspires with him
   else no creature: no other creature
256 **midnight weeds**: plants for the witches' brew gathered at
   midnight would be more effective
257 **Hecate's ban**: the curse of the goddess who presides over
   witchcraft
258 **dire property**: evil quality
259 **usurps**: intrudes on, infests
260 **estate**: position in life

HAMLET	O but she'll keep her word.
KING	Have you heard the argument? Is there no offence in't?
HAMLET	No, no, they do but jest, poison in jest, no offence i' th' world. 235
KING	What do you call the play?
HAMLET	The Mouse-trap. Marry how? Tropically. This play is the image of a murder done in Vienna. Gonzago is the duke's name, his wife, Baptista; you shall see anon; 'tis a knavish piece of work, but what o' 240 that? Your majesty and we that have free souls, it touches us not. Let the galled jade wince, our withers are unwrung.

Enter LUCIANUS

	This is one Lucianus, nephew to the king.
OPHELIA	You are as good as a chorus my lord. 245
HAMLET	I could interpret between you and your love, if I could see the puppets dallying.
OPHELIA	You are keen my lord, you are keen.
HAMLET	It would cost you a groaning to take off mine edge.
OPHELIA	Still better, and worse. 250
HAMLET	So you mis-take your husbands. Begin, murderer; pox, leave thy damnable faces, and begin. Come, 'the croaking raven doth bellow for revenge'.
LUCIANUS	Thoughts black, hands apt, drugs fit, and time agreeing; Confederate season, else no creature seeing; 255 Thou mixture rank, of midnight weeds collected, With Hecate's ban thrice blasted, thrice infected, Thy natural magic and dire property, On wholesome life usurps immediately. *[Pours the poison in his ears*
HAMLET	'A poisons him i' th' garden for his estate. His 260

As Hamlet tells Claudius the story of the play, the King rises, calls for lights and leaves – soon only Hamlet and Horatio remain. Hamlet is elated at the King's unease and they agree that the King has demonstrated his guilt.

261 is extant: still exists

265 false fire: guns firing blanks

270 Why, let...world away: a song or ballad
stricken: wounded in the hunt

271 ungalled: uninjured

272 watch: stay awake

274 forest of feathers: the plumes of feathers worn in men's hats, particularly as part of theatre costume

275 turn Turk with me: round on me, desert me

276 Provincial roses...razed shoes: roses of Provence – 'rosettes on my cut shoes'. Shoes were sometimes 'slashed' to leave a slit or show a coloured facing.

277 cry of players: Hamlet's collective noun for a troupe of actors, taken from the word for a pack of hounds. In lines 270–277 Hamlet, fired by his success at getting a reaction from Claudius, claims that he could make his living in the theatre.

280 O Damon dear: Damon and Pythias were inseparable friends in ancient Syracuse. Condemned to death by the ruler, Damon needed to sort out his affairs and Pythias stayed as hostage for him. When Damon returned, the tyrant, impressed, spared them both.

281 This realm...himself: the kingdom was stripped of Jove – the chief of the gods – Hamlet's father

283 peacock: Horatio says Hamlet could have rhymed, presumably with 'ass'. He seems to have chosen something worse. The 'peacock' was associated with vicious qualities. It is also read as 'pajock', or 'patchock' a brute, or 'paddock' a toad, thought then to be poisonous.

• *At which point does Claudius rise and stop the performance? Why did he not do so at a similar point in the Dumb Show? How does Hamlet react?*

name's Gonzago, the story is extant, and written in
very choice Italian. You shall see anon how the
murderer gets the love of Gonzago's wife.

OPHELIA   The King rises.

HAMLET   What, frighted with false fire!   265

QUEEN   How fares my lord?

POLONIUS   Give o'er the play.

KING   Give me some light – away!

ALL   Lights, lights, lights.
                              [*Exeunt all but* HAMLET *and* HORATIO

HAMLET   Why, let the stricken deer go weep,   270
               The hart ungalled play,
            For some must watch while some must sleep,
               So runs the world away.
            Would not this, sir, and a forest of feathers, if the
            rest of my fortunes turn Turk with me, with   275
            two Provincial roses on my razed shoes, get me a
            fellowship in a cry of players, sir?

HORATIO   Half a share.

HAMLET   A whole one, I.
            For thou dost know, O Damon dear,   280
               This realm dismantled was
            Of Jove himself, and now reigns here
               A very, very – peacock.

HORATIO   You might have rhymed.

HAMLET   O good Horatio, I'll take the ghost's word for   285
            a thousand pound. Didst perceive?

HORATIO   Very well, my lord.

HAMLET   Upon the talk of the poisoning?

HORATIO   I did very well note him.

HAMLET   Ah ha! Come, some music! Come, the
               recorders!   290
            For if the King like not the comedy,

Guildenstern comes in to say the King is out of sorts, angry at what has happened. Hamlet pretends at first to think Claudius is drunk, then talks of doctors. Guildenstern has been sent by Gertrude. Hamlet explains that he is not in his right mind.

292 perdy: Pardieu (by God), a mild oath

294 vouchsafe: grant

298 distempered: out of sorts, or drunk, which is the meaning Hamlet chooses to take up

300 choler: anger, Hamlet chooses the meaning 'bile'

303 purgation: both clearing of waste matter from the body by means of a laxative, and cleansing the soul of guilt by confession

305 put...frame: structure your conversation more logically

306 start not...from my affair: do not jump away so suddenly from my subject

307 tame: well–behaved, docile

313 wholesome: healthy – (here) sane, sensible

314 pardon: permission to go

320 command: have at your service

Why then belike, he likes it not, perdy.
Come, some music!

Enter ROSENCRANTZ *and* GUILDENSTERN

GUILDENSTERN Good my lord, vouchsafe me a word with you.

HAMLET   Sir, a whole history.   295

GUILDENSTERN The King, sir –

HAMLET   Ay sir, what of him?

GUILDENSTERN Is in his retirement marvellous distempered.

HAMLET   With drink sir?

GUILDENSTERN No my lord, rather with choler.   300

HAMLET   Your wisdom should show itself more richer to
           signify this to his doctor; for, for me to put him to
           his purgation would perhaps plunge him into far
           more choler.

GUILDENSTERN Good my lord, put your discourse into some   305
           frame, and start not so wildly from my affair.

HAMLET   I am tame sir, pronounce.

GUILDENSTERN The Queen your mother in most great
           affliction of spirit, hath sent me to you.

HAMLET   You are welcome.   310

GUILDENSTERN Nay good my lord, this courtesy is not of the
           right breed. If it shall please you to make me a
           wholesome answer, I will do your mother's
           commandment; if not, your pardon and my return
           shall be the end of my business.   315

HAMLET   Sir, I cannot.

GUILDENSTERN What, my lord?

HAMLET   Make you a wholesome answer; my wit's diseased.
           But sir, such answer as I can make, you shall
           command, or rather as you say, my mother: 320
           therefore no more, but to the matter. My mother,
           you say –

Rosencrantz tells Hamlet his mother wants to speak to him before he goes to bed. He accuses Hamlet of not being open with his friends, not sharing his troubles. Hamlet suggests they are trying to trap him. Picking up a recorder, Hamlet asks Guildenstern to play.

324 amazement and admiration: bewilderment and wonder
331 trade: dealings
333 pickers and stealers: hands. The reference is to the catechism in *The Book of Common Prayer*.
335 bar the door...liberty: if Hamlet keeps his problems bottled up, instead of confiding in his friend, he cannot free his mind
337 I lack advancement: Hamlet gives the reason that Rosencrantz originally suggested for his mood
340 'While the grass grows': completed by 'the horse starves'
342 To withdraw with you: Hamlet takes Rosencrantz aside
343 recover the wind...toil: get to windward of me again as if you wanted to drive me into a net. The fox, if he got the scent of a huntsman, would run away and this knowledge could be used to make him run into a net.
345 if my duty...unmannerly: if Hamlet finds the duty Guildenstern owes him too assertive, then love itself, from which duty stems, must be ill–mannered
347 I...that: it is Guildenstern's profession of love that Hamlet claims not to understand, not his whole remark
348 pipe: recorder

> • *Rosencrantz and Guildenstern are still observing Hamlet. What could they have learnt about his attitude to them if they had really listened?*

ROSENCRANTZ   Then thus she says, your behaviour hath
                struck her into amazement and admiration.

HAMLET   O wonderful son that can so stonish a mother!   325
                But is there no sequel at the heels of this mother's
                admiration? Impart.

ROSENCRANTZ   She desires to speak with you in her closet ere
                you go to bed.

HAMLET   We shall obey, were she ten times our mother.   330
                Have you any further trade with us?

ROSENCRANTZ   My lord, you once did love me.

HAMLET   So I do still, by these pickers and stealers.

ROSENCRANTZ   Good my lord, what is your cause of dis-
                temper? You do surely bar the door upon your   335
                own liberty, if you deny your griefs to your friend.

HAMLET   Sir, I lack advancement.

ROSENCRANTZ   How can that be, when you have the voice of
                the King himself for your succession in Denmark?

HAMLET   Ay sir, but 'While the grass grows' – the proverb 340
                is something musty.

                Enter PLAYERS *with recorders*

                O the recorders – let me see one. To withdraw with
                you – why do you go about to recover the wind of
                me, as if you would drive me into a toil?

GUILDENSTERN   O my lord, if my duty be too bold, my love   345
                is too unmannerly.

HAMLET   I do not well understand that. Will you play upon
                this pipe?

GUILDENSTERN   My lord, I cannot.

HAMLET   I pray you.   350

GUILDENSTERN   Believe me, I cannot.

HAMLET   I do beseech you.

GUILDENSTERN   I know no touch of it my lord.

When Guildenstern absolutely refuses to play, saying he does not know how to, Hamlet rebukes him for thinking he can manipulate him like a musical instrument. When Polonius comes by to give Hamlet the message that Gertrude wishes to speak to him, Hamlet again has fun at the old diplomat's expense.

354 ventages: holes
364 compass: range
366 little organ: the recorder
369 fret me: the frets are the raised bars under the strings of some instruments (lute, guitar) to regulate the fingering. The word *'fret'* (here) is the verb – to supply with frets, with a play on the meaning 'irritate'.
380 by and by: shortly
381 the top of my bent: my absolute limit

HAMLET	It is as easy as lying; govern these ventages with your fingers and thumb, give it breath with 355 your mouth, and it will discourse most eloquent music. Look you, these are the stops.

GUILDENSTERN But these cannot I command to any utterance
of harmony; I have not the skill.

HAMLET	Why look you now how unworthy a thing 360 you make of me. You would play upon me, you would seem to know my stops, you would pluck out the heart of my mystery, you would sound me from my lowest note to the top of my compass; and there is much music, excellent voice in this 365 little organ, yet cannot you make it speak. 'Sblood do you think I am easier to be played on than a pipe? Call me what instrument you will, though you can fret me, yet you cannot play upon me.

Enter POLONIUS

	God bless you sir. 370
POLONIUS	My lord, the Queen would speak with you, and presently.
HAMLET	Do you see yonder cloud that's almost in shape of a camel?
POLONIUS	By th' mass and 'tis, like a camel indeed. 375
HAMLET	Methinks it is like a weasel.
POLONIUS	It is backed like a weasel.
HAMLET	Or like a whale?
POLONIUS	Very like a whale.
HAMLET	Then I will come to my mother by and by. 380 They fool me to the top of my bent – I will come by and by.
POLONIUS	I will say so.
HAMLET	By and by is easily said. [*Exit* POLONIUS] Leave me friends. 385

Hamlet, now as sure as he can be of Claudius's guilt, tries to convince himself that he can take revenge. He prepares for the interview with his mother.

386 witching time: the time of night appropriate for witchcraft and other supernatural occurrences
388 Contagion: plague, pestilence
Now...hot blood: this sounds unlikely on Hamlet's lips, but by using the language of horror he hopes to nerve himself to murder
390 Soft: enough of this
391 nature: feelings of a son for his mother
392 Nero: a Roman emperor who arranged the death of his mother Agrippina. She had poisoned her husband.
396 How...shent: however she may be punished with words
397 To give...consent: may my soul never agree to these words becoming deeds

> • *Does Hamlet intend following the Ghost's instructions, as far as his mother is concerned?*

Claudius tells Rosencrantz and Guildenstern that because Hamlet is now clearly a danger they must take him to England at once. They tell the King that while the safety of any individual is important, it is vital that he, on whom so many depend, should not come to harm.

1 I like him not: I do not like the way he is behaving
with us: with me (the royal plural)
3 I your...dispatch: I will have your warrant quickly prepared
5 The terms of our estate: the circumstances of my position (royal plural again)
6 Hazard: danger
grow Out of his brows: is apparent from the way he looks
7 provide: equip
11 peculiar: individual
13 noyance: harm, injury
14 weal: well-being

[Exeunt all but HAMLET

'Tis now the very witching time of night,
When churchyards yawn, and hell itself breathes
   out
Contagion to this world. Now could I drink hot
   blood,
And do such bitter business as the day
Would quake to look on. Soft, now to my
   mother.   390
O heart, lose not thy nature, let not ever
The soul of Nero enter this firm bosom.
Let me be cruel, not unnatural,
I will speak daggers to her, but use none;
My tongue and soul in this be hypocrites,   395
How in my words somever she be shent,
To give them seals never my soul consent.   *[Exit*

Scene ❸

Enter KING, ROSENCRANTZ, *and* GUILDENSTERN

KING

I like him not, nor stands it safe with us
To let his madness range, therefore prepare you;
I your commission will forthwith dispatch,
And he to England shall along with you.
The terms of our estate may not endure   5
Hazard so near us as doth hourly grow
Out of his brows.

GUILDENSTERN   We will ourselves provide.
Most holy and religious fear it is
To keep those many many bodies safe
That live and feed upon your majesty.   10

ROSENCRANTZ The single and peculiar life is bound,
With all the strength and armour of the mind,
To keep itself from noyance, but much more
That spirit, upon whose weal depend and rest

Rosencrantz continues to praise the importance of kingship. The King wants to speed their journey. When they have left the King, Polonius arrives to say that Hamlet is on the way to his mother's room and that he will go and conceal himself so that a true version of their conversation can be told. Alone, Claudius is struck by the horror of his deed. His guilt makes him incapable of praying.

15 cess: cessation, death

16 gulf: whirlpool

17 massy: massive

20 mortised: fastened

21 Each small annexment: every small thing which is joined on
    consequence: attachment

22 bois'trous: violent and noisy

24 Arm you: get ready

27 closet: private room

28 arras: wall-hanging

29 the process: what goes on
    tax him home: take him to task, tell him the score

31 meet: appropriate, sensible

33 of vantage: from a convenient position

36 rank: foul, evil-smelling

37 primal eldest curse: God laid a curse on Cain for the
    murder of his brother Abel. The word *'primal'* is used
    because they were the sons of Adam and Eve (the book of
    Genesis in the *Bible*) and this is the first recorded curse of
    God on man.

39 Though inclination...intent: though my desire to pray is
    as strong as my determination to do so, my guilt , which is
    stronger still, defeats my intention

41 And...begin: like someone with two courses of action open
    to him, I pause, not knowing where to start. The word
    'bound' is taken to be in the sense of 'bound for a
    destination'. Here the two courses of action are 'to pray or
    not to pray' and echo Hamlet's own indecisions.

> • *Taking Claudius's speech which opens the scene, and
>   this soliloquy together, what do you make of the man?*

The lives of many. The cess of majesty   15
Dies not alone; but like a gulf doth draw
What's near it with it. It is a massy wheel
Fixed on the summit of the highest mount,
To whose huge spokes ten thousand lesser things
Are mortised and adjoined; which when it falls   20
Each small annexment, petty consequence,
Attends the boist'rous ruin. Never alone
Did the king sigh, but with a general groan.

KING   Arm you I pray you to this speedy voyage,
For we will fetters put upon this fear   25
Which now goes too free-footed.

ROSENCRANTZ ⎤
                                                    We will haste us.
GUILDENSTERN ⎦

Exeunt ROSENCRANTZ *and* GUILDENSTERN

Enter POLONIUS

POLONIUS   My lord, he's going to his mother's closet.
Behind the arras I'll convey myself
To hear the process. I'll warrant she'll tax him
      home,
And as you said, and wisely was it said,   30
'Tis meet that some more audience than a mother,
Since nature makes them partial, should o'erhear
The speech of vantage. Fare you well, my liege,
I'll call upon you ere you go to bed,
And tell you what I know.

KING   Thanks dear my lord. 35
                                          [*Exit* POLONIUS
O my offence is rank, it smells to heaven;
It hath the primal eldest curse upon't,
A brother's murder. Pray can I not,
Though inclination be as sharp as will.
My stronger guilt defeats my strong intent,   40
And like a man to double business bound,
I stand in pause when I shall first begin,

Claudius cannot be pardoned as he still enjoys all he gained from fratricide, and he cannot repent. He begs the angels for help. It would be easy to kill him, but he seems to be praying.

46 **Whereto...of offence**: what is God's mercy for, if not to come face to face with sin?

49 **To be forestalled...being down?**: to be prevented from falling – or having fallen, to be forgiven?

54 **effects**: those things and that position

56 **retain th' offence**: keep the gains. If you asked for pardon you should make what restitution you could, and not continue to benefit from your offence

58 **gilded**: supplied with money or gold
   shove by: push aside

60 **Buys out the law**: in this world corruption can override justice

61 **There**: above, in Heaven
   shuffling: evasiveness, deception
   the action lies: the case is before the court

62 **his**: its

63 **Even to the teeth...in evidence**: to give evidence about the worst aspects of our sins

64 **rests**: remains

65 **Try...can**: see what repentance can do

68 **limed**: birds were caught in a sticky substance (called birdlime) smeared on the branches.

69 **make assay**: make the attempt. An appeal to the angels, presumably including his own guardian angel, to intercede on his behalf.

73 **Now...pat**: now would be an opportune moment to do it.

75 **That...scanned**: either 'that needs further consideration' or, imagining the deed already done in these particular circumstances, 'people would interpret this "revenge" as...'

> • *What chiefly stands in the way of forgiveness and then repentance for Claudius?*

And both neglect. What if this cursed hand
Were thicker than itself with brother's blood,
Is there not rain enough in the sweet heavens   45
To wash it white as snow? Whereto serves mercy
But to confront the visage of offence?
And what's in prayer but this two-fold force,
To be forestalled ere we come to fall,
Or pardoned being down? Then I'll look up;   50
My fault is past. But o what form of prayer
Can serve my turn? 'Forgive me my foul murder'?
That cannot be since I am still possessed
Of those effects for which I did the murder,
My crown, mine own ambition, and my Queen. 55
May one be pardoned and retain th' offence?
In the corrupted currents of this world
Offence's gilded hand may shove by justice,
And oft 'tis seen the wicked prize itself
Buys out the law. But 'tis not so above;   60
There is no shuffling, there the action lies
In his true nature, and we ourselves compelled,
Even to the teeth and forehead of our faults
To give in evidence. What then? What rests?
Try what repentance can – what can it not?   65
Yet what can it, when one can not repent?
O wretched state, o bosom black as death,
O limed soul, that struggling to be free,
Art more engaged! Help, angels, make assay.
Bow stubborn knees, and heart with strings of
    steel,   70
Be soft as sinews of the new-born babe.
All may be well.   [*Kneels*

Enter HAMLET

HAMLET   Now might I do it pat, now he is praying;
And now I'll do 't – and so he goes to heaven;
And so am I revenged. That would be scanned: 75
A villain kills my father, and for that,

Hamlet compares what he knows of his father's murder with his proposed killing of Claudius. His father died without confession or absolution. It would be preferable, as vengeance, to kill a drunken or raging Claudius, not after confession and at prayer. Claudius rises, unable to pray.

79 this is...not revenge : this is reward, not revenge
80 grossly: in a state of gross sinfulness
81 broad blown: in full blossom
   flush: vigorous
82 audit: reckoning
83 in our...thought: as our thoughts go – in an indirect way. Shakespeare is using two nouns in place of a noun and an adjective
84 'Tis heavy with him: he is in a bad way
85 purging of his soul: confessing his sins
86 seasoned: prepared
88 Up: back in your scabbard
   hent: both 'grasp' and 'occasion' – the sword must wait to be used on an occasion which might be more likely to send Claudius straight to hell
91 At game: gambling
92 relish: trace
93 may kick at heaven: as he is forced to dive headfirst into hell
96 physic: medicine – ie being saved from death

> • *On a false premise, Hamlet lets his thoughts persuade him not to act. Are you disappointed?*

Polonius instructs Gertrude to be severe with Hamlet. He gets ready to hide as Hamlet calls out to his mother.

1 lay home to him: take him to task
2 pranks: outrageous tricks
4 silence me: hide myself and listen silently. Either ironic, since Polonius does not keep silent and thus invites his death, or a misreading.
5 round: direct

I his sole son do this same villain send
To heaven.
Why, this is hire and salary, not revenge.
'A took my father grossly full of bread,   80
With all his crimes broad blown, as flush as May,
And how his audit stands who knows save heaven?
But in our circumstance and course of thought,
'Tis heavy with him; and am I then revenged,
To take him in the purging of his soul,   85
When he is fit and seasoned for his passage?
No.
Up sword, and know thou a more horrid hent,
When he is drunk asleep, or in his rage,
Or in th' incestuous pleasure of his bed,   90
At game, a-swearing, or about some act
That has no relish of salvation in 't –
Then trip him that his heels may kick at heaven,
And that his soul may be as damned and black
As hell whereto it goes. My mother stays.   95
This physic but prolongs thy sickly days.   [*Exit*

KING   [*Rising*] My words fly up, my thoughts remain
                 below.
              Words without thoughts never to heaven go. [*Exit*

Scene 4

Enter QUEEN *and* POLONIUS

POLONIUS   'A will come straight. Look you lay home to him,
             Tell him his pranks have been too broad to bear
                with,
             And that your grace hath screened and stood
                between
             Much heat and him. I'll silence me even here.
             Pray you be round with him.   5

HAMLET   [*Within*] Mother, mother, mother!

Polonius hides as Hamlet enters. The Queen starts to rebuke him, but Hamlet will not accept what she says and in turn points out that she has made an illicit marriage. She is about to send for someone he will listen to, when Hamlet sits her down, promising to show her to herself. Alarmed she calls for help and Polonius, forgetting the need for silence, does so too. Hamlet pulls out his rapier and kills him, unseen, through the arras, thinking it might be Claudius.

11 idle: useless, silly
14 rood: the cross of Christ
17 I'll set...speak: I'll fetch people to whom you'll have to listen
24 Dead for a ducat: possibly a bet with himself that the thrust will kill the man, or an indication that someone who spies is not worth much anyway

- *Hamlet does not hesitate to kill the man behind the arras. What are the differences between the situations where he fails to kill Claudius, yet whips out his sword and kills whoever is hiding?*

QUEEN	I'll warrant you,

      Fear me not. Withdraw, I hear him coming.

               [POLONIUS *hides behind the arras*

Enter HAMLET

HAMLET   Now mother, what's the matter?

QUEEN   Hamlet, thou hast thy father much offended.

HAMLET   Mother, you have my father much offended.   10

QUEEN   Come, come, you answer with an idle tongue.

HAMLET   Go, go, you question with a wicked tongue.

QUEEN   Why, how now Hamlet!

HAMLET   What's the matter now?

QUEEN   Have you forgot me?

HAMLET   No by the rood, not so.

      You are the Queen, your husband's brother's

         wife,   15

      And would it were not so, you are my mother.

QUEEN   Nay, then I'll set those to you that can speak.

HAMLET   Come, come, and sit you down, you shall not

         budge.

      You go not till I set you up a glass

      Where you may see the inmost part of you.   20

QUEEN   What wilt thou do, thou wilt not murder me?

      Help, help, ho!

POLONIUS   [*Behind*] What ho, help, help, help!

HAMLET   [*Drawing*] How now! A rat? Dead for a ducat,

         dead.

                       [*Makes a pass through the arras*

POLONIUS   [*Behind*] O I am slain!   25

                       [*Falls and dies*

QUEEN   O me, what hast thou done?

HAMLET   Nay I know not,

      Is it the King?

Hamlet, having killed, likens the deed to his mother's actions. When he discovers he has killed Polonius he delivers a heartfelt epitaph, then turns to his mother. He sets out in blunt language to make her fully aware of what she has done, as he sees it. When she seems not to understand, he shows her the portraits of the two brothers.

30 As kill...brother: not necessarily an accusation of complicity in murder. This would be going far beyond the Ghost's brief. But in accepting the marriage with Claudius so soon after her husband's death she is almost an accessory after the fact.

38 brazed it: made it brazen, hammered it hard, like brass

39 proof and bulwark: tried and proved, a defence

43 the rose: the fresh bloom

45 blister: an indication of disease or a reference to the practice of branding prostitutes on the forehead

47 As from ...The very soul: as makes an empty farce of contracts (particularly the marriage vows)

49 rhapsody: a meaningless string of words

Heaven's face...solidity: the heavens flush red above the solid mass of the earth, and the earth itself, with glowing face, as though foretelling doomsday, is immensely distressed at the act. Alternative readings are 'Yea' for 'O'er' and 'tristful' (sad) for 'heated'.

53 index: table of contents, preface

55 counterfeit presentment: portrait

> • *We see here for the first time Hamlet's pent-up anger and frustration being vented directly at one of the guilty parties – not at his own inadequacy. Are you convinced that this is the first time that Gertrude has confronted her own dubious behaviour?*

QUEEN	O what a rash and bloody deed is this!
HAMLET	A bloody deed, almost as bad, good mother,
	As kill a king, and marry with his brother. 30
QUEEN	As kill a king?
HAMLET	Ay, lady, it was my word.

[*Lifts up the arras and discovers* POLONIUS

Thou wretched rash, intruding fool, farewell.
I took thee for thy better, take thy fortune;
Thou find'st to be too busy is some danger.
Leave wringing of your hands; peace, sit you
    down,   35
And let me wring your heart, for so I shall,
If it be made of penetrable stuff;
If damned custom have not brazed it so
That it be proof and bulwark against sense.

QUEEN   What have I done, that thou dar'st wag thy
    tongue   40
In noise so rude against me?

HAMLET   Such an act
That blurs the grace and blush of modesty,
Calls virtue hypocrite, takes off the rose
From the fair forehead of an innocent love,
And sets a blister there, makes marriage vows   45
As false as dicers' oaths, o such a deed
As from the body of contraction plucks
The very soul, and sweet religion makes
A rhapsody of words. Heaven's face does glow
O'er this solidity and compound mass   50
With heated visage, as against the doom,
Is thought-sick at the act.

QUEEN   Ay me, what act,
That roars so loud, and thunders in the index?

HAMLET   Look here upon this picture, and on this,
The counterfeit presentment of two brothers.   55
See what a grace was seated on this brow,

Hamlet makes a hard-hitting comparison between
Gertrude's two husbands. He asks what could possibly have
made her desert his father for his uncle. He seeks to shame
her and succeeds.

57 **front**: forehead
   Jove: the chief god in Roman mythology
59 **station**: stance, bearing
   Mercury: the messenger of the gods, usually depicted with
   wings on his heels
60 **New-lighted**: just alighted, having just landed
65 **mildewed ear**: diseased ear of corn
66 **Blasting**: infecting and destroying
67 **leave to feed**: stop grazing
68 **batten**: fatten yourself up
70 **hey-day in the blood**: excitement in passion, sexual drive
72 **Sense**: your senses
74 **apoplexed**: made numb
   madness...err: madness would not go so far astray
75 **Nor...thralled**: nor would the senses ever be made so
   captive by a state of hallucination
76 **But...difference**: but that they kept in reserve some
   capacity to choose between such different alternatives
78 **cozened you at hoodman-blind?**: deceived you into a
   game of blindman's buff?
80 **sans**: (French) without
82 **Could not so mope**: could not be so bewildered, so dazed
83 **Rebellious...own fire**: if the urge for sex, inspired by the
   devil, can still be so strong in a mature woman, there is no
   hope for virtue in passionate youth – it will just melt away
   like wax
84 **mutine**: mutiny
   matron: a married woman with the sense 'an older woman'
87 **compulsive...the charge**: irresistible passion signals the
   attack
88 **frost itself**: the older woman's passions, which should by
   rights be cold
89 **reason panders will**: reason procures what passion desires
91 **grained**: ingrained, dyed in

Hyperion's curls, the front of Jove himself,
An eye like Mars, to threaten and command,
A station like the herald Mercury,
New-lighted on a heaven-kissing hill,   60
A combination and a form indeed,
Where every god did seem to set his seal
To give the world assurance of a man.
This was your husband. Look you now what
      follows:
Here is your husband like a mildewed ear,   65
Blasting his wholesome brother. Have you eyes?
Could you on this fair mountain leave to feed,
And batten on this moor? Ha, have you eyes?
You cannot call it love, for at your age
The hey-day in the blood is tame, it's humble,   70
And waits upon the judgment; and what judgment
Would step from this to this? Sense sure you have,
Else could you not have motion; but sure that sense
Is apoplexed, for madness would not err,
Nor sense to ecstasy was ne'er so thralled   75
But it reserved some quantity of choice
To serve in such a difference. What devil was 't
That thus hath cozened you at hoodman-blind?
Eyes without feeling, feeling without sight,
Ears without hands or eyes, smelling sans all,   80
Or but a sickly part of one true sense
Could not so mope.
O shame, where is thy blush? Rebellious hell,
If thou canst mutine in a matron's bones,
To flaming youth let virtue be as wax,   85
And melt in her own fire. Proclaim no shame
When the compulsive ardour gives the charge,
Since frost itself as actively doth burn
And reason panders will.

QUEEN   O Hamlet speak no more,
Thou turn'st mine eyes into my very soul,   90
And there I see such black and grained spots

His mother now begs him to stop, but Hamlet is well launched on his theme – until the Ghost of his father reappears. Hamlet assumes the Ghost intends to chide him for not taking vengeance. Gertrude cannot see the Ghost, who tells Hamlet to speak to her. He does so.

92 **leave their tinct**: give up their colour, allow their colour to fade

93 **enseamed**: greasy

94 **Stewed**: bathed in sweat, with the secondary meaning of 'brothel'. These were commonly called 'stews'.
corruption: moral corruption and also putrefaction
honeying: using sweet words, talking fondly
making love: talking fondly – not the present meaning of indulging in the sexual act itself

98 **tithe**: a tenth part, also the annual payment due to the church or other authority

99 **precedent**: former
vice: another word for the clown, or jester, in dramas of the time, but also suggesting the idea of 'mischief' and 'villainy'

100 **cutpurse**: thief – when purses were bags on strings and could be cut off
rule: good government

104 **of shreds and patches**: literally made up of rags and scraps, and so unlike her first husband. But the phrase also recalls the multi-coloured or patchwork costume traditional for the vice or clown, who was also called 'the patch'.

106 **heavenly guards**: angels

108 **tardy**: slow to act, late

109 **lapsed in time and passion**: who has let slip time and moments of passionate hatred

112 **whet**: sharpen

113 **amazement**: bewilderment

115 **Conceit**: imagination

- *Why can Gertrude not see the Ghost? What effect does Hamlet's conversation with him have on her?*

As will not leave their tinct.

HAMLET   Nay but to live
In the rank sweat of an enseamed bed
Stewed in corruption, honeying, and making love
Over the nasty sty.

QUEEN   O, speak to me no more;   95
These words, like daggers, enter in mine ears;
No more, sweet Hamlet!

HAMLET   A murderer and a villain,
A slave that is not twentieth part the tithe
Of your precedent lord, a vice of kings,
A cutpurse of the empire and the rule,   100
That from a shelf the precious diadem stole
And put it in his pocket.

QUEEN   No more.

HAMLET   A king of shreds and patches –

Enter GHOST

Save me and hover o'er me with your wings,   105
You heavenly guards – what would your gracious
        figure?

QUEEN   Alas he's mad.

HAMLET   Do you not come your tardy son to chide,
That lapsed in time and passion lets go by
Th' important acting of your dread command?   110
O say.

GHOST   Do not forget, this visitation
Is but to whet thy almost blunted purpose.
But look, amazement on thy mother sits;
O step between her and her fighting soul –
Conceit in weakest bodies strongest works –   115
Speak to her Hamlet.

HAMLET   How is it with you lady?

QUEEN   Alas how is 't with you,
That you do bend your eye on vacancy,

Gertrude, alarmed to see Hamlet talking to the air, is convinced of his madness. He fears that pity for the Ghost will drive out vengeance. Gertrude must not make Hamlet's madness her excuse to continue in her sin.

119 **incorporal**: (incorporeal) without material existence, empty air

120 **Forth...peep**: the vital spirits were supposed to be subtle, highly refined substances which suffused the blood and, as here, in moments of great agitation might show themselves

121 **sleeping...alarm**: like soldiers raised suddenly from sleep when the trumpet calls to arms

122 **excrements**: in addition to the modern meaning of the word – what the body gets rid of – also what grows out of the body, like hair and nails. The *simile* (see GLOSSARY page 336) suggests that as though it were like the soldiers, Hamlet's hair suddenly stands on end.

126 **glares**: not necessarily an angry stare, but a fixed gaze.

127 **His form...capable**: at the sight of him, and knowing what has happened, even stones would be moved to action

128 **Do not...blood**: Hamlet begs to be spared another gaze from his father, fearing pity will take over from revenge

136 **habit**: clothes

137 **portal**: door

138 **very coinage**: mere creation

139 **This bodiless...cunning in**: madness is good at creating 'ghosts' or 'visions'
    ecstasy: madness, hallucination
    cunning: skilful;

145 **gambol from**: start away, shy away from

146 **unction**: ointment

148 **skin and film**: if skin grows over an abscess, the infection continuing underneath becomes more serious

---

- *Where is the irony in Gertrude's perception of Hamlet's madness in this scene?*
- *What is Hamlet's warning to his mother (lines 140–156)?*

	And with th' incorporal air do hold discourse?	
	Forth at your eyes your spirits wildly peep,	120
	And as the sleeping soldiers in th' alarm,	
	Your bedded hair like life in excrements	
	Start up and stand an end. O gentle son,	
	Upon the heat and flame of thy distemper	
	Sprinkle cool patience. Whereon do you look?	125
HAMLET	On him, on him. Look you how pale he glares.	
	His form and cause conjoined, preaching to stones,	
	Would make them capable. Do not look upon me,	
	Lest with this piteous action you convert	
	My stern effects; then what I have to do	130
	Will want true colour, tears perchance for blood.	
QUEEN	To whom do you speak this?	
HAMLET	Do you see nothing there?	
QUEEN	Nothing at all, yet all that is I see.	
HAMLET	Nor did you nothing hear?	
QUEEN	No, nothing but ourselves.	
HAMLET	Why look you there, look how it steals away –	135
	My father in his habit as he lived –	
	Look where he goes, even now out at the portal.	

[Exit GHOST

QUEEN	This is the very coinage of your brain;	
	This bodiless creation ecstasy	
	Is very cunning in.	
HAMLET	Ecstasy?	140
	My pulse as yours doth temperately keep time,	
	And makes as healthful music. It is not madness	
	That I have uttered; bring me to the test,	
	And I the matter will re-word, which madness	
	Would gambol from. Mother, for love of grace,	145
	Lay not that flattering unction to your soul,	
	That not your trespass, but my madness speaks.	
	It will but skin and film the ulcerous place,	
	Whiles rank corruption mining all within	

Hamlet begs his mother to change her ways, saying that
habit can replicate evil actions, but equally, if she stays apart
from Claudius for one night, it will be easier the second time
and so on until this abstinence becomes habit. Hamlet says
he repents of the killing of Polonius but in a rather offhand
way. Before he goes he answers his mother's request for
advice.

152 **do not...them ranker**: do not encourage the weeds to
   grow even more vigorously by spreading fertile soil on
   them. Hamlet is concerned that she is discounting her
   own misdeeds by comforting herself that what Hamlet has
   been saying to her are the words of a madman.
154 **fatness**: grossness
   pursy: fat, corpulent through self-indulgence
156 **curb**: (here) bow
157 **cleft**: split
162 **That monster custom...is put on**: habit is a monster
   because people get so used to their bad habits that they
   don't consider them any more – on the other hand the
   same can become true of good habits.
169 **use**: habitual practice
170 **either....the devil**: a verb is missing. The sense would
   seem to demand either a (one syllable) verb meaning
   'entertain', such as 'house' *or* 'get the better of' – 'quell'
   has been suggested.
176 **their scourge and minister**: 'heaven' has become 'the
   heavens' to produce the possessive 'their': administer their
   punishment
177 **bestow**: dispose of
   answer well: give a good account of
183 **bloat**: bloated, presumably with food and drink
184 **wanton**: lecherously

- *Hamlet approves of habit. What is his argument?*

Infects unseen. Confess yourself to heaven,   150
Repent what's past, avoid what is to come,
And do not spread the compost on the weeds
To make them ranker. Forgive me this my virtue,
For in the fatness of these pursy times
Virtue itself of vice must pardon beg,   155
Yea curb and woo for leave to do him good.

QUEEN O Hamlet thou hast cleft my heart in twain.

HAMLET O throw away the worser part of it,
And live the purer with the other half.
Good night: but go not to my uncle's bed,   160
Assume a virtue if you have it not.
That monster custom, who all sense doth eat
Of habits evil, is angel yet in this,
That to the use of actions fair and good
He likewise gives a frock or livery   165
That aptly is put on. Refrain tonight,
And that shall lend a kind of easiness
To the next abstinence, the next more easy;
For use almost can change the stamp of nature,
And either....the devil, or throw him out   170
With wondrous potency. Once more good night,
And when you are desirous to be blessed,
I'll blessing beg of you. For this same lord,
I do repent; but heaven hath pleased it so,
To punish me with this, and this with me,   175
That I must be their scourge and minister.
I will bestow him, and will answer well
The death I gave him. So again good night.
I must be cruel only to be kind.
Thus bad begins, and worse remains behind.   180
One word more good lady.

QUEEN   What shall I do?

HAMLET Not this by no means that I bid you do:
Let the bloat king tempt you again to bed,
Pinch wanton on your cheek, call you his mouse,

Hamlet forbids Gertrude to tell Claudius the truth about his madness. Rosencrantz and Guildenstern are to escort him to England. He shows her he knows they are his enemies. He drags Polonius's body away with a fitting obituary.

185 reechy: filthy, squalid

186 paddling in: fondling

187 ravel...out: disentangle

189 in craft: by design

190 For who...hide: what good, beautiful, clever queen, such as you, would keep matters of such relevant concern from a toad, a bat, a tomcat? These three creatures are familiars of witches and sorcerers.

194 Unpeg the basket...neck down: there was a fable where an ape let birds fly from a wicker cage or basket on the roof and then himself got into the cage and tried to repeat the performance, assuming that he too could fly out. This whole set of instructions to Gertrude is, of course, governed by line 182 *'Not...that I bid you do'*.

205 bear the mandate: have their instructions from the king
   sweep my way: clear my path

206 marshal me to knavery: lead me on to their trickery
   enginer: engineer, designer of military machines to use in war, particularly to end sieges

208 Hoist with his own petard: blown up by his own bomb. A petard was a metal or wooden container of explosive, fired by a fuse, used for blowing in doors or gates, or making large holes in castle walls
   and 't: and it

211 in one line...directly meet: plot and counter-plot meet

212 This man...packing: the fact that he has killed Polonius will speed his departure

217 to draw...with you: bring our association to an end

- *Why does Gertrude put up with Hamlet's treatment of her? Is she relieved he is going to England?*
- *Note that Hamlet can confide in her about his enemies.*

	And let him for a pair of reechy kisses,	185
	Or paddling in your neck with his damned fingers,	
	Make you to ravel all this matter out	
	That I essentially am not in madness,	
	But mad in craft. 'Twere good you let him know,	
	For who that's but a queen, fair, sober, wise,	190
	Would from a paddock, from a bat, a gib,	
	Such dear concernings hide, who would do so?	
	No, in despite of sense and secrecy,	
	Unpeg the basket on the house's top,	
	Let the birds fly, and like the famous ape,	195
	To try conclusions in the basket creep,	
	And break your own neck down.	

QUEEN   Be thou assured, if words be made of breath,
           And breath of life, I have no life to breathe
           What thou hast said to me.   200

HAMLET   I must to England, you know that?

QUEEN   Alack,
           I had forgot. 'Tis so concluded on.

HAMLET   There's letters sealed, and my two schoolfellows,
           Whom I will trust as I will adders fanged,
           They bear the mandate; they must sweep my
               way,   205
           And marshal me to knavery. Let it work,
           For 'tis the sport to have the enginer
           Hoist with his own petard; and 't shall go hard
           But I will delve one yard below their mines,
           And blow them at the moon. O 'tis most sweet   210
           When in one line two crafts directly meet.
           This man shall set me packing.
           I'll lug the guts into the neighbour room.
           Mother, good night. Indeed this counsellor
           Is now most still, most secret, and most grave,   215
           Who was in life a foolish prating knave.
           Come sir, to draw towards an end with you.
           Good night, mother.
                                [*Exit* HAMLET *dragging in* POLONIUS

CTIVITIES

Keeping track

Scene 1

1 This scene opens with Rosencrantz and Guildenstern reporting back to Claudius and Gertrude after their attempt to discover the reasons for Hamlet's madness. What do they have to tell Claudius and Gertrude? Is there anything new in this?

2 What is Polonius suggesting when he says that *'with devotion's visage'* we *'sugar o'er the devil himself'* (lines 47–49)?

3 How does Claudius react to this comment and what is revealed about him here?

4 Hamlet's third soliloquy shows him once more in a mood of brooding introspection. What is troubling Hamlet at this point in the play? What conclusions does he reach?

5 Lines 88–191 are often referred to as 'the nunnery scene'. This encounter has been deliberately contrived by Polonius. What is the plan, and what exactly is Polonius trying to prove?

6 It is not clear whether Hamlet knows he is being overheard. Do you think it makes any difference to the dramatic effect? Can you find any evidence to suggest that Hamlet knows that Claudius and Polonius are listening?

7 How does Hamlet behave towards Ophelia? Does his behaviour affect your thoughts and feelings about him? How does Ophelia react to Hamlet in this part of the scene?

8 What conclusion does Claudius reach and what action does he decide to take?

9 What is Polonius's reaction to what they have overheard?

Scene 2

1 The first part of this scene shows Hamlet offering advice to the Players on the subject of acting. Can you see any ways in which his words are relevant to his own situation?

2 In his conversation with Horatio (lines 55–94), Hamlet reveals his plan to trap Claudius. Why do you think he does this?

3 He also defines the 'ideal man': how does he define this ideal? How close is Hamlet to his own ideal?

4 Just before the beginning of the 'inner play', Hamlet continues his attack on Ophelia. What is his mood here? How and why does he attack Ophelia? What do you think of his behaviour?

5 The Dumb Show enacts the events surrounding the murder of Hamlet's father. Claudius does not appear to react. Why do you think this is?

6 The inner play also enacts the events leading to the murder of Hamlet's father. Much of the emphasis is on the words of the Player Queen. How does Gertrude react? What does Claudius learn from the inner play? What does Hamlet learn?

7 How does Hamlet react to the success of the inner play?

8 What does he plan to do when he speaks to his mother?

Scene 3

1 At the beginning of this scene Claudius confirms his decision to remove Hamlet to England. What insight do we gain into his private thoughts and feelings in his soliloquy? Does this change your view of Claudius in any way? Why does his attempt to pray for forgiveness fail?

2 When the king is kneeling in prayer, Hamlet appears to have the perfect opportunity to exact his revenge. However, he does not take his chance. What reasons does he give for not killing Claudius? In what way is this ironic? Do you accept his reasons?

Scene 4

1 This encounter is the result of a plan constructed by Polonius. What is the plan? Why has it been set up and what part is Polonius going to play in it?

2 Hamlet has obeyed the summons come to his mother's closet and, in doing so, missed an opportunity to kill Claudius. Does this tell us anything about Hamlet's real priorities? Is Claudius the only target of his bloody thoughts? Is he the main target?

3 How does Gertrude try to begin the scene and how does Hamlet attempt to seize the initiative? Does he succeed?

4 Why does Gertrude think that Hamlet is going to murder her?

5 Who does Hamlet think he is stabbing?

6 How does he justify his action? What are his feelings about what he has done?

7 When Gertrude asks, 'What have I done', Hamlet launches into a denunciation of her conduct. How would you describe his tone? What has made him speak to her in this way?

8 How does Gertrude respond to Hamlet's attack on her?

9 What advice does Hamlet give to his mother and how does she react to this advice?

10 Has Gertrude been changed by this encounter?

Drama

1 Imagine you are psychologists dealing with the young Hamlet.
You have acquired a diary entry which contains the famous
soliloquy *To be, or not to be'*.

Work through the speech analysing the patient's mental
health and report back to a case conference on your findings.
Some of you could be working in an unprejudiced manner, but
others could have been employed by Claudius.

Having discussed the patient, you could then interview him
to try to help your diagnosis. You could have Hamlet played by
a varying number of people to represent the different voices in
his head: the revengeful son, the doubting fearer of damnation,
the woman/mother-hater, the playful word-player, etc.

2 Imagine one of the servants is present at the play. The press are
desperate to know what went on, but official channels are
playing it down. Improvise the telephone conversation between
one of you as the servant, and a partner as a newspaper reporter
looking for some royal scandal. Write up the ensuing article
using exaggeration and sensationalist language.

3 Work in two groups: some of you rehearse and perform the
Dumb Show, while others rehearse the reactions of the royal
audience. Bring the two together.

4 Work in threes on the exchanges between Hamlet, Rosencrantz
and Guildenstern (Act 3 scene 2 lines 294–369). Choose a
section and work on getting the level of vicious wordplay –
compare this with their earlier exchanges.

5 In pairs, learn the exchange between Hamlet and Gertrude
(Act 3 scene 4 lines 8–21).

Rehearse this scene to explore the complex relationship
between mother and son. As an audience, we have a very good
idea of what is going on in Hamlet's mind, but what is
Gertrude thinking? We only have her public utterances to help
us. Did she recognize herself in the *Murder of Gonzago*?

What was the relationship like between mother and son before
the death of the father? Hotseat the two characters to help you.

6 Using Act 3 scene 4 lines 54–89 work in groups of about six. One
person should represent Gertrude, while the other five represent
five Hamlets all attacking her using the words as weapons.

7 Use FORUM THEATRE (see page 297) to explore these key
moments:
• the moment when Hamlet says *'No, not I, I never gave you
aught.'* (Act 3 scene 1 line 95)
• the moment when *'The King rises.'* (Act 3 scene 2 line 264)
• the arrival of the Ghost (Act 3 scene 4 line 104).

Key elements

In Act 3 these are:
- the third soliloquy
- the 'nunnery scene'
- the inner play
- Claudius at prayer
- the closet scene.

The key scene

Hamlet's third soliloquy: Act 3 scene 1

Keying it in

1 This speech is Hamlet's first appearance after his decision to unmask Claudius by using the inner play. Look back across the opening two acts of the play.
   - What moods has Hamlet experienced so far?
   - Is there any pattern to his feelings?

The speech itself

1 Critics have debated what *'the question'* actually is and it is probably fair to say that this famous soliloquy is by no means transparent in meaning.
   - What do you think he means by *'To be, or not to be'*? Look at lines 56–65.
   - How does Hamlet describe life in these lines?
   - How do the language and imagery convey his feelings about life?
   - How does Hamlet describe death in these lines?
   - How do the language and imagery convey his feelings about death?
   - In which direction is the argument leading?
2 Look at lines 66–82.
   In this part of the speech, the argument changes direction: life is still presented as an inescapable torment.
   - What exactly are the torments of life?
   - How does the language convey Hamlet's feelings?
   However, Hamlet recognizes the fact that we endure the agony of existence, even though death offers an escape from 'the heart-ache' of life.
   - Why do we choose to go on living, according to Hamlet?
   - Choose two quotations which illustrate this point.

3 Look at lines 83–88.

In these lines Hamlet reaches two conclusions:
'conscience does make cowards of us all, '
and
  'the native hue of resolution
Is sicklied o'er with the pale cast of thought'.
- What do you understand by the word *'conscience'* here?
- Is there any significant difference between these two conclusions?
- Is it possible that *'thought'* and *'conscience'* mean much the same thing to Hamlet?
- What is the effect of *'thought'* on *'resolution'*?
- How does Hamlet's choice of language indicate his attitude to the result of *'thought'*?

Overview

In this soliloquy the keynote is the mood of despair and frustration as Hamlet grapples with apparently insoluble contradictions. Inaction – the product of conscience and thought – makes us cowards, but action – the product of blood and instinct – makes us less than human. Hamlet feels trapped in that paradox.
- Compare this soliloquy with *'O that this too too solid flesh'* and *'O what a rogue and peasant slave am I!'*
- What connections can you find between these three speeches?
- Taken together what do they reveal about Hamlet?
- How far do they explain his 'delay' in killing Claudius?

Close study

Act 3 scene 3 lines 73–96
1 How difficult does the task of killing Claudius appear at first?
2 What does Hamlet mean when he says *'That would be scanned'*?
3 Compare what is happening here with Hamlet's conclusions in the *'To be, or not to be'* soliloquy.
4 In what way would killing Claudius at prayer be *'hire and salary'*?
5 In what circumstances does Hamlet say he wants to kill Claudius?
6 How does the language indicate Hamlet's inner feelings?
7 Dr Johnson commented that this speech was 'too terrible to be read or uttered'.
   - In what ways is it 'terrible'?
   - Why do you think Dr Johnson felt like that?
     Do you agree with him?
8 How do you react to Hamlet at this point in the play?

Hamlet and revenge

1 At the end of Act 2 Hamlet had expressed a need for proof of Claudius' guilt, but he did seem to have discovered a sense of purpose and a momentum of a kind. However, the third soliloquy returns to a mood of brooding introspection as Hamlet struggles to make sense of his feelings and his situation.

   The attack on Ophelia in the 'nunnery scene' reveals that his problems go beyond just killing Claudius. He has not succeeded in achieving the sustained, single-minded fury of the conventional revenger and his anger does not have a single focus.
   - Why does he attack Ophelia so cruelly?
   - What makes this scene so painful?

2 The success of the inner play rouses Hamlet to a mood where he could '*drink hot blood*' and perform '*bitter business*'.
   - Is he pleased or alarmed by this?
   - Do you want him to be like the figure of Pyrrhus?

3 At this point Hamlet is presented with an opportunity to kill Claudius. However, he does not kill him.
   - Why does he not kill him?
   - Is it significant that he is on his way to his mother's closet?
   - Does this reveal something about Hamlet's real priorities?

4 Interestingly the confrontation with Gertrude seems to give a release to much of Hamlet's frustration. He agrees to go to England without protest.
   - Why do you think he agrees to this so readily?
   - Where does this leave his revenge on Claudius?

5 By the end of Act 3, Hamlet has fulfilled the Ghost's demands as far as Gertrude is concerned and he has proved beyond any doubt that Claudius is a murderer. However, he is still entangled in the intellectual and moral complexities of revenge and the King is still alive and dangerous. It is worth noting that Hamlet's killing of Polonius has also made him an object of revenge and that Claudius, as a result of the inner play, now knows that Hamlet is aware of his guilt.

Assignments

Essays

1 Look at the inner play. What dramatic opportunities does this scene offer?
2 Look at the closet scene. Where do your sympathies lie in this scene?
3 Why has Hamlet not killed Claudius by the end of Act 3?

When Rosencrantz and Guildenstern have left the King and Queen together, Gertrude explains her distress. Claudius immediately sees that he was the potential target when Polonius was killed and blames himself for not having restricted Hamlet's movements. He wants to know where Hamlet is.

  1 **There's…must translate**: you must explain the cause of these heavy sighs
  4 **Bestow this place on us**: leave us
11 **brainish apprehension**: deluded conviction
13 **It…there**: I would have been his victim if I'd been hiding there. (The royal plural again, as throughout this speech.)
17 **laid to us**: blamed on me
    providence: foresight
18 **kept short**: kept on a short rein
    out of haunt: away from places where people gather
22 **divulging**: becoming generally known
23 **pith**: essential tissue
25 **ore**: precious metal, often gold

- *Is Gertrude keeping faith with Hamlet, or telling Claudius what she really belives?*
- *We can learn a lot from the order of priorities in Claudius's speech on this page …*

Act four

Scene 1 ─────────────

Enter KING, ROSENCRANTZ, *and* GUILDENSTERN

KING There's matter in these sighs, these profound
     heaves.
You must translate, 'tis fit we understand them.
Where is your son?

QUEEN Bestow this place on us a little while.
     [*Exeunt* ROSENCRANTZ *and* GUILDENSTERN
Ah mine own lord, what have I seen tonight! 5

KING What, Gertrude? How does Hamlet?

QUEEN Mad as the sea and wind when both contend
Which is the mightier. In his lawless fit,
Behind this arras hearing something stir,
Whips out his rapier, cries, 'A rat, a rat!' 10
And in this brainish apprehension kills
The unseen good old man.

KING   O heavy deed!
It had been so with us, had we been there.
His liberty is full of threats to all;
To you yourself, to us, to every one. 15
Alas, how shall this bloody deed be answered?
It will be laid to us, whose providence
Should have kept short, restrained and out of haunt
This mad young man; but so much was our love,
We would not understand what was most fit, 20
But like the owner of a foul disease,
To keep it from divulging, let it feed
Even on the pith of life. Where is he gone?

QUEEN To draw apart the body he hath killed,
O'er whom his very madness, like some ore 25

While Gertrude speaks of Hamlet's remorse, Claudius is planning to get him out of the country. He tells Rosencrantz and Guildenstern to find Hamlet and the body of Polonius, which must be taken to the chapel. His next thought is to talk things over with trusted friends, to find a way of ensuring that no blame may attach to him.

26 mineral: mine
    metals base: not precious metals
32 countenance: face up to, acknowledge
41 the world's diameter: from one end of the world to the other
42 blank: either the white mark in the centre of a target (cf French 'blanc' – white) or 'point-blank' – on a level line of fire

Hamlet, having temporarily disposed of the corpse, hears Rosencrantz and Guildenstern calling him.

Among a mineral of metals base,
Shows itself pure; 'a weeps for what is done.

KING   O Gertrude, come away.
The sun no sooner shall the mountains touch,
But we will ship him hence, and this vile deed   30
We must with all our majesty and skill,
Both countenance and excuse. Ho Guildenstern!

Enter ROSENCRANTZ *and* GUILDENSTERN

Friends both, go join you with some further aid.
Hamlet in madness hath Polonius slain,
And from his mother's closet hath he dragged
     him.   35
Go seek him out, speak fair, and bring the body
Into the chapel; I pray you haste in this.
     [*Exeunt* ROSENCRANTZ *and* GUILDENSTERN
Come Gertrude, we'll call up our wisest friends;
And let them know both what we mean to do
And what's untimely done; so haply slander –   40
Whose whisper o'er the world's diameter,
As level as the cannon to his blank,
Transports his poisoned shot, may miss our name,
And hit the woundless air. O come away,
My soul is full of discord and dismay.   45 [*Exeunt*

Scene ❷

Enter HAMLET

HAMLET   Safely stowed.

ROSENCRANTZ   ⎫   [*Within*] Hamlet, Lord Hamlet!
GUILDENSTERN ⎭

HAMLET   But soft, what noise? Who calls on Hamlet? O here
they come.

Enter ROSENCRANTZ *and* GUILDENSTERN

When Rosencrantz and Guildenstern ask Hamlet where the corpse is, he answers ambiguously, making it clear at the same time that he knows the King is using them as informers. The three of them go to the King.

6 **Compounded**: mixed

11 **keep your...mine own**: keep your secret and not my own. Hamlet is sure that Rosencrantz and Guildenstern have 'plans' for him. He will not reveal what his counter-measures might be.

12 **demanded**: questioned

13 **replication**: reply

15 **countenance**: expressions of favour

18 **in the corner of his jaw**: some apes have cheek pouches where they store food for eating later

20 **it is...dry again**: presumably, once an agent has served a king in this way, he may be of no further use...or even dangerous

23 **a knavish speech...ear**: Hamlet makes this sound like a proverb, but he means: you are probably too stupid to understand my carefully crafted insult

27 **The body...body**: Polonius's body is in the same building as the King, but the King is not dead, he is not in the same state as the body

28 **The King is a thing**: since he lacks any proper authority to be the King, Claudius is – nothing

30 **Hide fox, and all after**: omitted in Q2. Probably a reference to a children's game like hide-and-seek.

- *Why do both Rosencrantz and Guildenstern apparently refuse to understand Hamlet's potentially dangerous dislike of them?*

ROSENCRANTZ What have you done my lord with the dead
body?   5

HAMLET   Compounded it with dust whereto 'tis kin.

ROSENCRANTZ Tell us where 'tis that we may take it thence,
And bear it to the chapel.

HAMLET   Do not believe it.

ROSENCRANTZ Believe what?   10

HAMLET   That I can keep your counsel, and not mine own.
Besides, to be demanded of a sponge, what
replication should be made by the son of a king?

ROSENCRANTZ Take you me for a sponge my lord?

HAMLET   Ay sir, that soaks up the King's countenance, his   15
rewards, his authorities. But such officers do the
King best service in the end; he keeps them like an
ape in the corner of his jaw, first mouthed to be last
swallowed. When he needs what you have gleaned,
it is but squeezing you, and, sponge, you shall   20
be dry again.

ROSENCRANTZ I understand you not my lord.

HAMLET   I am glad of it; a knavish speech sleeps in a foolish
ear.

ROSENCRANTZ My lord, you must tell us where the body is, and   25
go with us to the King.

HAMLET   The body is with the King, but the King is not with
the body. The King is a thing –

GUILDENSTERN A thing my lord!

HAMLET   Of nothing. Bring me to him. Hide fox, and all   30
after.

[*Exeunt*

The King, attended possibly by those he has been consulting, is musing on the fact that Hamlet is popular with the people. Claudius has decided that sending Hamlet away is best on all counts. Hamlet is now guarded. When he is brought in, he jokes about the supper-dish Polonius is providing for the worms.

4 distracted: bewildered

6 scourge: punishment. The severity of the punishment is considered, but not the gravity of the offence.

7 To bear...and even: to manage matters so that everything runs smoothly

9 Deliberate pause: well-weighed reflection, consideration
Diseases...relieved: a proverb – desperate ills need desperate remedies

21 convocation: assembly
politic: shrewd, with the additional sense of diplomatic, or meddling in politics
e'en: at this very moment

22 Your worm...for diet: possibly a reminder of the Diet of Worms – every pupil's joke, but they have been beaten to it by Hamlet. Emperor Charles V called a meeting (diet) in the German city of Worms, in 1521. At this convocation Martin Luther was excommunicated for refusing to deny his Reformist beliefs.

22 we fat...fat us: generally we fatten up animals so that they can feed us

Scene 3

Enter KING, *attended*

KING   I have sent to seek him, and to find the body.
How dangerous is it that this man goes loose.
Yet must not we put the strong law on him.
He's loved of the distracted multitude,
Who like not in their judgment, but their eyes,   5
And where 'tis so, th' offender's scourge is
     weighed,
But never the offence. To bear all smooth and even,
This sudden sending him away must seem
Deliberate pause. Diseases desperate grown
By desperate appliance are relieved,   10
Or not at all.

Enter ROSENCRANTZ

          How now, what hath befallen?

ROSENCRANTZ   Where the dead body is bestowed, my lord,
We cannot get from him.

KING   But where is he?

ROSENCRANTZ   Without, my lord, guarded, to know your
     pleasure.

KING   Bring him before us.   15

ROSENCRANTZ   Ho Guildenstern, bring in my lord.

Enter HAMLET *and* GUILDENSTERN

KING   Now Hamlet, where's Polonius?

HAMLET   At supper.

KING   At supper? Where?

HAMLET   Not where he eats, but where 'a is eaten; a   20
certain convocation of politic worms are e'en at
him. Your worm is your only emperor for diet; we

Hamlet, again playing with words and ideas when Claudius is present, eventually hints at Polonius's whereabouts, and servants are sent to find the body. Claudius tells Hamlet he must leave immediately for England, suggesting that he has his reasons. Hamlet hints in return that he is aware of them.

25 variable service: different courses
32 progress: as in 'royal progress' – where the king or queen travels through the kingdom
35 seek him...yourself: a roundabout way of saying 'Go to hell'.
37 nose: smell
42 tender: care about
45 bark: ship
at help: in the right quarter
46 associates tend: the escorts are waiting
bent: set, ready to leave
52 I see...sees them: Hamlet manages to suggest not only that he suspects something of Claudius' purposes, but also that heaven has its eye on him, too.

> • *Should Claudius sense a threat to himself in Hamlet's word-play concerning maggots, kings and beggars?*

fat all creatures else to fat us, and we fat ourselves
for maggots; your fat king and your lean beggar is
but variable service, two dishes, but to one   25
table – that's the end.

KING   Alas, alas!

HAMLET   A man may fish with the worm that hath eat of a
king, and eat of the fish that hath fed of that worm.

KING   What dost thou mean by this?   30

HAMLET   Nothing but to show you how a king may go a
progress through the guts of a beggar.

KING   Where is Polonius?

HAMLET   In heaven. Send thither to see; if your messenger
find him not there, seek him i' th' other place   35
yourself. But if indeed you find him not within this
month, you shall nose him as you go up the stairs
into the lobby.

KING   Go seek him there.   [*To some* ATTENDANTS

HAMLET   'A will stay till you come.   40
[*Exeunt* ATTENDANTS

KING   Hamlet, this deed, for thine special safety –
Which we do tender, as we dearly grieve
For that which thou hast done – must send thee
hence
With fiery quickness. Therefore prepare thyself.
The bark is ready, and the wind at help,   45
Th' associates tend, and every thing is bent
For England.

HAMLET   For England.

KING   Ay Hamlet.

HAMLET   Good.   50

KING   So is it if thou knew'st our purposes.

HAMLET   I see a cherub that sees them. But come, for
England. Farewell dear mother.

Claudius tries to ensure early departure for Hamlet. In a
soliloquy he reveals his instructions for Hamlet's execution.
Then he will be able to relax.

55 My mother...my mother: Hamlet says goodbye to his
mother who is not present, not to Claudius, who is.
Making use of the concept of man and woman in marriage
as one flesh, he points up their crime.
58 at foot: close behind, close on his heels
60 every thing...th' affair: everything else that depends on
this business has been completed
62 England: he is addressing the King of England
if...aught: if you set any store by my good will
63 As my...sword: my power should make you see the sense
of securing my goodwill, since your country still smarts
from wounds inflicted by Denmark
64 cicatrice: scar
65 free awe: unforced reverence or respect
66 coldly set...process: look upon our royal mandate with
indifference
67 imports at full: gives directions for
68 congruing: agreeing
69 present: immediate
70 hectic: fever
72 haps: fortunes

> • *Note the first mention of letters ordering Hamlet's
> death.*

Fortinbras and his army arrive, claiming the promised
permission to march across Denmark.

2 licence: permission
3 Craves the conveyance: requests safe passage
6 express...his eye: pay our respects in his presence
7 And...so: please tell him this

> • *Once again we are reminded of the presence in the
> wings of Fortinbras.*

KING   Thy loving father, Hamlet.

HAMLET   My mother – father and mother is man and wife, 55
              man and wife is one flesh; and so, my mother.
              Come, for England.   [*Exit*

KING   Follow him at foot, tempt him with speed
                 aboard,
              Delay it not; I'll have him hence tonight.
              Away, for every thing is sealed and done   60
              That else leans on th' affair; pray you make haste.
                    [*Exeunt* ROSENCRANTZ *and* GUILDENSTERN
              And England, if my love thou hold'st at aught –
              As my great power thereof may give thee sense,
              Since yet thy cicatrice looks raw and red
              After the Danish sword, and thy free awe   65
              Pays homage to us – thou mayst not coldly set
              Our sovereign process, which imports at full,
              By letters congruing to that effect,
              The present death of Hamlet. Do it, England,
              For like the hectic in my blood he rages,   70
              And thou must cure me. Till I know 'tis done,
              Howe'er my haps, my joys were ne'er begun.
                                                        [*Exit*

Scene 4

Enter FORTINBRAS, *with his army over the stage*

FORTINBRAS   Go captain, from me greet the Danish King;
              Tell him that by his licence Fortinbras
              Craves the conveyance of a promised march
              Over his kingdom. You know the rendezvous.
              If that his majesty would aught with us,   5
              We shall express our duty in his eye,
              And let him know so.

CAPTAIN   I will do't my lord.

Hamlet meets one of the Norwegian army captains. The army is on its way to do battle for a small patch of ground in Poland. Both the captain and Hamlet are cynical about the point of this. Rosencrantz tries to hurry Hamlet along, as instructed.

8 **softly**: carefully
9 **powers**: troops
11 **How purposed**: this has the force of both 'Where are they going?' and 'What are their intentions?'
15 **main**: whole country
17 **addition**: exaggeration
22 **ranker**: higher
   sold in fee: sold outright
26 **debate**: dispute, contest
   this straw: this worthless issue
27 **imposthume**: abcess.
32 **all occasions...against me**: everything that happens seems to point up my failings
34 **market of his time**: the use to which he puts his time

- *Again we have a glimpse of what Hamlet might have been like as king. Would he have refused to fight pointless battles, or would he have been pushed into it by 'reasons of state', 'need to keep the army employed' etc, etc? Can a crown prince afford to think too much, to plan either his love life or his statecraft?*

FORTINBRAS	Go softly on. [*Exeunt* FORTINBRAS *and* SOLDIERS

Enter HAMLET, ROSENCRANTZ, GUILDENSTERN, *and others*

HAMLET	Good sir, whose powers are these?	
CAPTAIN	They are of Norway sir.	10
HAMLET	How purposed sir I pray you?	
CAPTAIN	Against some part of Poland.	
HAMLET	Who commands them sir?	
CAPTAIN	The nephew to old Norway, Fortinbras.	
HAMLET	Goes it against the main of Poland sir,	15
	Or for some frontier?	
CAPTAIN	Truly to speak, and with no addition,	
	We go to gain a little patch of ground	
	That hath in it no profit but the name.	
	To pay five ducats, five, I would not farm it;	20
	Nor will it yield to Norway or the Pole	
	A ranker rate, should it be sold in fee.	
HAMLET	Why then the Polack never will defend it.	
CAPTAIN	Yes, it is already garrisoned.	
HAMLET	Two thousand souls and twenty thousand ducats	25
	Will not debate the question of this straw.	
	This is th' imposthume of much wealth and peace,	
	That inward breaks, and shows no cause without	
	Why the man dies. I humbly thank you sir.	
CAPTAIN	God buy you sir.	
	[*Exit*	
ROSENCRANTZ	Will't please you go my lord?	30
HAMLET	I'll be with you straight, go a little before.	
	[*Exeunt all except* HAMLET	
	How all occasions do inform against me,	
	And spur my dull revenge! What is a man,	
	If his chief good and market of his time	
	Be but to sleep and feed? A beast, no more.	35

In a soliloquy, Hamlet considers again the possible reasons for his inaction in the task of vengeance. He looks at the army assembled to fight for nothing worth having – except the honour. He sees his shame, when with honour at stake he has done nothing. Again he promises bloody thoughts.

36 discourse: powers of reasoning
39 fust: go stale, moulder
40 bestial oblivion: the heedlessness of animals
   craven scruple: cowardly hesitation
41 the event: the outcome
45 Sith: since
46 gross: plain, obvious
47 this army...charge: this enormous and costly army
48 delicate and tender: sensitive, young
50 Makes mouths: pulls faces at, scorns
   invisible event: outcome which cannot yet be seen
53 Rightly...at the stake: it is true that to be great is not to avoid taking a stand when the quarrel is over something petty, but to enter a quarrel even for something insignificant when it is one's honour that is at stake
62 fight for...the slain?: fight for a small piece of land of an area scarcely large enough to contain the fighting-men or to accommodate the graves of all who are killed

- *As a man of action Fortinbras ('strong of arms') is an impossible role model for Hamlet. Hamlet much admires his ability not to have scruples about the outcome, but to act, when honour is at stake.*
- *Are we convinced by Hamlet's latest resolution (lines 65–66)? Is he?*

Sure he that made us with such large discourse,
Looking before and after, gave us not
That capability and god-like reason
To fust in us unused. Now whether it be
Bestial oblivion, or some craven scruple   40
Of thinking too precisely on the event –
A thought which quartered hath but one part
    wisdom,
And ever three parts coward – I do not know
Why yet I live to say 'This thing's to do',
Sith I have cause, and will, and strength, and
    means   45
To do 't. Examples gross as earth exhort me:
Witness this army of such mass and charge,
Led by a delicate and tender prince;
Whose spirit with divine ambition puffed
Makes mouths at the invisible event,   50
Exposing what is mortal, and unsure
To all that fortune, death, and danger dare,
Even for an egg-shell. Rightly to be great
Is not to stir without great argument,
But greatly to find quarrel in a straw   55
When honour's at the stake. How stand I then,
That have a father killed, a mother stained,
Excitements of my reason and my blood,
And let all sleep, while to my shame I see
The imminent death of twenty thousand men,   60
That for a fantasy and trick of fame
Go to their graves like beds, fight for a plot
Whereon the numbers cannot try the cause,
Which is not tomb enough and continent
To hide the slain? O from this time forth,   65
My thoughts be bloody, or be nothing worth.[*Exit*

It is clear that Ophelia has asked for an audience with the Queen. Gertrude has refused but as a gentleman of the court explains what a state of distress and near-madness Ophelia is in, the Queen agrees to see her. This seems to her another ominous development.

1 **importunate**: persistent
2 **distract**: mad
2 **Her mood...pitied**: her state of mind must give rise to pity
5 **hems**: clears her throat
6 **Spurns...straws**: spitefully rejects whatever is said to her, however unimportant *or* takes offence easily
   in doubt: where the meaning is not clear
7 **nothing**: nonsense
8 **Yet...collection**: but the very dislocated nature of it makes those who hear her want to piece it together
9 **they aim at it**: they guess at it
13 **unhappily**: too close for comfort
15 **conjectures**: suspicions
   ill-breeding minds: minds which ferment mischief
17 **as...is**: sin's true nature is that it is a sickness of the soul
18 **toy**: trifle, insignificant happening
   amiss: calamity
   artless: clumsy, foolish
19 **jealousy**: mistrust
20 **spills**: destroys

> • *Taking the Gentleman's observation of Ophelia as accurate, make sure that – whatever performance or video you may have seen – you have a clear picture* from the text *of the change that has come over Ophelia before she enters.*

Scene 5

Enter QUEEN, HORATIO, *and a* GENTLEMAN

QUEEN	I will not speak with her.
GENTLEMAN	She is importunate,

Indeed distract. Her mood will needs be pitied.

QUEEN   What would she have?

GENTLEMAN She speaks much of her father, says she hears
There's tricks i' th' world, and hems, and beats her
    heart,   5
Spurns enviously at straws, speaks things in doubt
That carry but half sense. Her speech is nothing,
Yet the unshaped use of it doth move
The hearers to collection; they aim at it,
And botch the words up fit to their own
    thoughts,   10
Which as her winks, and nods, and gestures yield
    them,
Indeed would make one think there might be
    thought,
Though nothing sure, yet much unhappily.

HORATIO   'Twere good she were spoken with, for she may
    strew
Dangerous conjectures in ill-breeding minds.   15

QUEEN   Let her come in.   [*Exit* GENTLEMAN
To my sick soul, as sin's true nature is,
Each toy seems prologue to some great amiss.
So full of artless jealousy is guilt,
It spills itself in fearing to be spilt.   20

Enter GENTLEMAN *with* OPHELIA

OPHELIA   Where is the beauteous majesty of Denmark?

QUEEN   How now Ophelia!

When Ophelia comes in she is distractedly singing snatches of songs about true love and death. These themes are so intermingled that they can be seen to refer to the loss of the man she loved, Hamlet, and her father's death and possibly, as the King enters, even to the death of Hamlet's father, for whom Gertrude hardly wept.

25 cockle hat: the original tradition was that a pilgrim to the shrine of St James at Compostella wore a scallop shell (not a cockle shell) on his hat. Scallop shells carved in stone also still decorate many of the churches on the pilgrim routes to Compostella.

26 shoon: shoes. Ophelia, in her mad unhappiness adapts the ballad form of the love song to her needs. The reference to a pilgrim recalls the famous Walsingham ballad where a pilgrim to the shrine at Walsingham is met by a lover enquiring for his 'true love'.

36 Larded: decorated, covered with. Larded is still used in the culinary sense, to put strips of fat in or over meat which is likely to be dry.

37 Which bewept...showers: *'not'* is likely to be a pointed alteration by Ophelia – it puts one syllable too many in the line. Neither her father nor Hamlet's was properly mourned.

40 God dild you: a corruption of 'God yield you (thanks)' – thank you

the owl was a baker's daughter: according to legend Christ went into a baker's shop to ask for something to eat. The baker's wife immediately put a cake into the oven for him, but her daughter said it was too large and reduced it by half. The dough, however, swelled to an enormous size, and the daughter cried out 'Heugh! heugh! heugh!' and was transformed into an owl.

43 Conceit upon: fanciful ideas about

51 dupped: ('dup' is a contraction of 'do up') here: opened

- *Compare what you have seen of Hamlet's madness and Ophelia's.*

OPHELIA	[*Sings*] How should I your true love know
	From another one?
	By his cockle hat and staff, 25
	And his sandal shoon.

QUEEN   Alas sweet lady, what imports this song?

OPHELIA   Say you? Nay, pray you mark.
          [*Sings*] He is dead and gone lady,
                    He is dead and gone,   30
                    At his head a grass-green turf,
                    At his heels a stone.
          Oho!

QUEEN   Nay but Ophelia, –

OPHELIA   Pray you mark.
          [*Sings*] White his shroud as the mountain snow –

          Enter KING

QUEEN   Alas, look here my lord.   35

OPHELIA   [*Sings*] Larded all with sweet flowers,
                    Which bewept to the grave did not go
                    With true-love showers.

KING   How do you pretty lady?

OPHELIA   Well, God dild you. They say the owl was a   40
          baker's daughter. Lord, we know what we are, but
          know not what we may be. God be at your table.

KING   Conceit upon her father.

OPHELIA   Pray let's have no words of this, but when they ask
          you what it means, say you this: 45
          [*Sings*] Tomorrow is Saint Valentine's day,
                    All in the morning betime,
                    And I a maid at your window,
                    To be your Valentine.
                    Then up he rose, and donned his clothes, 50
                    And dupped the chamber door,
                    Let in the maid, that out a maid,
                    Never departed more.

Soon Ophelia's singing is providing echoes of Hamlet's bawdy conversation with her and of her brother's and her father's warnings. Claudius, having sent Horatio to keep an eye on Ophelia, briefly interprets her madness as the result of grief. He then goes on to list the recent misfortunes and to regret that Polonius's burial was done in secret, as he fears the reaction.

56 Gis: Jesus
 Saint Charity: not a real saint
58 do't: have sexual intercourse
59 By Cock: a common avoidance of the oath 'By God' but also with a sexual reference
60 tumbled me: lay with me, had intercourse with me
76 spies: scouts, reconnoitering ahead of the main army
79 muddied: agitated, stirred up like a muddy pool
81 greenly: foolishly (because of unripe, immature judgement)
82 hugger-mugger: secretly
83 Divided...mere beasts: a repetition of the idea that without reason human beings are no different from animals, mere figures
85 as much containing: as of much significance

> • *Claudius is again forced to consider the reasons for the madness of a young person at his court. How quickly does this turn to thoughts for himself?*

KING   Pretty Ophelia.

OPHELIA   Indeed without an oath I'll make an end on't.   55
                                              [*Sings*

              By Gis and by Saint Charity,
                  Alack and fie for shame,
              Young men will do't if they come to't,
                  By Cock, they are to blame.
              Quoth she, before you tumbled me,   60
                  You promised me to wed.
              He answers,
                  So would I 'a done by yonder sun,
                  An thou hadst not come to my bed.

KING   How long hath she been thus?   65

OPHELIA   I hope all will be well. We must be patient, but I
              cannot choose but weep to think they should lay
              him i' th' cold ground. My brother shall know of it,
              and so I thank you for your good counsel. Come,
              my coach. Good night ladies, good night,   70
              sweet ladies, good night, good night.   [*Exit*

KING   Follow her close; give her good watch I pray you.
                                        [*Exit* HORATIO
              O this is the poison of deep grief, it springs
              All from her father's death. And now behold
              O Gertrude, Gertrude,   75
              When sorrows come, they come not single spies,
              But in battalions. First her father slain,
              Next, your son gone, and he most violent author
              Of his own just remove, the people muddied,
              Thick and unwholesome in their thoughts and
                  whispers,   80
              For good Polonius' death. And we have done but
                  greenly
              In hugger-mugger to inter him. Poor Ophelia
              Divided from herself and her fair judgment,
              Without the which we are pictures, or mere beasts.
              Last, and as much containing as all these,   85

A further concern for Claudius is that Laertes has come back secretly from France. He, Claudius fears, will find it all too easy to blame him for his father's death and hasty burial. The angry Laertes and his armed followers, proposing Laertes for king, approach noisily and rush in.

87 **his wonder**: his bewilderment
   keeps himself in clouds: wraps himself in suspicion
88 **wants not buzzers**: does not lack tale-bearers
90 **Wherein necessity...and ear**: so that, lacking true facts, the need to find a scapegoat will stop at nothing to accuse me, first in one ear and then the other
93 **murdering-piece**: small cannon which fired a scattering charge: it was also called a 'murderer'
94 **superfluous**: because any one of the pieces of shot could have killed him
95 **Attend**: listen
96 **Switzers**: Swiss mercenaries were often employed as guards – and still do guard the Vatican
98 **overpeering of its list**: rising above its furthest limits
99 **flats**: mudflats, shallows
   impiteous: pitiless. Some editions prefer '*impetuous*', with the suggestion of violence.
100 **in a riotous head**: leading a rebellious force. This does also continue the metaphor of the ocean rushing in, '*riotous head*' suggesting a tumultuous head of water.
101 **O'erbears**: overwhelms
102 **as**: as if
103 **Antiquity forgot...every word**: precedent and custom both forgotten, which back up and support our every word
109 **counter**: in hunting, the hounds run counter when they trace the scent backwards, in the wrong direction.
112 **give me leave**: leave me

> • *Now that Claudius has broken the expected succession to the throne, it is easier for people to put up any likely candidates as king.*

Her brother is in secret come from France,
Feeds on his wonder, keeps himself in clouds,
And wants not buzzers to infect his ear
With pestilent speeches of his father's death;
Wherein necessity, of matter beggared,   90
Will nothing stick our person to arraign.
In ear and ear. O my dear Gertrude, this
Like to a murdering-piece in many places
Gives me superfluous death.   [*A noise within*

QUEEN   Alack, what noise is this?

KING   Attend.   95
              Where are my Switzers? Let them guard the door.

              Enter MESSENGER

              What is the matter?

MESSENGER   Save yourself my lord:
              The ocean overpeering of his list
              Eats not the flats with more impiteous haste
              Than young Laertes in a riotous head   100
              O'erbears your officers. The rabble call him lord,
              And as the world were now but to begin,
              Antiquity forgot, custom not known,
              The ratifiers and props of every word,
              They cry 'Choose we! Laertes shall be king':   105
              Caps, hands, and tongues applaud it to the clouds:
              'Laertes shall be king, Laertes king.'

QUEEN   How cheerfully on the false trail they cry.
              O this is counter, you false Danish dogs.

KING   The doors are broke.   110
                                          [*Noise within*

              Enter LAERTES *and other* DANES, *armed*

LAERTES   Where is this King? Sirs, stand you all without.

DANES   No let's come in.

LAERTES   I pray you give me leave.

Laertes, insisting that his followers stay outside, confronts the King. Gertrude tries to calm him. The King invokes the divinity of kingship and acts with some dignity. Laertes is furious over his father's death and wants to take revenge, even if his own damnation results.

114 Keep: guard
116 That drop...true mother: if a single drop of Laertes's blood remains calm, then it is to declare that his father was made unfaithful by his whore of a mother. (See note on branding prostitutes Act 3 scene 4 line 45.) Laertes is saying 'If I stay calm, then I am not my father's son'.
121 fear: fear for
122 There's such...will: kingship is so protected by its divine nature that treason scarcely dares attempt what it has in mind to do
131 grace: God's free gift to man, without which there is no salvation or heaven after death
132 To this point...for my father: I stick at this point, that both this world and the next can go hang, let happen whatever will happen, I will be thoroughly revenged for my father
136 My will...world's: (by) my will, not all the world's (will)
137 And for my means...little: however difficult it may appear, I'll find a way to do it
139 the certainty...father: the facts about your father's death

- *Compare Laertes's angry declaration of intent to avenge his father with those made by Hamlet.*

DANES	We will, we will. [*Exeunt* FOLLOWERS
LAERTES	I thank you. Keep the door. O thou vile King,
	Give me my father.
QUEEN	Calmly, good Laertes 115
LAERTES	That drop of blood that's calm proclaims me
	bastard,
	Cries cuckold to my father, brands the harlot
	Even here between the chaste unsmirched brows
	Of my true mother.
KING	What is the cause, Laertes,
	That thy rebellion looks so giant-like? 120
	Let him go Gertrude, do not fear our person.
	There's such divinity doth hedge a king,
	That treason can but peep to what it would,
	Acts little of his will. Tell me Laertes,
	Why thou art thus incensed – let him go
	Gertrude. 125
	Speak man.
LAERTES	Where is my father?
KING	Dead.
QUEEN	But not by him.
KING	Let him demand his fill.
LAERTES	How came he dead? I'll not be juggled with.
	To hell allegiance, vows to the blackest devil 130
	Conscience and grace to the profoundest pit!
	I dare damnation. To this point I stand,
	That both the worlds I give to negligence,
	Let come what comes, only I'll be revenged
	Most throughly for my father.
KING	Who shall stay you? 135
LAERTES	My will, not all the world's.
	And for my means, I'll husband them so well,
	They shall go far with little.
KING	Good Laertes,
	If you desire to know the certainty

Claudius manages to calm Laertes a little, to the point where he is prepared to grant that the King may not be guilty of Polonius's death. At this Ophelia comes in. Laertes is both distressed and angry at the sight of what she has become. Ophelia sings about a funeral. Laertes claims that her madness moves him to revenge more than any persuasion would.

141 swoopstake: sweepstake. You will take all the stakes, ie you will be revenged on friend and foe alike

145 pelican: traditionally the pelican was supposed to peck its own breast to feed its young with blood

146 Repast: feed

149 most sensibly: with deep emotion

155 Burn out...mine eye: burn out the sensitivity and the function of my eye, ie destroy my sight

157 Till our scale turn the beam: till the weight on our side tilts the scales. The beam is the bar which links the two sides of old-style scales.

161 fine: sensitive. This sensitivity is so acute that human nature loses some part of itself to the loved one when he or she goes away. Ophelia's mind has gone, with her father's death and possibly with the loss of Hamlet.

164 They bore him...nonny: Ophelia sings lines from a ballad lamenting a death, but incongruously adds a cheerful chorus line, more suitable for a love-song.

- *How does Claudius set about changing Laertes's angry and accusatory mood?*

	Of your dear father, is't writ in your revenge, 140
	That, swoopstake, you will draw both friend and
	foe,
	Winner and loser?
LAERTES	None but his enemies.
KING	Will you know them then?
LAERTES	To his good friends thus wide I'll ope my arms,
	And like the kind life-rendering pelican, 145
	Repast them with my blood.
KING	Why now you speak
	Like a good child, and a true gentleman.
	That I am guiltless of your father's death,
	And am most sensibly in grief for it,
	It shall as level to your judgment 'pear 150
	As day does to your eye.
DANES	[*Within*] Let her come in.
LAERTES	How now, what noise is that?

Enter OPHELIA

	O heat, dry up my brains, tears seven times salt
	Burn out the sense and virtue of mine eye. 155
	By heaven, thy madness shall be paid with weight,
	Till our scale turn the beam. O rose of May,
	Dear maid, kind sister, sweet Ophelia –
	O heavens, is't possible a young maid's wits
	Should be as mortal as an old man's life? 160
	Nature is fine in love, and where 'tis fine,
	It sends some precious instance of itself
	After the thing it loves.
OPHELIA	[*Sings*]
	They bore him barefaced on the bier;
	Hey non nonny, nonny, hey nonny, 165
	And in his grave rained many a tear –
	Fare you well my dove.
LAERTES	Hadst thou thy wits, and didst persuade revenge,

Ophelia distributes wild flowers and herbs she has picked.
Laertes, seized by grief, is persuaded by Claudius to go with
him so that they may talk.

170 A-down a-down: a frequent refrain in country songs
171 the wheel: the wheel of Fortune; the spinning-wheel; a
wheeling dance step, or 'wheel' used as a refrain. All
would suggest the idea of a recurring pattern.
172 the false...daughter: no ballad or story can be found to
fit, but there are many instances in the play of the betrayal
of trust.
173 This nothing's...matter: this nonsense means more than
a lot of 'sense'
174 There's rosemary: supposed to strengthen the memory,
rosemary was also used both at weddings and funerals,
and meant 'fidelity in love'. There are no stage directions
indicating who should receive any of these flowers. It is
assumed that rosemary and pansies are offered to Laertes,
possibly with some confusion on Ophelia's part that he
also represents her love for Hamlet.
175 pansies: in French 'pensée' means 'pansy' and 'thought'
177 document: lesson
179 fennel and **columbines**: 'flattery' and 'infidelity in
marriage'
180 rue: a small greeny-grey evergreen shrub with bitter-
tasting leaves. It stands for repentance and regret – 'rue'.
182 a difference: in heraldry a term used for a distinguishing
mark on the arms adopted by a junior family member
daisy: symbol of changeable and inconstant love
183 violets: stand for faithfulness
185 For...all my joy: a line from a popular song on the
subject of love and unfaithful love
186 Thought: sorrow
passion: suffering
187 favour: attraction
188 And...come again: a lament for her dead father, possibly
mingling in her crazed grief with the loss of Hamlet's love
194 All flaxen was his poll: his hair was white
196 we cast away moan: we stop lamenting – it is pointless
200 commune with: talk to you about

	It could not move thus.	
OPHELIA	You must sing 'A-down a-down', an you call	170
	him a-down-a. O how the wheel becomes it! It is	
	the false steward that stole his master's daughter.	
LAERTES	This nothing's more than matter.	
OPHELIA	There's rosemary, that's for remembrance –	
	pray you love, remember – and there is pansies,	175
	that's for thoughts.	
LAERTES	A document in madness, thoughts and	
	remembrance fitted.	
OPHELIA	There's fennel for you, and columbines. There's	
	rue for you, and here's some for me; we may	180
	call it herb of grace a Sundays – o you must wear	
	your rue with a difference. There's a daisy, I would	
	give you some violets, but they withered all when	
	my father died – they say 'a made a good end –	
	[*Sings*] For bonny sweet Robin is all my joy.	185
LAERTES	Thought and affliction, passion, hell itself,	
	She turns to favour and to prettiness.	

OPHELIA   [*Sings*] And will 'a not come again?
      And will 'a not come again?
          No, no, he is dead,   190
          Go to thy death-bed,
      He never will come again.

      His beard was as white as snow,
      All flaxen was his poll.
          He is gone, he is gone,   195
          And we cast away moan.
      God ha' mercy on his soul!
And of all Christian souls I pray God. God buy you.
                    [*Exit*

LAERTES	Do you see this o God?	
KING	Laertes, I must commune with your grief,	200
	Or you deny me right. Go but apart,	
	Make choice of whom your wisest friends you will,	

Claudius tells Laertes he may choose friends of his to judge where the blame for Polonius's death lies – if with him, he will offer full satisfaction. If the guilt is elsewhere, Claudius will join with Laertes for vengeance. Laertes agrees, mentioning again the hasty and secret nature of his father's funeral.

204 by direct…hand: if I am found to be involved directly or indirectly

209 we shall…content: I shall work with your deepest emotions to give you satisfaction

211 His means of death: the way he died

212 hatchment: coat of arms

213 ostentation: show, ceremony

Sailors come to Horatio with letters.

8 'A shall sir an't please him: he shall sir, if it please him

And they shall hear and judge 'twixt you and me:
If by direct or by collateral hand
They find us touched, we will our kingdom give, 205
Our crown, our life, all that we call ours
To you in satisfaction; but if not,
Be you content to lend your patience to us,
And we shall jointly labour with your soul
To give it due content.

LAERTES   Let this be so.   210
His means of death, his obscure funeral,
No trophy, sword, nor hatchment o'er his bones,
No noble rite nor formal ostentation,
Cry to be heard as 'twere from heaven to earth,
That I must call 't in question.

KING   So you shall;   215
And where th' offence is let the great axe fall.
I pray you go with me.   [*Exeunt*

Scene 6

Enter HORATIO *and a* SERVANT

HORATIO   What are they that would speak with me?

SERVANT   Sea-faring men sir, they say they have letters for
               you.

HORATIO   Let them come in.   [*Exit* SERVANT
               I do not know from what part of the world
               I should be greeted, if not from Lord Hamlet.   5

Enter SAILORS

FIRST SAILOR God bless you sir.

HORATIO   Let him bless thee too.

FIRST SAILOR 'A shall sir an't please him. There's a letter for you
               sir, it comes from th' ambassador that was bound

The letter to Horatio is from Hamlet. It tells him that their ship was attacked by pirates. When Hamlet boarded the pirate ship, it drew away, so that he became their only prisoner. Hamlet did a deal with them. He has been landed on Danish soil in exchange for favours to the pirates. Horatio will give the sailors access to the King and they will tell Horatio where to find Hamlet.

12 overlooked: scanned, read
13 means: access
17 the grapple: (now grapnel) as the ships closed, Hamlet's captain decided the only solution was the 'brave' one ('*a compelled valour*'). Grappling irons – like small anchors with several metal claws on them – were used to haul the ships close enough for the enemy ship to be boarded.
21 knew what they did: it was clear, from his dress and bearing, that Hamlet was an aristocratic and probably wealthy prize
23 repair thou to me: come to me
26 the bore of the matter: the bore refers to the diameter of a cannon. Hamlet is saying that his words are (necessarily, in a letter which might be intercepted) far too insignificant for the important subject he needs to tell him about, as small shot would be to a great cannon.

Claudius and Laertes have spoken and Laertes, while allowing that Hamlet may have tried to kill Claudius, asks why no action was taken against him.

1 my acquittance seal: release me from any suggestion of guilt
3 knowing: understanding

> • *Laertes is coming closer and closer to siding with Claudius. What does this tell us about Claudius?*

for England, if your name be Horatio, as I am let 10
to know it is.

HORATIO   [*Reads*] 'Horatio, when thou shalt have overlooked
this, give these fellows some means to the King,
they have letters for him. Ere we were two days old
at sea, a pirate of very warlike appointment gave   15
us chase. Finding ourselves too slow of sail, we put
on a compelled valour, and in the grapple I
boarded them, on the instant they got clear of our
ship, so I alone became their prisoner. They have
dealt with me like thieves of mercy, but they   20
knew what they did, I am to do a good turn for
them. Let the King have the letters I have sent, and
repair thou to me with as much speed as thou
wouldst fly death. I have words to speak in thine
ear will make thee dumb, yet are they much too   25
light for the bore of the matter. These good fellows
will bring thee where I am. Rosencrantz and
Guildenstern hold their course for England, of
them I have much to tell thee. Farewell.

He that thou knowest thine,   30
                                  HAMLET.'
Come, I will give you way for these your letters,
And do't the speedier that you may direct me
To him from whom you brought them.   [*Exeunt*

Scene 7

Enter KING *and* LAERTES

KING   Now must your conscience my acquittance seal,
And you must put me in your heart for friend,
Sith you have heard, and with a knowing ear,
That he which hath your noble father slain
Pursued my life.

LAERTES   It well appears. But tell me   5
Why you proceeded not against these feats,

Claudius has to explain to Laertes why, if he knew that
Hamlet meant to kill him, he has taken no action against
him. He cites Gertrude's love for Hamlet, his own love for
his wife, and Hamlet's popularity with the general public.
Laertes has to comfort himself with the thought that he will
avenge his father's death and Ophelia's madness.

7 **capital**: punishable by death
10 **unsinewed**: feeble
12 **Lives...looks**: lives for the sight of him
13 **My virtue...either which**: be it good or bad, whichever
14 **so conjunctive**: so closely joined
15 **moves not but in his sphere**: can only move in its
   appointed orbit
   sphere: astronomers believed that concentric hollow globes
   (spheres) revolved round the earth, carrying the various
   heavenly bodies (sun, moon, planet and fixed stars)
16 **I could...by her**: I could only exist by her side
17 **count**: legal indictment
18 **general gender**: common people
20 **Would...stone**: there are natural springs which in time will
   coat objects left in their flow with a deposit like stone
21 **gyves**: fetters, and so the offences which caused a man to
   be put in chains
   graces: virtues
22 **Too slightly timbered**: made of too light a wood
23 **reverted**: turned back
27 **go back again**: go back to earlier days
28 **Stood challenger...perfections**: such were her qualities
   that on a peak of perfection she stood above all others of
   her time
29 **Break not your sleeps for that**: do not lose any sleep over
   that
31 **flat**: spiritless
32 **with danger**: with what threatens danger

- *'The Queen his mother lives almost by his looks'. If this
  is true, and there are other indications that it is, what
  light does this throw on the 'closet' scene?*

So criminal and so capital in nature,
As by your safety, greatness, wisdom, all things else,
You mainly were stirred up.

KING   O for two special reasons,
Which may to you perhaps seem much
        unsinewed,   10
But yet to me th' are strong. The Queen his
        mother
Lives almost by his looks, and for myself –
My virtue or my plague, be it either which –
She is so conjunctive to my life and soul,
That as the star moves not but in his sphere,   15
I could not but by her. The other motive,
Why to a public count I might not go,
Is the great love the general gender bear him;
Who dipping all his faults in their affection,
Would like the spring that turneth wood to
        stone   20
Convert his gyves to graces, so that my arrows,
Too slightly timbered for so loud a wind,
Would have reverted to my bow again,
And not where I had aimed them.

LAERTES   And so have I a noble father lost,   25
A sister driven into desperate terms,
Whose worth, if praises may go back again,
Stood challenger on mount of all the age
For her perfections. But my revenge will come.

KING   Break not your sleeps for that; you must not
        think   30
That we are made of stuff so flat and dull,
That we can let our beard be shook with danger,
And think it pastime. You shortly shall hear more.
I loved your father, and we love ourself,
And that I hope will teach you to imagine –   35

Enter a MESSENGER

How now, what news?

The messenger hands over Hamlet's letters to the King, one for him and one for Gertrude. Hamlet reveals that he is back in the country. Laertes is glad that he will be able to tax him with the murder of Polonius. The King makes it clear that he too has plans, if Hamlet will not go to England.

44 naked: destitute, stripped of everything he had
50 abuse: deception
  no such thing: nothing of the sort has really happened
51 hand: handwriting
  character: handwriting
54 devise me: work it out for me
58 Thus didst thou: some editions emend *'didst'* to *'diest'* and those advocating *'didst'* want a mimed sword thrust to accompany *'Thus'*. However, *'Thus didst thou'* seems sufficient, without any decoration. An essential part of revenge is to make sure the offender knows that you know his offence, and face to face (*'to his teeth'*) to watch him understand that you know, before the vengeance is carried out.
63 checking: whether borrowed from falconry or horsemanship, it means balking suddenly or shying, in mid-flight, mid-gallop
65 ripe in my device: just come to completion, to fruition, in my mind

MESSENGER	Letters my lord, from Hamlet
	This to your majesty; this to the Queen.
KING	From Hamlet? Who brought them?
MESSENGER	Sailors my lord they say, I saw them not;
	They were given me by Claudio, he received
	them 40
	Of him that brought them.
KING	Laertes, you shall hear them.
	Leave us. [*Exit* MESSENGER
	[*Reads*] 'High and mighty, you shall know I am set
	naked on your kingdom. Tomorrow shall I beg
	leave to see your kingly eyes, when I shall, first 45
	asking your pardon thereunto, recount the occasion
	of my sudden and more strange return.
	HAMLET.'
	What should this mean? Are all the rest
	come back?
	Or is it some abuse, and no such thing? 50
LAERTES	Know you the hand?
KING	'Tis Hamlet's character.
	'Naked?'
	And in a postscript here, he says 'alone'.
	Can you devise me?
LAERTES	I'm lost in it my lord. But let him come; 55
	It warms the very sickness in my heart,
	That I shall live and tell him to his teeth,
	'Thus didst thou'.
KING	If it be so Laertes –
	As how should it be so? How otherwise? –
	Will you be ruled by me?
LAERTES	Ay my lord, 60
	So you will not o'errule me to a peace.
KING	To thine own peace. If he be now returned,
	As checking at his voyage, and that he means
	No more to undertake it, I will work him
	To an exploit, now ripe in my device, 65

Laertes asks to be the means of bringing revenge on Hamlet. Claudius has heard from a Norman acquaintance of Laertes who has visited the court that Laertes is a most accomplished swordsman. When Hamlet had heard this he had been full of envy. The Norman was a brilliant rider and Laertes identifies him as Lamord.

66 **shall not choose**: cannot help
68 **uncharge the practice**: acquit the stratagem of any guilt
71 **organ**: perpetrator, the doer of the deed
77 **the unworthiest siege**: of the least significance
78 **very riband**: mere ribbon
79 **for youth...graveness**: the light and careless fashions are no less suitable for youth than furs and garments for mature age, indicating a concern for well-being and for dignity
85 **can well**: are very skilful
88 **incorpsed and demi-natured with**: of one body and half the nature of, like the centaurs of Greek mythology who were half-man, half-horse. Wise, strong and gifted, they brought up and trained many of the Greek heroes of myth and fable.
89 **So far he...thought**: he exceeded so far what I had imagined to be possible
90 **in forgery...tricks**: in conceiving displays and feats of horsemanship
93 **Lamord**: if names are in fact significant, then Lamord is very close to French 'la mort' (death) and Lamord's remarks have suggested to Claudius the means of Hamlet's death
94 **the brooch...gem**: the very ornament, the jewel

> • *Claudius has brought matters so far, that instead of blaming him for Polonius's death, Laertes is now his eager accomplice and instrument for revenge on Hamlet. What has precipitated Claudius's plans for vengence?*

Under the which he shall not choose but fall.
And for his death no wind of blame shall
    breathe
But even his mother shall uncharge the practice,
And call it accident.

LAERTES   My lord, I will be ruled,
The rather if you could devise it so   70
That I might be the organ.

KING   It falls right.
You have been talked of since your travel much.
And that in Hamlet's hearing, for a quality
Wherein they say you shine. Your sum of parts
Did not together pluck such envy from him   75
As did that one, and that in my regard
Of the unworthiest siege.

LAERTES   What part is that my lord?

KING   A very riband in the cap of youth,
Yet needful too, for youth no less becomes
The light and careless livery that it wears   80
Than settled age his sables and his weeds
Importing health and graveness. Two months
since, Here was a gentleman of Normandy –
I have seen myself, and served against the French,
And they can well on horseback, but this gallant 85
Had witchcraft in 't, he grew unto his seat,
And to such wondrous doing brought his horse,
As had he been incorpsed and demi-natured
With the brave beast. So far he topped my thought,
That I in forgery of shapes and tricks   90
Come short of what he did.

LAERTES   A Norman was't?

KING   A Norman.

LAERTES   Upon my life, Lamord.

KING   The very same.

LAERTES   I know him well, he is the brooch indeed
And gem of all the nation.   95

Hamlet had said he would like to try his duelling skills with Laertes. Claudius tries to make sure that Laertes has the will to avenge his father.

96 He made...you: he declared your skill

98 For art and exercise: of your brilliant accomplishments

101 The scrimers: the master fencers

102 He swore...eye: he claimed he had no skill in movement, guarding nor quickness of eye

104 envenom: literally 'poison' – foreshadowing Act 5

112 love is begun by time: there is a moment which triggers the beginnings of love

113 passages of proof: examples which prove this

114 qualifies: lessens, diminishes

115 There lives...abate: love contains within itself the seeds of its own decay

116 snuff: the part of the wick already burnt

117 And nothing...still: and nothing remains in a similar state of goodness all the time

118 For goodness...too much: love, in excess, consumes itself (*'too much'* is here used as a noun meaning 'excess')
   plurisy: (1) excess (2) a disease involving inflammation of membranes around the lungs, believed in Shakespeare's time to be caused by excess of humours

119 That we would...delays: something which we have the will to do, we ought to carry out while the will is still strong, for the intention changes and is subject to being diminished and delayed

122 tongues, hands, accidents: all ways in which the intention can be brought to nothing

123 spendthrift's sigh: it was believed that each sigh cost a loss of blood from the heart. A spendthrift wastes money on extravagance. Claudius suggests that if we don't act promptly, the duty becomes painful, as breathing is to someone with pleurisy.

124 to the quick of th' ulcer: to the heart of the trouble.

- *Claudius's remarks about the will to action growing cold is an interesting, if unwitting comment on Hamlet.*

LAERTES	To cut his throat i' th' church.
KING	No place indeed should murder sanctuarize;
	Revenge should have no bounds. But good Laertes,
	Will you do this, keep close within your chamber. 130
	Hamlet returned shall know you are come home;
	We'll put on those shall praise your excellence,
	And set a double varnish on the fame
	The Frenchman gave you, bring you in fine together
	And wager on your heads; he being remiss, 135
	Most generous, and free from all contriving,
	Will not peruse the foils, so that with ease,
	Or with a little shuffling, you may choose
	A sword unbated, and in a pass of practice
	Requite him for your father.
LAERTES	I will do 't. 140
	And for that purpose I'll anoint my sword.
	I bought an unction of a mountebank,
	So mortal, that but dip a knife in it,
	Where it draws blood no cataplasm so rare,
	Collected from all simples that have virtue 145
	Under the moon, can save the thing from death
	That is but scratched withal. I'll touch my point
	With this contagion, that if I gall him slightly,
	It may be death.
KING	Let's further think of this,
	Weigh what convenience both of time and
	means 150
	May fit us to our shape. If this should fail,
	And that our drift look through our bad
	performance,
	'Twere better not assayed; therefore this project
	Should have a back or second, that might hold
	If this did blast in proof. Soft, let me see – 155
	We'll make a solemn wager on your cunnings –
	I ha 't!
	When in your motion you are hot and dry,
	As make your bouts more violent to that end.

When Hamlet is hot and thirsty from the fencing, there will
be a poisoned drink already prepared, in case the poisoned
foil does not kill him. At this point Gertrude comes in to tell
them that Ophelia has drowned. The account she gives is
that Ophelia fell in while climbing up to hang a garland on a
willow tree. The water weighed down her clothes and she
drowned.

160 **I'll...him**: I'll have him offered
161 **for the nonce**: for this particular occasion
162 **stuck**: sword-thrust
168 **askant**: aslant, slanting over
169 **hoar**: grey-white
170 **Therewith**: with these ie. with pliable twigs of willow
171 **crowflowers**: ragged robin
    nettles: presumably the white or yellow flowers of the
    'dead' nettle which does not sting
    long purples: a kind of wild orchis, with long purple
    flowers and with roots like blanched fingers. The *'grosser
    name'* alluded to, is prompted by the suggestion that the
    roots spread from a tuberous mass which looks like
    testicles.
172 **liberal**: (here) free-spoken
173 **cold**: (here) modest
174 **pendent**: hanging
    crownet weeds: coronets of wild flowers
175 **envious sliver**: spiteful, malicious slender branch. The
    word *'sliver'* normally refers to a piece which has already
    been cut or split off.
176 **trophies**: usually weapons, helmets etc. captured by the
    victorious army and hung on a memorial
180 **incapable of**: not realizing
181 **a creature...element**: an aquatic creature, fitted for living
    in water
184 **melodious lay**: tuneful song

> • *If all these details are known about Othelia's death
> why didn't anybody rescue her?*

And that he calls for drink, I'll have preferred
    him   160
A chalice for the nonce, whereon but sipping,
If he by chance escape your venomed stuck,
Our purpose may hold there. But stay, what noise?

Enter QUEEN

How sweet Queen!

QUEEN   One woe doth tread upon another's heel,   165
So fast they follow: your sister's drowned,
    Laertes.

LAERTES   Drowned! O where?

QUEEN   There is a willow grows askant the brook,
That shows his hoar leaves in the glassy stream;
Therewith fantastic garlands did she make,   170
Of crowflowers, nettles, daisies, and long
    purples
That liberal shepherds give a grosser name,
But our cold maids do dead men's fingers call them.
There on the pendent boughs her crownet weeds
Clamb'ring to hang, an envious sliver broke,   175
When down her weedy trophies and herself
Fell in the weeping brook. Her clothes spread
wide, And mermaid-like awhile they bore her up,
Which time she chanted snatches of old tunes,
As one incapable of her own distress,   180
Or like a creature native and indued
Unto that element; but long it could not be
Till that her garments, heavy with their drink,
Pulled the poor wretch from her melodious lay
To muddy death.

LAERTES   Alas, then she is drowned?   185

QUEEN   Drowned, drowned.

LAERTES   Too much of water has thou poor Ophelia,
And therefore I forbid my tears, but yet

Laertes cannot help his tears at Ophelia's death, but underneath, his anger blazes. When Laertes has left, Claudius tells Gertrude he is afraid that this news has undone all the calming effect he has had on Laertes.

189 It is our trick: it is the way with us
191 The woman will be out: the female element in my nature will be played out
193 this folly: his tears

* *What does Claudius fear after this news?*

It is our trick, nature her custom holds,
Let shame say what it will; when these are
    gone,   190
The woman will be out. Adieu my lord.
I have a speech of fire that fain would blaze,
But that this folly drowns it.   [*Exit*

KING   Let's follow, Gertrude.
How much I had to do to calm his rage!
Now fear I this will give it start again,   195
Therefore let's follow.
                              [*Exeunt*

Keeping track

Scene 1

1 The scene opens with Gertrude in some distress and Claudius anxious to know what has happened in her encounter with Hamlet. How accurate is Gertrude's account of the killing of Polonius?
2 What conclusions do you draw from her behaviour here?
3 How does Claudius react to the death of Polonius?
4 Why is he so anxious now to remove Hamlet from Elsinore?

Scene 2

This short scene has a narrative function in that we see Hamlet being summoned into the presence of Claudius. However, it also reinforces our understanding of Hamlet's thoughts and feelings about his 'friends', Rosencrantz and Guildenstern.
1 What are his thoughts and feelings about them?
2 Do you agree with him?

Scene 3

1 What 'reasons' does Claudius give for sending Hamlet away rather than allowing the *'strong law'* to apprehend him?
2 What do you think are his real 'reasons'?
3 When Hamlet enters he has slipped once more into his *'antic disposition'*. Why do you think he has done this?
4 What do his words reveal about his attitude towards Polonius?
5 How does he behave towards Claudius?
6 What does Claudius's short soliloquy at the end of the scene reveal about his plan to deal with the problem of Hamlet for once and for all?
7 What is the role of Rosencrantz and Guildenstern in this plot?

Scene 4

1 As Hamlet prepares to leave for England he encounters Fortinbras and his army returning to do battle for *'a little patch of ground'*. What is Hamlet's conclusion about this military action?
2 Hamlet's soliloquy (lines 31–66) is prompted by the sight of so many men prepared to risk their lives for no obvious reason or reward. What

accusations does Hamlet make at himself in this speech? In what ways does this speech echo the 'To be, or not to be' soliloquy?

Scene 5

1 Why do you think Gertrude is unwilling to see Ophelia at first and why does she eventually agree to admit her?
2 What does Gertrude's aside (lines 17–20) reveal about her? Do you find your attitude towards her changing?
3 Ophelia's songs show her madness. Can you detect any underlying themes in her words? How do you react to the sight of Ophelia like this?
4 How does Claudius react to the situation?
5 The entrance of Laertes shows another reaction to the killing of a father. In what ways does he form a contrast with Hamlet? What effect does his arrival have on Ophelia?

Scene 6

1 What is the purpose of this short scene?
2 What questions does this scene leave unanswered?
3 Why do you think Hamlet has written to Claudius?

Scene 7

1 At the beginning of this scene Claudius has succeeded in directing Laertes's fury towards Hamlet. How do you think he did this?
2 How does Laertes react to Hamlet's letter?
3 What is the plan agreed between Claudius and Laertes?
4 Gertrude enters this scene bringing news of Ophelia's death. How does she describe her death?
5 How does Laertes respond to the news of Ophelia's death?
6 What do you make of Claudius's reaction?

Drama

1 • Rehearse Act 4 scene 3 lines 17–57. Think about how Claudius deals with this situation which is potentially damaging to his position: a royal member of the family has apparently murdered a loyal Councillor in the Queen's bedchamber – on top of which, Hamlet now seems to be completely mad. Work at the moves and gestures which will show the tension in Claudius.
  • Work with a partner: one of you, as a royal spokesperson, tells the other, a cynical reporter, what happened to Polonius in the palace that day.

2 Look at Claudius's speech in Act 4 scene 5 lines 75–94. What is Gertrude doing? In pairs, work out how Gertrude deals with this speech, after what happened between her and Hamlet. Does Claudius realize anything has changed? How does she hide her feelings?

3 Use FORUM THEATRE to explore the moment when Gertrude comes in on Claudius with Laertes in Act 4 scene 7 line 164 *'How sweet Queen!'*. Consider the contrast between their secret plotting and the Queen's news. Neither party knows what the other knows. What does Gertrude think is going on? Do they think she has overheard them? How can she tell Laertes the news?

Key elements

In Act 4 these are:
- Hamlet's soliloquy: *'How all occasions do inform against me'*
- Ophelia's madness and death
- Laertes's revenge plot.

The key scene

Claudius and Laertes: Act 4 scene 7.

Keying it in

Laertes returns to the play in Act 4 scene 5.
- What is his mood?
- How does he form a contrast with Hamlet?
- Who is the object of his desire for revenge?
- In what way is this ironic?
- How does he justify his demand for blood?
- What are your thoughts and feelings about Laertes up to this point in the play?

The scene itself

1 At the beginning of the scene Claudius has apparently succeeded in persuading Laertes that he is not guilty of Polonius's death.
   - What else has he suggested to Laertes?
   - How has he persuaded Laertes?
   - In what ways is this clever?

- Is it typical of Claudius? How?
2 Look at lines 5–24.
   - Laertes asks an obvious and reasonable question. What is it?
   - What answers does Claudius give?
   - Do you believe him?
3 Look at lines 25–35.
   Laertes seems to accept what Claudius has said but he is still determined to have his revenge.
   - What is Claudius's intention now?
   - Do you think he sees an opportunity to solve his problems?
   - What do you think he is about to tell Laertes when he is interrupted by the messenger?
4 Look at lines 36–60.
   - Why is Claudius so shocked to receive a letter from Hamlet?
   - How does he react to the content of the letter?
   - What is Laertes's response to this unexpected development?
   - Claudius is quick to seize the initiative here. When he says *'Will you be ruled by me?'* he obviously intends to use Laertes for his own purposes.
5 Look at lines 62–107.
   - What is Claudius suggesting here?
   - How does Laertes react?
6 Look at lines 108–163.
   Claudius changes his approach at this point as he lures Laertes into his plan.
   - Why does he ask *'was your father dear to you?'*
   - What is he suggesting in the speech from lines 111–127?
   - What effect does this have on Laertes?
   - What does Laertes's claim that he would *'cut his throat i' th' church'* reveal about his mood and character?
   - Claudius says, *'Revenge should have no bounds.'* (line 129) Do you agree with him?
   - Does the fact that it is Claudius who says this affect your reaction? He also describes Hamlet as *'Most generous and free from all contriving'*.
   - Is this an accurate description?
   - Do you find it ironic that Claudius should say this?
   Laertes's approach to revenge has changed under the influence of Claudius.
   - How has it changed?
   - What does he suggest in lines 140–149?
   - How does Claudius respond to the suggestion?
   - Do you find their plan ironic, or perhaps typical?

Overview

In this scene, Claudius is desperately, and perhaps skilfully, trying to contain a dangerous situation which threatens his security. He manipulates the enraged Laertes and draws him into his own devious scheme.

However, the 'corrupting' of Laertes sheds some interesting light on the whole issue of revenge and acts as a prompt to the audience to consider their attitude to revenge.

Think about the implications of these quotations:
'I dare damnation.'
'To cut his throat i' th' church.
No place indeed should murder sanctuarize;
Revenge should have no bounds.'

Close study

Act 4 scene 2 lines 6–31
- When Hamlet mentions Polonius's body, what is his tone?
- What does this reveal about his attitude to the killing?
- Do you approve of Hamlet's behaviour?
- What does the word *'sponge'* reveal about Hamlet's attitude to Rosencrantz?
- What warning does he give Rosencrantz in these lines?
  Look at Act 3 scene 2 lines 342–369.
- What similarities can you find in these exchanges?
- Do you admire Hamlet's handling of his spying 'friends'?

Hamlet and revenge

After the success of the inner play in Act 3, Hamlet did perform *'bitter business'*, but it was directed against Polonius and his mother. In Act 4, the rage appears to have subsided once more and he confronts Claudius more in a mood of scornful contempt than violent outrage.

The encounter with Fortinbras and his army forces Hamlet to explore, yet again, the issue of revenge and his own failure to take direct action. It is entirely possible that an audience could see Fortinbras's expedition as a form of senseless bravado, an example of masculine pride posing as 'honour'. However, Hamlet sees it as courage and a damning indictment of his own cowardice. Not for the first time in the play, Hamlet reproaches himself with failure to act like a man because of *'Bestial oblivion'* or *'thinking too precisely'*. To have 'scruples' is to be *'craven'* and this speech echoes the *'To be, or not to be'* soliloquy.

The reactions of Ophelia and Laertes to the violent death of Polonius are also illuminating. Ophelia is driven to madness and suicide as the 'violence' of grief goes inward and destroys her; Laertes is driven to treachery and damnation as his violence lashes outward. In a way, they enact the alternatives in responding to such powerful emotion. You might like to think about the parallels between Hamlet and Laertes and Ophelia. The 'violence' in Hamlet seems to go both inward and outward at different times.

Assignments

Essays

1 Look at the two soliloquies 'To be, or not to be' and 'How all occasions do inform against me'. How do these speeches develop your understanding of Hamlet's difficulties as a revenger?
2 Compare the reactions of Laertes and Ophelia to the death of Polonius. In what ways do they illuminate Hamlet's situation?

The sexton and his mate are discussing the fact that the coroner at the inquest has said Ophelia is to be allowed a Christian burial, when as far as they know, she committed suicide. They discuss what constitutes deliberate drowning and come to the conclusion that if she had not been a lady of the court she would not have been buried in sacred ground.

1 **christian burial**: Christians would normally be buried in sanctified ground, usually a churchyard. If a person had committed suicide the burial would take place outside consecrated ground, sometimes at a crossroads and with a stake through the body.

4 **straight**: straightaway
crowner: coroner

6 **in her own defence**: this would have been, and still is, a plea in a murder case, likely if proved, to reduce the sentence. Since suicide was regarded by the church as self-murder, there is a certain logic attaching to it in the speaker's mind.

8 **found**: decided in court

9 **se offendendo**: a mistake for 'se defendendo' (in self-defence), or possibly a deliberate coining of a pseudo-Latin phrase, since his argument has been throughout that she killed herself knowingly

11 **wittingly**: knowingly – possibly why Gertrude has made the point that Ophelia did not realize the danger she was in
three branches: a reference to the legal argument used in a real court case over a suicide

12 **argal**: mistake for 'ergo' Latin for 'therefore'

14 **goodman delver**: master digger

23 **quest**: inquest

26 **out**: outside, without

> • *The 'ordinary people' in Shakespeare's plays are often credited merely with producing 'comic relief' to lighten the tragic proceedings. Look carefully at what the two grave-diggers say and do. What kind of people are they? What effect do they seem to you to have?*

Act five

Scene 1

Enter two CLOWNS, *the* SEXTON, *and his* MATE

1ST CLOWN   Is she to be buried in christian burial when
she wilfully seeks her own salvation?

2ND CLOWN   I tell thee she is, and therefore make her grave
straight. The crowner hath sat on her, and finds it
christian burial.   5

1ST CLOWN   How can that be, unless she drowned herself in
her own defence?

2ND CLOWN   Why, 'tis found so.

1ST CLOWN   It must be 'se offendendo', it cannot be else.
For here lies the point, if I drown myself   10
wittingly, it argues an act, and an act hath three
branches; it is to act, to do, and to perform: argal
she drowned herself wittingly.

2ND CLOWN   Nay, but hear you goodman delver –

1ST CLOWN   Give me leave. Here lies the water – good.   15
Here stands the man – good. If the man go to this
water and drown himself, it is, will he, nill he, he
goes, mark you that. But if the water come to him,
and drown him, he drowns not himself; argal, he
that is not guilty of his own death, shortens not   20
his own life.

2ND CLOWN   But is this law?

1ST CLOWN   Ay marry is 't, crowner's quest law.

2ND CLOWN   Will you ha' the truth on 't? If this had not
been a gentlewoman, she would have been   25
buried out a christian burial.

The two men consider that it is unfair that a suicide from the court circle should still be entitled to a Christian burial. They have a jokey conversation about digging and then about grave-digging. Horatio and Hamlet are seen in the distance.

28 countenance: permission
29 even-christian: fellow-Christians
30 ancient: traditional, from earliest times
34 bore arms: usually 'had a coat of arms' but here used punningly, as line 38 will reveal
40 confess thyself: 'and be hanged' completes the proverb
44 frame: structure
53 unyoke: unyoke the oxen from the plough, come to the end of the day's work
57 Cudgel: beat
58 mend his pace: speed up

1ST CLOWN	Why, there thou say'st, and the more pity that great folk should have countenance in this world to drown or hang themselves, more than their even-christian. Come my spade. There is no ancient gentlemen but gardeners, ditchers, and grave-makers, they hold up Adam's profession. 30
2ND CLOWN	Was he a gentleman?
1ST CLOWN	'A was the first that ever bore arms.
2ND CLOWN	Why he had none. 35
1ST CLOWN	What, art a heathen? How dost thou understand the Scripture? The Scripture says 'Adam digged'. Could he dig without arms? I'll put another question to thee; if thou answerest me not to the purpose, confess thyself – 40
2ND CLOWN	Go to.
1ST CLOWN	What is he that builds stronger than either the mason, the shipwright, or the carpenter?
2ND CLOWN	The gallows-maker, for that frame outlives a thousand tenants. 45
1ST CLOWN	I like thy wit well in good faith; the gallows does well, but how does it well? It does well to those who do ill; now thou dost ill to say the gallows is built stronger than the church; argal, the gallows may do well to thee. To 't again, come. 50
2ND CLOWN	'Who builds stronger than a mason, a shipwright, or a carpenter?'
1ST CLOWN	Ay, tell me that and unyoke.
2ND CLOWN	Marry now I can tell.
1ST CLOWN	To 't. 55
2ND CLOWN	Mass I cannot tell.

Enter HAMLET *and* HORATIO *afar off*

| 1ST CLOWN | Cudgel thy brains no more about it, for your dull ass will not mend his pace with beating; and, when |

While one of the men goes off to fetch a drink the other starts to sing as he digs the grave. As he digs, he uncovers a skull and throws it out. Hamlet considers whose head this might have been in life.

61 Yaughan: Johann, John
62 stoup: jar (a measure containing approximately two litres)
63 In youth...meet: the grave-digger's version of a popular song, turned into the rhythm of a work-song, while he digs
65 contract-a...behove: to pass the time to my advantage
66 meet: so fitting, suitable
69 Custom...easiness: he is so used to digging graves that the thought of why he is digging does not bother him at all
70 the hand...daintier sense: someone who has a good deal of leisure can afford more delicate feelings
77 jowls: knocks
78 Cain's jawbone: again a reminder of the theme of fratricide
79 pate: head
80 o'er-reaches: takes advantage of
circumvent: get the better of
89 chopless: without the lower jaw
90 mazzard: head

> • *To Hamlet's introspection is now added a physical realization of mortality. How does this affect him?*

you are asked this question next, say 'a grave-
maker', the houses that he makes last till   60
doomsday. Go, get thee to Yaughan: fetch me a
stoup of liquor.

> [*Exit* 2ND CLOWN
> [*He digs, and sings*

In youth when I did love, did love,
   Methought it was very sweet,
To contract-a the time, for-a my behove,   65
   O methought there-a was nothing-a meet.

HAMLET   Has this fellow no feeling of his business, that 'a
sings at grave-making?

HORATIO   Custom hath made it in him a property of easiness.

HAMLET   'Tis e'en so, the hand of little employment hath   70
the daintier sense.

1ST CLOWN   [*Sings*]
But age with his stealing steps
   Hath clawed me in his clutch,
And hath shipped me into the land,
   As if I had never been such.   75

> [*Throws up a skull*

HAMLET   That skull had a tongue in it, and could sing once,
how the knave jowls it to the ground, as if 'twere
Cain's jawbone, that did the first murder. This
might be the pate of a politician, which this ass now
o'er-reaches; one that would circumvent God,   80
might it not?

HORATIO   It might my lord.

HAMLET   Or of a courtier, which could say 'Good morrow
sweet lord, how dost thou good lord?' This might
be my lord such-a-one, that praised my lord -   85
sucha-one's horse when 'a meant to beg it,
might it not?

HORATIO   Ay my lord.

HAMLET   Why e'en so, and now my Lady Worm's; chopless,
and knocked about the mazzard with a sexton's   90

Hamlet broods on the thought that everyone, however clever, wealthy, busy or pompous, comes to this end.

92 Did these bones...with them?: was the creation and raising of these people of so little importance that their bones should be used to play games?

93 loggats: a game where wooden clubs were thrown at a stake fixed in the ground. The nearest was the winner.

99 Why: not a question-word, but an exclamation

100 quiddities, quillities: quibbling, fussy legal arguments

101 tenure: the legal title by which property is held

103 sconce: (here) head, a jokey use

104 action of battery: a legal term 'action for assault'

106 statutes...recoveries: jargon used in land deals; 'statute' bond which secured for the creditor the mortgaged land and goods if the debtor could not pay; *'recognizances'* the bonds acknowledging the debt; *'double vouchers'* a voucher was the person called upon to warrant a tenant's title – two warrantors made the process even more secure

106 his fines...his recoveries: fine and recovery – the method by which the entail on an estate, which prevented the current owner disposing of it as he wished, could be converted into outright ownership

107 fine: final result – play on the word *'fine'*, as also in:

108 fine pate: clever head

109 fine dirt: well-sifted soil

110 purchases: the obtaining of property other than by inheritance; acquisition

111 pair of indentures: an agreement between two or more parties of which two or more copies were made. Originally they were written on one large sheet and separated by the cutting of a zig-zag line. They should thus fit together exactly, making forgery difficult.

113 inheritor: the man who has acquired, not inherited, the land. Now in his coffin, he occupies no more space than the documents.

118 They are...in that: only fools would assume that any document would be 'proof' against death
assurance: legal proof

120 sirrah: form of address to servants, etc

spade; here's fine revolution an we had the trick
to see 't. Did these bones cost no more the
breeding, but to play at loggats with them? Mine
ache to think on 't.

1ST CLOWN [*Sings*]
A pick axe, and a spade, a spade,   95
    For and – a shrouding sheet,
O a pit of clay for to be made
    For such a guest is meet.

[*Throws up another skull*

HAMLET There's another. Why may not that be the skull
of a lawyer? Where be his quiddities now, his   100
quillities, his cases, his tenures, and his tricks? Why
does he suffer this rude knave now to knock him
about the sconce with a dirty shovel, and will not
tell him of his action of battery? Hum! This fellow
might be in 's time a great buyer of land, with   105
his statutes, his recognizances, his fines, his double
vouchers, his recoveries. Is this the fine of his fines,
and the recovery of his recoveries, to have his fine
pate full of fine dirt? Will his vouchers vouch him
no more of his purchases, and double ones   110
too, than the length and breadth of a pair of
indentures? The very conveyances of his lands will
scarcely lie in this box; and must the inheritor
himself have no more, ha?

HORATIO Not a jot more my lord.   115

HAMLET Is not parchment made of sheep-skins?

HORATIO Ay my lord, and of calves' skins too.

HAMLET They are sheep and calves which seek out assurance
in that. I will speak to this fellow. Whose grave's
this sirrah?   120

1ST CLOWN Mine sir.
[*Sings*] O a pit of clay for to be made
    For such a guest is meet.

Hamlet asks for whom the grave is being dug. The grave-digger proves very pedantic in his answers, but Hamlet learns that a woman is to be buried. The man does not recognize Hamlet, but tells him he has been a grave-digger since Hamlet's birth. Hamlet, he says, has gone mad and been sent to England.

124 thou liest: the first of the *puns* (see GLOSSARY page 335) on telling lies and lying
129 the quick: the living
140 absolute: exact
   by the card: accurately, according to precise rules; the compass card, on which the 32 points of the compass are marked, used for accurate naval navigation
141 equivocation: the using of a word in more than one sense and the ambiguity that may thus come about
143 picked: finicky, fussy
145 galls his kibe: rubs his chilblain. The lower orders are treading so close on the heels of the aristocracy in manners, that there will soon be little to choose between them.

> • *What do you notice about Hamlet's duel of words with the grave-digger, compared with those he tries to start at court?*

HAMLET	I think it be thine indeed, for thou liest in 't.
1ST CLOWN	You lie out on 't sir, and therefore 'tis not 125 yours; for my part I do not lie in 't, yet it is mine.
HAMLET	Thou dost lie in 't, to be in 't and say it is thine. 'Tis for the dead, not for the quick; therefore thou liest. 130
1ST CLOWN	'Tis a quick lie sir, 'twill away again from me to you.
HAMLET	What man dost thou dig it for?
1ST CLOWN	For no man sir.
HAMLET	What woman then? 135
1ST CLOWN	For none neither.
HAMLET	Who is to be buried in 't?
1ST CLOWN	One that was a woman sir, but rest her soul she's dead.
HAMLET	How absolute the knave is! We must speak by 140 the card, or equivocation will undo us. By the Lord, Horatio, these three years I have took note of it – the age is grown so picked, that the toe of the peasant comes so near the heel of the courtier he galls his kibe. How long hast thou been grave- 145 maker?
1ST CLOWN	Of all the days i' th' year I came to 't that day that our last King Hamlet overcame Fortinbras.
HAMLET	How long is that since?
1ST CLOWN	Cannot you tell that? Every fool can tell that; 150 it was that very day that young Hamlet was born – he that is mad and sent into England.
HAMLET	Ay marry, why was he sent into England?
1ST CLOWN	Why because 'a was mad. 'A shall recover his wits there, or if 'a do not, 'tis no great matter there. 155
HAMLET	Why?

According to the sexton, Hamlet's madness will not be
noticed in England, where everyone is mad. The sexton has
been doing his job for thirty years, he says. Hamlet asks how
long a body may lie in the ground before it decomposes.
Picking up a skull the sexton says it has been in the earth for
23 years. It was the skull of Yorick, the King's jester. As a
child Hamlet had known him and enjoyed his company.

165 thirty years: this seems to put Hamlet's age at thirty, or it
may just mean 'many, many years'
168 pocky: infected with the pox, usually referring to the
venereal disease syphilis
hold the laying in: last through until the burial
174 whoreson: (here) wretched – used to indicate a jokey
familiarity

1ST CLOWN	'Twill not be seen in him there, there the men are as mad as he.
HAMLET	How came he mad?
1ST CLOWN	Very strangely they say. 160
HAMLET	How strangely?
1ST CLOWN	Faith e'en with losing his wits.
HAMLET	Upon what ground?
1ST CLOWN	Why here in Denmark. I have been sexton here man and boy thirty years. 165
HAMLET	How long will a man lie i' the earth ere he rot?
1ST CLOWN	Faith if 'a be not rotten before 'a die, as we have many pocky corses nowadays that will scarce hold the laying in, he will last you some eight year, or nine year. A tanner will last you nine year. 170
HAMLET	Why he more than another?
1ST CLOWN	Why sir, his hide is so tanned with his trade that 'a will keep out water a great while; and your water is a sore decayer of your whoreson dead body. Here's a skull now hath lien you i' th' earth three and 175 twenty years.
HAMLET	Whose was it?
1ST CLOWN	A whoreson mad fellow's it was, whose do you think it was?
HAMLET	Nay I know not. 180
1ST CLOWN	A pestilence on him for a mad rogue, 'a poured a flagon of Rhenish on my head once; this same skull sir, was sir, Yorick's skull, the King's jester.
HAMLET	This?
1ST CLOWN	E'en that. 185
	[Takes the skull
HAMLET	Let me see. Alas poor Yorick! I knew him Horatio, a fellow of infinite jest, of most excellent fancy; he hath borne me on his back a thousand

Hamlet is fascinated and horrified by the thought that when flesh covered Yorick's skull he knew the man, and as a child was carried on his shoulder, kissed him and laughed at his jokes. His mother, however thickly she may paint her face, must come to this state. Even the greatest men, Alexander and Caesar, came to dust at last. Ophelia's funeral procession enters.

189 abhorred: it is a terrible thought that he once rode on the back of what is now a heap of bones

190 my gorge rises: I feel like retching

195 chop-fallen: dispirited, crestfallen. Also (here) literally with the lower jaw hanging loose, or missing

207 bung-hole: the hole in a barrel which is tapped for the beer to be drawn

208 too curiously: too closely

210 modesty: moderation
likelihood to lead it: the likelihood of what will be found leads the expectation on

213 loam: a clayey earth made into a kind of mortar by the addition of sand and straw

218 flaw: squall

> • *Why does the knowledge that he is handling Yorick's skull provoke more horror in Hamlet than the other deaths?*

times, and now how abhorred in my imagination it
is – my gorge rises at it. Here hung those lips   190
that I have kissed I know not how oft. Where be
your gibes now? Your gambols, your songs, your
flashes of merriment, that were wont to set the
table on a roar? Not one now to mock your own
grinning? Quite chop-fallen? Now get you to   195
my lady's chamber, and tell her, let her paint an
inch thick, to this favour she must come. Make her
laugh at that. Prithee Horatio tell me one thing.

HORATIO   What's that my lord?

HAMLET   Dost thou think Alexander looked a this   200
fashion i' th' earth?

HORATIO   E'en so.

HAMLET   And smelt so? Pah!   [*Puts down the skull*

HORATIO   E'en so my lord.

HAMLET   To what base uses we may return, Horatio!   205
Why may not imagination trace the noble dust of
Alexander, till 'a find it stopping a bung-hole?

HORATIO   'Twere to consider too curiously to consider so.

HAMLET   No faith, not a jot, but to follow him thither with
modesty enough, and likelihood to lead it;   210
as thus – Alexander died, Alexander was buried,
Alexander returneth to dust, the dust is earth, of
earth we make loam, and why of that loam whereto
he was converted might they not stop a beer barrel?
   Imperious Cæsar, dead and turned to clay,   215
   Might stop a hole to keep the wind away.
   O that that earth which kept the world in awe
   Should patch a wall t' expel the winter's flaw!
But soft, but soft awhile – here comes the King,

Enter the KING, QUEEN, LAERTES *in funeral procession
following the corpse of* OPHELIA, *then the* DOCTOR *of*
DIVINITY *and* LORDS

Hamlet and Horatio move aside as the funeral procession approaches. From the lack of full ceremony, Hamlet deduces that it is the funeral of a suicide of some rank. He recognizes Laertes to whom the priest explains that even this ceremonial and the burial in sanctified ground is an exception. Laertes angrily refers to his sister as an angel and Hamlet realizes whose funeral this is. The Queen says farewell to the girl who might have become her son's wife.

221 maimed: incomplete
223 Fordo: do away with
    estate: rank
224 Couch we awhile: let's stay hidden. Couch usually means 'lie'.
228 obsequies...warranty: the arrangements for her funeral have been made as extensive as we have been allowed
229 warranty: permission, authorization
    Her death: the way she met her death
230 great command: the permission of our superiors
    the order: the normal practice
232 For: instead of
233 Shards: broken pieces of pottery
234 virgin crants: garlands or wreaths carried in front of a virgin's coffin and then hung up in the church
235 strewments: flowers strewn on her coffin
    bringing home of bell and burial: bringing to her last resting-place with the sound of church bells and with a proper funeral
238 profane the service of the dead: desecrate the burial service
239 sage requiem: solemn funeral hymns
241 unpolluted: chaste
244 When...howling: in his anger and hurt Laertes suggests that while Ophelia will become an angel of Heaven, the priest will be suffering the torments of Hell
245 Sweets: sweet-smelling flowers

> • *We have heard Hamlet theorizing about suicide, now we learn about the Church's strictures from a priest. Is Laertes a consistent character in his reactions to perceived wrongs?*

	The Queen, the courtiers. Who is this they	
	follow?	220

The Queen, the courtiers. Who is this they
   follow? 220
And with such maimed rites? This doth
   betoken,
The corse they follow did with desperate hand
Fordo it own life. 'Twas of some estate.
Couch we awhile and mark.   [*Retires with* HORATIO

LAERTES   What ceremony else? 225

HAMLET   That is Laertes, a very noble youth. Mark.

LAERTES   What ceremony else?

DOCTOR   Her obsequies have been as far enlarged
As we have warranty. Her death was doubtful,
And but that great command o'ersways the
   order, 230
She should in ground unsanctified been lodged
Till the last trumpet. For charitable prayers,
Shards, flints, and pebbles should be thrown on her;
Yet here she is allowed her virgin crants,
Her maiden strewments, and the bringing
   home 235
Of bell and burial.

LAERTES   Must there no more be done?

DOCTOR   No more be done.
We should profane the service of the dead,
To sing sage requiem and such rest to her
As to peace-parted souls.

LAERTES   Lay her i' th' earth: 240
And from her fair and unpolluted flesh
May violets spring. I tell thee churlish priest,
A minist'ring angel shall my sister be
When thou liest howling.

HAMLET   ·What, the fair Ophelia!

QUEEN   Sweets to the sweet. Farewell. [*Scatters flowers* 245
I hoped thou shouldst have been my Hamlet's
   wife.

Laertes, in his grief, curses Hamlet for killing Polonius and thus driving Ophelia mad. He leaps into the grave and tells them to bury him alive with his dead sister. Hamlet find this grief excessive in a brother and they struggle. They are parted and Hamlet declares how he had loved Ophelia.

250 thy most ingenious sense: your sensitivity of mind, your precious reason
254 flat: level ground, plain
255 Pelion: a mountain in Thessaly, Greece
256 Olympus: the mountain in Thessaly where the Greek gods lived
257 emphasis: intensity of feeling
phrase: phraseology, expression
258 wandering stars: planets
259 wonder-wounded: transfixed with astonishment, astounded
263 splenitive: quick to anger, irascible
269 wag: move, blink

- *Laertes has cursed a priest; a lover and a brother fight each other physically and with words at Ophelia's funeral. What atmosphere might we expect this to project over the rest of the play?*

I thought thy bride-bed to have decked, sweet
 maid,
And not have strewed thy grave.

LAERTES   O treble woe
Fall ten times treble on that cursed head,
Whose wicked deed thy most ingenious sense   250
Deprived thee of! Hold off the earth awhile,
Till I have caught her once more in mine arms;
          [*Leaps into the grave*
Now pile your dust upon the quick and dead,
Till of this flat a mountain you have made,
T'o'ertop old Pelion or the skyish head   255
Of blue Olympus.

HAMLET [*Advancing*]   What is he whose grief
Bears such an emphasis, whose phrase of sorrow
Conjures the wandering stars, and makes them
 stand
Like wonder-wounded hearers? This is I,
Hamlet the Dane.   260
          [*Leaps into the grave*

LAERTES The devil take thy soul.
          [*Grapples with him*

HAMLET   Thou pray'st not well.
I prithee take thy fingers from my throat,
For, though I am not splenitive and rash,
Yet have I something in me dangerous,
Which let thy wisdom fear. Hold off thy hand. 265

KING Pluck them asunder.

QUEEN   Hamlet, Hamlet!

ALL Gentlemen, –

HORATIO   Good my lord, be quiet.
       [*The* ATTENDANTS *part them, and*
          they come out of the grave

HAMLET Why, I will fight with him upon this theme
Until my eyelids will no longer wag.

Hamlet challenges a brother's love for Ophelia with his own, which sounds extreme. The Queen explains this excess as one of his mad fits, giving him time to calm down and leave. At the King's request Horatio goes after Hamlet. Claudius reminds Laertes of their earlier talk and urges patience.

275 forbear him: leave him be

276 thou 't: thou wilt – you will
   woo't: wilt thou – will you

278 eisel: vinegar

284 the burning zone: the path of the sun between the tropics of Cancer and Capricorn

285 Ossa: another mountain in Thessaly. When, in Greek mythology the giants tried to climb into heaven, they piled Pelion (see note on line 255) on Ossa, in the hope of reaching high enough.

289 golden couplets are disclosed: the dove lays two eggs, out of which golden yellow chicks hatch

290 His silence...drooping: he will be quiet again with head bowed like the dove over her chicks

293 Let Hercules...day: *either*: 'even Hercules (a mythical Greek hero of great strength and cleverness) would not be able to stop you, cats and dogs must act according to their nature' *or*: whatever Laertes, in the pretended guise of a Hercules does, my day will come

297 present push: immediate action

299 living: lasting, enduring – possibly also a reference to the death of Hamlet, already arranged between them

> • *How did Hamlet treat Ophelia the last time he was with her? How can you square this with his declarations of love now?*

QUEEN	O my son, what theme? 270
HAMLET	I loved Ophelia, forty thousand brothers Could not, with all their quantity of love, Make up my sum – what wilt thou do for her?
KING	O he is mad, Laertes.
QUEEN	For love of God forbear him. 275
HAMLET	'Swounds, show me what thou 't do. Woo't weep, woo't fight, woo't fast, woo't tear thyself? Woo't drink up eisel, eat a crocodile? I'll do't. Dost come here to whine, To outface me with leaping in her grave? 280 Be buried quick with her, and so will I. And if thou prate of mountains, let them throw Millions of acres on us, till our ground, Singeing his pate against the burning zone, Make Ossa like a wart. Nay an thou'lt mouth, 285 I'll rant as well as thou.
QUEEN	This is mere madness, And thus awhile the fit will work on him; Anon as patient as the female dove When that her golden couplets are disclosed, His silence will sit drooping.
HAMLET	Hear you sir, 290 What is the reason that you use me thus? I loved you ever – but it is no matter. Let Hercules himself so what he may, The cat will mew, and dog will have his day. [*Exit*

KING	I pray thee, good Horatio, wait upon him. 295
	                [*Exit* HORATIO
	[*To Laertes*] Strengthen your patience in our last
	   night's speech,
	We'll put the matter to the present push.
	Good Gertrude, set some watch over your son.
	This grave shall have a living monument.

Alone with Horatio, Hamlet tells him about the events on board ship. Unable to sleep, Hamlet put on his coat and went to the cabin of Rosencrantz and Guildenstern. He found and took away their sealed instructions from Claudius. These, giving reasons of state and the danger of Hamlet's continued existence, ordered that he should be beheaded. Hamlet shows the commission to the astonished Horatio.

2 circumstance: details

6 mutines in the bilboes: mutineers in their chains
   bilbo: a long iron bar, with sliding shackles to confine the ankles of prisoners, and a lock by which one end of the bar could be fixed to the floor or the ground
   Rashly: suddenly (cf modern German 'rasch' – quickly, swiftly) or recklessly. Either 'on a sudden impulse' or 'recklessly' would fit here. He was after all going to burgle the cabin of his two gaolers while they were asleep.

7 let us know...pall: let us acknowledge that our impetuousity sometimes does us a good turn when the careful plots we have laid grow stale

9 learn: teach (cf modern French 'apprendre', which can mean either 'learn' or 'teach')

10 There's a divinity...how we will: there's a divine power which directs our destiny – however we may start shaping it ourselves

13 My sea-gown scarfed about me: my sea-going coat over my shoulders

15 Fingered: stole
   in fine: in conclusion

20 Larded: see note to Act 4 scene 5 line 36

21 Importing: concerning

22 bugs: bogeys, terrifying creatures

23 on the...bated: having read this, without delay ('*supervise*' is the Latin-based version of 'o'erlook')

24 stay: wait for

An hour of quiet shortly shall we see,   300
Till then in patience our proceeding be.   [*Exeunt*

Scene 2

Enter HAMLET *and* HORATIO

HAMLET   So much for this sir, now shall you see the other –
                You do remember all the circumstance?

HORATIO   Remember it my lord!

HAMLET   Sir, in my heart there was a kind of fighting,
                That would not let me sleep; methought I lay   5
                Worse than the mutines in the bilboes. Rashly –
                And praised be rashness for it; let us know,
                Our indiscretion sometimes serves us well
                When our deep plots do pall: and that should
                    learn us
                There's a divinity that shapes our ends,   10
                Rough-hew them how we will –

HORATIO   That is most certain.

HAMLET   Up from my cabin,
                My sea-gown scarfed about me, in the dark
                Groped I to find out them, had my desire,
                Fingered their packet, and in fine withdrew   15
                To mine own room again; making so bold,
                My fears forgetting manners, to unseal
                Their grand commission; where I found, Horatio –
                O royal knavery – an exact command,
                Larded with many several sorts of reasons,   20
                Importing Denmark's health, and England's too,
                With ho, such bugs and goblins in my life,
                That on the supervise, no leisure bated,
                No not to stay the grinding of the axe,
                My head should be struck off.

HORATIO   Is 't possible?   25

Hamlet rewrote the commission from Claudius, with his minders as the victims, resealing the letter with his father's seal. The next day the pirates struck.

29 be-netted round: snared, trapped

30 Ere...the play: before I could instruct my brains about the prologue (a speech or poem used as an introduction to a play) they were working on the play itself

33 statists: statesmen

34 A baseness: beneath my dignity

36 yeoman's: a faithful servant's

38 earnest conjuration: solemn appeal

39 tributary: he paid him tribute (the Danegeld of Act 3 scene 1 line 173)

41 wheaten garland: peace traditionally wore a garland of full ears of wheat, to stand for the plenty she would bring

42 And stand...amities: just as the comma is the punctuation which offers least pause, so are their nations as close as can be, without being joined

43 And...charge: Hamlet has enjoyed writing in a style which he despises

As'es: a possible pun on 'asses'

47 Not shriving time allowed: with no time allowed for confession and absolution

48 even in that...ordinant: even here Heaven directed the course of events

49 signet: a stone with his father's crest engraved on it, or the same, set in a ring. Seals were used to make an impression in soft sealing-wax across the join of a folded letter. This then hardened and it was clear (1) who the letter came from (2) that it had not been tampered with.

50 the model of: exactly like

52 Subscribed: signed

53 changeling: usually a baby or child substituted by the fairies for the human child they have stolen

56 go to 't: are going to their deaths

- *Hamlet answers Horatio's implied reproach (l. 56)
  with 'They are not near my conscience'. Why not?*

HAMLET	Here's the commission; read it at more leisure.
	But wilt thou hear now how I did proceed?
HORATIO	I beseech you.
HAMLET	Being thus be-netted round with villanies –

HAMLET   Here's the commission; read it at more leisure.
But wilt thou hear now how I did proceed?

HORATIO   I beseech you.

HAMLET   Being thus be-netted round with villanies –
Ere I could make a prologue to my brains,   30
They had begun the play – I sat me down,
Devised a new commission, wrote it fair –
I once did hold it as our statists do,
A baseness to write fair, and laboured much
How to forget that learning, but, sir, now   35
It did me yeoman's service – wilt thou know
Th' effect of what I wrote?

HORATIO   Ay, good my lord.

HAMLET   An earnest conjuration from the King,
As England was his faithful tributary,
As love between them like the palm might
    flourish,   40
As peace should still her wheaten garland wear
And stand a comma 'tween their amities,
And many such-like 'As'es' of great charge,
That on the view and knowing of these contents,
Without debatement further more or less,   45
He should the bearers put to sudden death,
Not shriving time allowed.

HORATIO   How was this sealed?

HAMLET   Why even in that was heaven ordinant.
I had my father's signet in my purse,
Which was the model of that Danish seal;   50
Folded the writ up in form of th' other,
Subscribed it, gave 't the impression, placed it
    safely,
The changeling never known. Now the next day
Was our sea-fight, and what to this was sequent
Thou knowest already.   55

HORATIO   So Guildenstern and Rosencrantz go to 't.

Horatio, shaken by proof of Claudius's attempt on Hamlet's life, points out that news will soon come from England of its failure. Hamlet regrets his behaviour with Laertes, now seeing similarities in their fate.

57 they did...employment: they were happy to be used
58 defeat: destruction, ruin
59 by their own insinuation grow: the fact that they insinuated themselves into the King's favour helped bring about their destruction
60 'Tis dangerous...baser nature: it is not a good idea for insignificant people to come between the angry sword thrusts of great opponents
63 Does it not...now upon: does it not now rest on me
65 Popped in...my hopes: come between the election (of the new king) and my hopes
66 Thrown out...proper life: cast his fishing line to catch my own life
67 cozenage: deception
68 quit: repay
69 canker: (here) cancer, disease
come In: engage in, enter upon
73 interim: the period until that time
74 And a man's...say 'One': a man's life is over in the time it takes to count 'One'
77 by the image...his: Hamlet sees his state of mind and circumstances reflected in Laertes. They have both had a father murdered and have both lost Ophelia.
79 bravery: spectacular demonstration
82 water-fly: fly that hovers over water, without any obvious direction, or possibly the water-boatman, a fly that skates aimlessly around on the surface
84 gracious: blessed

> • *Hamlet seems to have reasoned himself into an acceptance that his conscience should also approve the killing of Claudius (lines 63–70). He is relying on Horatio for a reassuring answer. Does he get it?*

HAMLET	Why man, they did make love to this employment.
	They are not near my conscience, their defeat
	Does by their own insinuation grow.
	'Tis dangerous when the baser nature comes 60
	Between the pass and fell incensed points
	Of mighty opposites.
HORATIO	Why, what a King is this!
HAMLET	Does it not, think thee, stand me now upon –
	He that hath killed my king, and whored my
	mother;
	Popped in between the election and my hopes, 65
	Thrown out his angle for my proper life,
	And with such cozenage – is 't not perfect
	conscience
	To quit him with this arm? And is 't not to be
	damned,
	To let this canker of our nature come
	In further evil? 70
HORATIO	It must be shortly known to him from England
	What is the issue of the business there.
HAMLET	It will be short; the interim is mine,
	And a man's life's no more than to say 'One'.
	But I am very sorry, good Horatio, 75
	That to Laertes I forgot myself;
	For by the image of my cause, I see
	The portraiture of his; I'll court his favours.
	But sure the bravery of his grief did put me
	Into a towering passion.
HORATIO	Peace, who comes here? 80

Enter OSRIC

OSRIC	Your lordship is right welcome back to Denmark.
HAMLET	I humbly thank you sir. Dost know this water-fly?
HORATIO	No my good lord.
HAMLET	Thy state is the more gracious, for 'tis a vice to
	know him. He hath much land, and fertile. 85

Osric, long-winded and affected, anxious to please, tells Hamlet of the wager Claudius has laid on a duel with Laertes. Hamlet finds Osric ridiculous and enjoys using similar language to him.

86 **Let a beast...mess**: as long as an animal owns many other animals, his manger will stand beside the King's table
  crib: the manger from which farm animals eat

87 **chough**: either a bird of the crow family, and therefore talkative or (usual spelling 'chuff') a boorish fellow. The word 'chuff' could also mean buttocks or arse.
  spacious in the possession of dirt: the bird would have plenty of dirt to scratch around in; the boor might boast of owning much land, or (see the note on 'chuff' above) 'talking a lot of shit'

92 **bonnet**: hat or cap

95 **indifferent**: fairly

97 **complexion**: constitution

103 **for my ease**: Osric politely insists on keeping his hat off

105 **excellent differences**: accomplishments quite out of the ordinary

106 **of very soft society**: well-mannered
  great showing: distinguished appearance

107 **card or calendar**: map or directory

108 **you shall find...would see**: he contains in himself all the attributes a gentleman could wish to find

110 **his definement**: the definition of the qualities you offer
  perdition: loss (cf modern French 'perdre'– to lose)

111 **to divide him inventorially**: to make a list (an inventory) of his qualities, one by one, to catalogue

112 **dozy**: make dizzy, confuse
  and yet...sail: it's no good going off at a tangent to try and get close to him because he is so far ahead
  yaw: divert from a straight course

113 **in the verity of extolment**: to speak truth in praising him

114 **of great article**: with many items

115 **his infusion...rareness**: his essence of such rare value

116 **as...true diction of him**: to speak the truth about
  his semblable...umbrage: the only one like him is his mirror image; only his shadow can follow at his heels

Let a beast be lord of beasts, and his crib shall stand
at the king's mess. 'Tis a chough, but as I say,
spacious in the possession of dirt.

OSRIC   Sweet lord, if your lordship were at leisure, I should
impart a thing to you from his majesty.   90

HAMLET   I will receive it sir, with all diligence of spirit. Put
your bonnet to his right use, 'tis for the head.

OSRIC   I thank your lordship, it is very hot.

HAMLET   No believe me, 'tis very cold, the wind is northerly.

OSRIC   It is indifferent cold my lord, indeed.   95

HAMLET   But yet methinks it is very sultry, and hot for my
complexion.

OSRIC   Exceedingly my lord, it is very sultry – as 'twere – I
cannot tell how. But my lord, his majesty bade me
signify to you that 'a has laid a great wager on   100
your head. Sir, this is the matter –

HAMLET   I beseech you remember –
                [HAMLET *moves him to put on his hat*

OSRIC   Nay good my lord, for my ease in good faith. Sir,
here is newly come to court Laertes; believe me an
absolute gentleman, full of most excellent   105
differences, of very soft society and great showing;
indeed to speak feelingly of him, he is the card or
calendar of gentry, for you shall find in him the
continent of what part a gentleman would see.

HAMLET   Sir, his definement suffers no perdition in you,   110
though I know to divide him inventorially would
dozy th' arithmetic of memory, and yet but yaw
neither, in respect of his quick sail. But in the verity
of extolment, I take him to be a soul of great
article, and his infusion of such dearth and   115
rareness, as to make true diction of him, his
semblable is his mirror, and who else would trace
him, his umbrage, nothing more.

Osric seems rather taken aback by Hamlet's parodying of him and in much briefer exchanges Hamlet learns what the wager is – six Barbary horses against six French rapiers and daggers and all the pieces of equipment belonging to them.

120 concernancy: how does this concern us?
Why...breath?: why are we talking about this gentleman?
123 Is 't...sir really: is it not possible to understand in a different language? You will get there in the end.
125 nomination: naming
127 His purse...spent: taking Osric's *'golden words'* as coins in a purse – he has run out of currency
131 it would not much approve me: it would not say much for me
134 I dare not...himself: Hamlet suggests that to recognize excellence in another person, you must be capable of that excellence yourself – so in a sense you would be boasting of your own qualities
137 but...unfellowed: (with this punctuation) according to what those in his service say about him, he's unmatched; (with the comma after *'them'*) according to what they say about him, in excellence he is unmatched
140 Rapier and dagger: this was two-handed fighting, with the dagger (poniard) in the left hand warding off the opponent's rapier thrusts, while attempting to make hits with one's own rapier
142 Barbary: Arab
143 he has imponed: placed a bet
145 assigns: appurtenances, attachments
girdle: sword-belt
hangers: straps from which the rapier hung on the sword-belt
and so: and so on
146 carriages: another word for 'hangers' based on the original sense of 'gun carriages'
very dear to fancy...liberal conceit: matching the hilts, finely and imaginatively crafted
150 I knew...had done: I knew you'd need an explanation in the margin

OSRIC	Your lordship speaks most infallibly of him.
HAMLET	The concernancy sir? Why do we wrap the 120 gentleman in our more rawer breath?
OSRIC	Sir?
HORATIO	Is 't not possible to understand in another tongue? You will do 't sir really.
HAMLET	What imports the nomination of this gentleman? 125
OSRIC	Of Laertes?
HORATIO	His purse is empty already, all's golden words are spent.
HAMLET	Of him sir.
OSRIC	I know you are not ignorant – 130
HAMLET	I would you did sir, yet in faith if you did, it would not much approve me. Well sir?
OSRIC	You are not ignorant of what excellence Laertes is –
HAMLET	I dare not confess that, lest I should compare with him in excellence; but, to know a man well, 135 were to know himself.
OSRIC	I mean sir for his weapon, but in the imputation laid on him by them in his meed, he's unfellowed.
HAMLET	What's his weapon?
OSRIC	Rapier and dagger. 140
HAMLET	That's two of his weapons – but well.
OSRIC	The King sir, hath wagered with him six Barbary horses, against the which he has imponed, as I take it, six French rapiers and poniards, with their assigns, as girdle, hangers, and so. Three of the 145 carriages in faith are very dear to fancy, very responsive to the hilts, most delicate carriages, and of very liberal conceit.
HAMLET	What call you the carriages?
HORATIO	I knew you must be edified by the margent ere 150 you had done.

The wager is that in a duel of twelve bouts, Laertes will not score three more hits than Hamlet. Hamlet replies that he will win for the King if he can. Osric leaves to convey this message to the King, and Hamlet and Horatio again amuse themselves at his expense.

153 german: (or 'germane') relevant

154 cannon: a reference to note on line 146

160 The King...twelve for nine: a wager against Laertes scoring more than three hits over Hamlet is easy to understand – but the additional arithmetic in this speech makes the details obscure. Of course, the King and Laertes know that the match will never go the full length, and Hamlet seems casually concerned merely to do whatever is required of him.

169 breathing time: time for exercise

174 re-deliver you e'en so?: take this back as your answer?

175 after what...will: with whatever embellishment your nature will allow

177 I commend...lordship: leave–taking phrase

179 commend: Hamlet chooses to take 'commend' in the set phrase as 'recommend' 'advocate' and goes on to say that no one else is likely to do so.

181 This lapwing...its head: lapwings nest on the ground, often in exposed positions and just a few hours after hatching, the young are led away to safety. They are used here as a *metaphor* (see GLOSSARY page 335) for young people who are quick off the mark.
shell on his head: so recently hatched that a piece of shell still sticks to its head

183 'A did...his dug: he used to flatter his mother's (or more likely his wet-nurse's) teat

185 drossy age: frivolous times
got the tune of the time: only learnt to parrot the prevailing tune. Hamlet is commenting on people like Osric who take for themselves other people's thoughts and opinions and ape their behaviour. When they are really put to the test their trivial nature is revealed.

186 outward habit of encounter: external appearance of behaviour

OSRIC	The carriages sir, are the hangers.
HAMLET	The phrase would be more german to the matter, if we could carry cannon by our sides; I would it might be hangers till then. But on – six 155 Barbary horses against six French swords, their assigns, and three liberal-conceited carriages; that's the French bet against the Danish. Why is this 'imponed', as you call it?
OSRIC	The King sir, hath laid sir, that in a dozen 160 passes between yourself and him, he shall not exceed you three hits; he hath laid on twelve for nine; and it would come to immediate trial, if your lordship would vouchsafe the answer.
HAMLET	How if I answer 'no'? 165
OSRIC	I mean, my lord, the opposition of your person in trial.
HAMLET	Sir, I will walk here in the hall. If it please his majesty, it is the breathing time of day with me; let the foils be brought, the gentleman willing, and 170 the King hold his purpose, I will win for him an I can; if not, I will gain nothing but my shame and the odd hits.
OSRIC	Shall I re-deliver you e'en so?
HAMLET	To this effect sir, after what flourish your 175 nature will.
OSRIC	I commend my duty to your lordship.
HAMLET	Yours, yours. [*Exit* OSRIC] He does well to commend it himself, there are no tongues else for 's turn. 180
HORATIO	This lapwing runs away with the shell on his head.
HAMLET	'A did comply with his dug, before 'a sucked it. Thus has he, and many more of the same breed that I know the drossy age dotes on, only got 185 the tune of the time, and outward habit of

A courtier comes to enquire whether Hamlet accepts the duel and to announce that the King and Queen and the court are coming down. Horatio warns Hamlet that he will lose the wager and Hamlet, although he thinks he can win, admits to some foreboding. Horatio offers to help him withdraw, but Hamlet insists that fate will take its course.

187 **yeasty collection**: superficial bunch – the image is of
   frothy bubbles of yeast once they start working
189 **winnowed**: sifted and sorted out
   do but...trial: once they are put to the test – once you
   blow at the bubbles, they disappear
191 **commended him to you**: sent his compliments
196 **I...purposes**: I stand by what I say I'll do
197 **If...ready**: whatever time is convenient for him, it will be
   so for me
200 **In happy time**: at an appropriate moment
201 **use some gentle entertainment**: receive with courtesy
211 **gain-giving**: misgiving, ominous feeling
213 **forestall their repair hither**: stop their coming here
214 **we defy augury**: Hamlet rejects his feeling of foreboding.
   An *'augury'* is the interpretation of signs which seem to
   foretell what is to come.
   there is...a sparrow: a reference to the *Bible* (*Matthew
   10.29*). God has charge of everything that happens, so
   that even a sparrow's death is taken account of.
215 **it**: death. In these lines Hamlet sets out the inevitability of
   fate.

> • *How would you describe Hamlet's mood at this stage?*
> • *How does Shakespeare increase the tensions before the
>   duel?*

encounter, a kind of yeasty collection, which carries
them through and through the most profound
and winnowed opinions; and do but blow them
to their trial, the bubbles are out.   190

Enter a LORD

LORD   My lord, his majesty commended him to you by
            young Osric, who brings back to him, that you
            attend him in the hall. He sends to know if your
            pleasure hold to play with Laertes, or that you will
            take longer time.   195

HAMLET   I am constant to my purposes. They follow the
            King's pleasure. If his fitness speaks, mine is ready;
            now or whensoever, provided I be so able as now.

LORD   The King and Queen and all are coming down.

HAMLET   In happy time.   200

LORD   The Queen desires you to use some gentle
            entertainment to Laertes before you fall to play.

HAMLET   She well instructs me.   [*Exit* LORD

HORATIO   You will lose this wager my lord.

HAMLET   I do not think so. Since he went into France,   205
            I have been in continual practice; I shall win at the
            odds. But thou wouldst not think how ill all 's
            here about my heart – but it is no matter.

HORATIO   Nay my good lord, –

HAMLET   It is but foolery, but it is such a kind of   210
            gain-giving as would perhaps trouble a woman.

HORATIO   If your mind dislike any thing, obey it. I will
            forestall their repair hither, and say you are not fit.

HAMLET   Not a whit, we defy augury; there is special
            providence in the fall of a sparrow. If it be now,   215
            'tis not to come; if it be not to come, it will be
            now; if it be not now, yet it will come – the

The audience, consisting of the King, Queen and court enters with Laertes. The King gets Hamlet and Laertes to shake hands and Hamlet excuses himself to Laertes for killing Polonius, saying it was his madness. Laertes answers politely.

218 readiness is all: the most important thing is to be prepared
  Since...betimes: since no one knows what life would have held, if he'd lived, it is no hardship to die early
223 presence: those assembled here
225 a sore distraction: madness which is hard to bear
226 exception: dislike
229 If Hamlet...denies it: if Hamlet is not himself, because he has lost his mind, and in this state wrongs Laertes, then it is not really Hamlet who does the wrong and he denies responsibility for it.
  ta'en: taken
233 faction: party
236 Let my...evil: let my assertion that I meant no wrong
239 in nature: as far as my natural feelings go
240 Whose motive...revenge: and it is those which in the present circumstance should most move me to revenge
241 in my...honour: as far as the question of honour goes
242 I stand...ungored: I will keep myself at a distance and reject any reconciliation until from some elders, seen as men of honour, I may have a judgement and precedent for reconciliation to keep my name undamaged
247 And will not wrong it: Hamlet has not told Laertes how Polonius came to die. Laertes is not being frank with Hamlet now.

> • *Compare Hamlet's and Laertes's public reconciliation. Who is the more honest?*

readiness is all. Since no man knows aught of what
he leaves, what is 't to leave betimes? Let be.

A table prepared, Trumpets, Drums, and OFFICERS
with Cushions. KING, QUEEN, *and all the state, foils,
daggers, and* LAERTES

KING   Come Hamlet, come and take this hand from
    me.   220
     [*The* KING *puts* LAERTES' *hand into* HAMLET'S

HAMLET   Give me your pardon sir, I've done you wrong;
    But pardon 't as you are a gentleman.
    This presence knows,
    And you must needs have heard, how I am
     punished
    With a sore distraction. What I have done 225
    That might your nature, honour, and exception
    Roughly awake, I here proclaim was madness.
    Was 't Hamlet wronged Laertes? Never Hamlet.
    If Hamlet from himself be ta'en away,
    And when he's not himself does wrong Laertes, 230
    Then Hamlet does it not, Hamlet denies it.
    Who does it then? His madness. If 't be so,
    Hamlet is of the faction that is wronged,
    His madness is poor Hamlet's enemy.
    Sir, in this audience,   235
    Let my disclaiming from a purposed evil
    Free me so far in your most generous thoughts,
    That I have shot my arrow o'er the house,
    And hurt my brother.

LAERTES   I am satisfied in nature,
    Whose motive in this case should stir me most 240
    To my revenge; but in my terms of honour
    I stand aloof, and will no reconcilement
    Till by some elder masters of known honour
    I have a voice and precedent of peace,
    To keep my name ungored. But till that time 245
    I do receive your offered love like love,
    And will not wrong it.

Hamlet and Laertes seem reconciled for the moment, but Laertes is still very touchy. Osric fetches the foils and Laertes rejects the first one offered to him and chooses another. Hamlet is satisfied with his. The King orders goblets of wine to be set ready. At Hamlet's success the cannon shall sound, and he will drink to Hamlet's health and throw a rich pearl into Hamlet's cup. He orders the match to begin.

248 frankly: freely, with an open mind

250 foil: (here) setting for a jewel and a pun on the foils they will fight with

252 Stick fiery off: blaze out

256 laid the odds: laid your bet

258 but since...therefore odds: but since he is generally considered to be the better, we have the advantage of the handicap

262 stoups: drinking-vessels, cups, flaggons, tankards

264 Or quit...exchange: makes a convincing comeback in the third bout

266 better breath: staying power

267 union: rich pearl

270 kettle: kettledrum

HAMLET	I embrace it freely,
	And will this brother's wager frankly play.
	Give us the foils. Come on.
LAERTES	Come, one for me.
HAMLET	I'll be your foil Laertes, in mine ignorance 250
	Your skill shall like astar i' th' darkest night
	Stick fiery off indeed.
LAERTES	You mock me sir.
HAMLET	No by this hand.
KING	Give them the foils, young Osric. Cousin Hamlet,
	You know the wager?
HAMLET	Very well, my lord. 255
	Your grace hath laid the odds a th' weaker side.
KING	I do not fear it, I have seen you both;
	But since he is bettered, we have therefore odds.
LAERTES	This is too heavy. Let me see another.
HAMLET	This likes me well. These foils have all a length? 260
	[They prepare to play
OSRIC	Ay my good lord.
KING	Set me the stoups of wine upon that table.
	If Hamlet give the first or second hit,
	Or quit in answer of the third exchange,
	Let all the battlements their ordnance fire. 265
	The King shall drink to Hamlet's better breath,
	And in the cup an union shall he throw,
	Richer than that which four successive kings
	In Denmark's crown have worn. Give me the cups,
	And let the kettle to the trumpet speak, 270
	The trumpet to the cannoneer without,
	The cannons to the heavens, the heaven to earth,
	'Now the King drinks to Hamlet'. Come, begin;
	And you the judges bear a wary eye.
	[Trumpets the while
HAMLET	Come on sir. 275

Hamlet scores two hits and at the second the trumpets give the signal for the cannons to sound. The King drinks to Hamlet, at the same time putting the pearl in a cup and offering it to Hamlet, who refuses to drink yet. Gertrude drinks to Hamlet from this poisoned cup before Claudius can stop her. Laertes is about to wound Hamlet – though his conscience protests. Hamlet challenges him to play more decisively.

280 palpable: evident, obvious
287 fat: sweaty *or* out of condition. From internal evidence – 'take my napkin, rub thy brows' the former seems more likely. Also Hamlet has claimed (line 206) that he has been practising.
288 napkin: handkerchief
289 carouses: drinks a health
297 you but dally: you are only playing about
298 pass: thrust
299 you make a wanton of me: you are treating me like a spoilt child
302 Have at you now! : the challenge preceding a fresh thrust

- *Why is Claudius unable to prevent Gertrude drinking from the poisoned cup? How would you stage this?*
- *Is Laertes having second thoughts?*

LAERTES	Come my lord.	*[They play*
HAMLET	One.	
LAERTES	No.	
HAMLET	Judgment.	
OSRIC	A hit, a very palpable hit.	280
LAERTES	Well, again.	
KING	Stay, give me drink. Hamlet, this pearl is thine,	
	Here's to thy health.	

[Trumpets sound, and cannon shot off within
Give him the cup.

HAMLET	I'll play this bout first, set it by awhile.	
	Come – another hit. What say you?	285
LAERTES	A touch, a touch, I do confess 't.	
KING	Our son shall win.	
QUEEN	He's fat and scant of breath.	
	Here Hamlet, take my napkin, rub thy brows.	
	The Queen carouses to thy fortune, Hamlet.	
HAMLET	Good madam.	
KING	Gertrude do not drink.	290
QUEEN	I will my lord, I pray you pardon me.	
KING	[*Aside*] It is the poisoned cup; it is too late.	
HAMLET	I dare not drink yet madam – by and by.	
QUEEN	Come, let me wipe thy face.	
LAERTES	My lord, I'll hit him now.	
KING	I do not think 't.	295
LAERTES	[*Aside*] And yet 'tis almost against my conscience.	
HAMLET	Come, for the third Laertes, you but dally.	
	I pray you pass with your best violence;	
	I am afeared you make a wanton of me.	
LAERTES	Say you so, come on.	*[They play*	300
OSRIC	Nothing neither way.	
LAERTES	Have at you now!	

Laertes wounds Hamlet and in the ensuing scuffle they exchange rapiers and Laertes is hurt with the poisoned foil. The Queen dies, a victim of the poisoned wine she has drunk. Hamlet orders the doors to be locked and the perpetrator found. Laertes confesses to the poisoned rapier and blames the King for Gertrude's death. Having learnt about the poisoned weapon, Hamlet stabs the King and then forces him to drink the poison. Claudius dies. Laertes suggests that he and Hamlet forgive one another.

303 incensed: furiously angry

308 as a...springe: like a woodcock caught in my own snare

310 swounds: faints

319 envenomed: poisoned

323 The point envenomed too!: Hamlet has already learnt the foil is unbated, since he has been wounded

325 Treason, treason!: anyone laying hand on the King would be guilty of treason. Of those present (and still alive) only Hamlet and Horatio know the whole story of the King's wickedness; Laertes knows only the latest manifestation of it. Of these three, two are as good as dead.

328 union: double meaning – the pearl/poison capsule and the 'incestuous' and ill–fated union with his mother

330 tempered: compounded, mixed

> • *With the deaths of the main characters achieved or imminent, a different concern will take centre stage, triggered by the bystanders' cry of 'Treason'. What is it?*

[LAERTES *wounds* HAMLET; *then, in scuffling, they*
change rapiers, and HAMLET *wounds* LAERTES

KING   Part them, they are incensed.

HAMLET   Nay come, again.   [*The* QUEEN *falls*

OSRIC   Look to the Queen there, ho!   305

HORATIO   They bleed on both sides. How is it my lord?

OSRIC   How is 't Laertes?

LAERTES   Why as a woodcock to mine own springe, Osric.
            I am justly killed with mine own treachery.

HAMLET   How does the Queen?

KING   She swounds to see them
            bleed.   310

QUEEN   No, no, the drink, the drink – o my dear Hamlet –
            The drink, the drink! I am poisoned.   [*Dies*

HAMLET   O villany! Ho, let the door be locked. Treachery!
            Seek it out.

LAERTES   It is here, Hamlet. Hamlet, thou art slain.   315
            No medicine in the world can do thee good,
            In thee there is not half an hour of life.
            The treacherous instrument is in thy hand,
            Unbated and envenomed. The foul practice
            Hath turned itself on me; lo here I lie,   320
            Never to rise again. Thy mother's poisoned –
            I can no more – the King, the King's to blame.

HAMLET   The point envenomed too!
            Then, venom, to thy work.   [*Stabs the* KING

ALL   Treason, treason!   325

KING   O yet defend me friends, I am but hurt.

HAMLET   Here, thou incestuous, murderous, damned Dane,
            Drink off this potion. Is thy union here?
            Follow my mother.   [KING *dies*

LAERTES   He is justly served,
            It is a poison tempered by himself.   330
            Exchange forgiveness with me noble Hamlet.

Laertes dies as he expresses the hope of mutual forgiveness, which Hamlet grants, as he asks Horatio to report the true motives behind these deaths. Horatio protests that he will follow Hamlet into death by drinking the remaining poison. Hamlet begs him to restore honour to his name by telling the true story. There are sounds of an army approaching. Fortinbras is coming. Hamlet is dying but gives Fortinbras his vote in the election to King of Denmark.

337 mutes: characters in a play without speaking parts. Hamlet has shown before that he considers he could be an actor. Now that his revenge has come out of the darkness of his troubled thoughts and has been enacted before the whole court, it must seem as real/unreal to him as if it were a play. He also now needs Horatio to perform the functions of chorus (see note Act 3 scene 2 line 245) and epilogue (a speech or short poem delivered by one of the actors to the spectators after a play is over).

338 fell: cruel

sergeant: sheriff's officer; an officer of the court with powers of arrest

342 the unsatisfied: those who need a satisfactory explanation of Hamlet's strange conduct

343 more an antique Roman: more inclined to regard suicide in such a case as a noble act, worthy of admiration, rather than inviting shame and damnation

349 Absent thee from felicity awhile: put off for a while the happiness death brings

355 o'er-crows: triumphs over, crows over – as the winning cock in a cockfight

359 th' occurrents more or less: all the happenings, important and unimportant

- *What is it that persuades Horatio not to follow Hamlet immediately into death?*
- *Why, in spite of all his previous reservations about death, does Hamlet now call it 'felicity'?*

	Mine and my father's death come not upon thee, Nor thine on me. [*Dies*
HAMLET	Heaven make thee free of it. I follow thee. I am dead, Horatio. Wretched Queen, adieu. 335 You that look pale and tremble at this chance, That are but mutes or audience to this act, Had I but time, as this fell sergeant death Is strict in his arrest, o I could tell you – But let it be. Horatio, I am dead, 340 Thou livest; report me and my cause aright To the unsatisfied.
HORATIO	Never believe it; I am more an antique Roman than a Dane. Here's yet some liquor left.
HAMLET	As thou 'rt a man, Give me the cup – let go, by heaven I'll ha't. 345 O God, Horatio, what a wounded name, Things standing thus unknown, shall leave behind me! If thou didst ever hold me in thy heart, Absent thee from felicity awhile, And in this harsh world draw thy breath in pain, 350 To tell my story. [*March afar off, and shot within* What warlike noise is this?

Enter OSRIC

OSRIC	Young Fortinbras, with conquest come from Poland, To th' ambassadors of England gives This warlike volley.
HAMLET	O I die Horatio, The potent poison quite o'er-crows my spirit. 355 I cannot live to hear the news from England, But I do prophesy the election lights On Fortinbras, he has my dying voice; So tell him, with th' occurrents more and less

Hamlet dies. Fortinbras, accompanied by martial music and
the English ambassadors, enters. He has heard of the deaths.
The English ambassadors expect thanks for achieving the
deaths of Rosencrantz and Guildenstern and learn that it was
not Claudius who gave the order. Horatio asks for the
bodies to be placed on view while he tells the assembled
company the background to what has happened.

360 **have solicited**: have caused (this result)
366 **quarry**: heap of the dead – normally the 'bag' after a hunt
    havoc: originally in the call 'Havoc!' an incitement to a
    victorious army to pillage. Here, wholesale destruction or
    slaughter.
367 **feast**: the idea that Death will feast on the dead bodies
    toward: being planned
    eternal: sometimes used, as here, for 'infernal', 'damned'
377 **jump**: immediately
    question: strife
383 **Of carnal...inventors' heads**: this is a catalogue, a trail,
    for the story Hamlet has asked Horatio to tell. While
    many of the items in the list can be applied to more than
    one death, some of the applications may be as follows:
    'carnal' refers to the *'incestuous'* marriage, which was
    itself possibly one of the motives for the *'unnatural'* killing
    of a brother; *'accidental judgments'* – sentences apparently
    carried out by accident, as that on Gertrude; *'casual*
    slaughters' – chance killings – Polonius and possibly
    Ophelia, Laertes; deaths *'put on by cunning and forced*
    cause' – Hamlet's intended execution in England and the
    actual deaths there of Rosencrantz and Guildenstern, and
    Hamlet's own death.
385 **put on**: set up
    forced cause: contrivance
386 **in this upshot**: in this event – the upshot was the final
    shot in an archery match
    purposes mistook...heads: methods of carrying out their
    intentions which misfired and destroyed those who had
    thought them up

Which have solicited. The rest is silence.   360

[*Dies*

HORATIO   Now cracks a noble heart. Good night sweet
    prince,
And flights of angels sing thee to thy rest.
Why does the drum come hither?

Enter FORTINBRAS *with Drum and colours, the*
ENGLISH AMBASSADORS, *and others*

FORTINBRAS Where is this sight?

HORATIO   What is it ye would see?
If aught of woe or wonder, cease your search.   365

FORTINBRAS This quarry cries on havoc. O proud death,
What feast is toward in thine eternal cell,
That thou so many princes at a shot
So bloodily hast struck?

FIRST
AMBASSADOR   The sight is dismal,
And our affairs from England come too late.   370
The ears are senseless that should give us hearing,
To tell him his commandment is fulfilled,
That Rosencrantz and Guildenstern are dead.
Where should we have our thanks?

HORATIO   Not from his mouth
Had it th' ability of life to thank you;   375
He never gave commandment for their death.
But since, so jump upon this bloody question,
You from the Polack wars, and you from England,
Are here arrived, give order that these bodies
High on a stage be placed to the view,   380
And let me speak to the yet unknowing world
How these things came about; so shall you hear
Of carnal, bloody, and unnatural acts,
Of accidental judgments, casual slaughters,
Of deaths put on by cunning and forced cause,   385
And, in this upshot, purposes mistook

Horatio finishes sketching out what he will have to tell and
Fortinbras takes control, while Horatio points out that
Fortinbras has Hamlet's vote, which will attract that of
others. Fortinbras orders Hamlet's body to be placed by four
captains on a raised platform and speaks of the potential he
seemed to have as the future king. The other bodies too are
carried up, and cannons are fired.

391 **rights of memory:** possibly a reference to the claims of
Fortinbras in Act 1 scene 1, which were threatening to
cause a war
392 **my vantage:** the advantage I now have
394 **whose voice will draw on more:** Hamlet's dying
declaration for the election of Fortinbras will influence
others
396 **wild:** in disarray
397 **On:** on top of
399 **had he been put on:** ie if he had been made king
400 **passage:** passing from this world
401 **rite of war:** martial ceremonies
404 **Becomes the field:** is fitting for the battlefield

- *'Something is rotten in the state of Denmark'. Has
  this rottenness now been purged, in preparation for a
  fresh start?*
- *What might Hamlet's dying hopes for Denmark have
  been in his choice of Fortinbras for king?*

- *Estimate the importance of Horatio's role in the play.*
- *Fortinbras makes a judgement about Hamlet's
  potential as king. What is yours?*

Fall'n on the inventors' heads. All this can I
Truly deliver.

FORTINBRAS   Let us haste to hear it,
And call the noblest to the audience.
For me, with sorrow I embrace my fortune.   390
I have some rights of memory in this kingdom,
Which now to claim my vantage doth invite me.

HORATIO   Of that I shall have also cause to speak,
And from his mouth whose voice will draw on
          more.
But let this same be presently performed,   395
Even while men's minds are wild, lest more
          mischance
On plots and errors happen.

FORTINBRAS   Let four captains
Bear Hamlet like a soldier to the stage,
For he was likely, had he been put on,
To have proved most royal: and for his passage,   400
The soldiers' music and the rite of war
Speak loudly for him.
Take up the bodies – such a sight as this
Becomes the field, but here shows much amiss.
Go bid the soldiers shoot.   405
          [*Exeunt marching, after which a peal of ordnance is*
                                                    shot off

 **CTIVITIES**

Keeping track

Scene 1

1 The scene begins with the 'humorous' discussion between the grave-diggers on the subject of whether or not Ophelia is entitled to a 'Christian burial'. What is the attitude of the grave-diggers to the death of Ophelia?
2 Why do you think Shakespeare introduces these 'comic' figures? Is it simply a matter of 'light relief'?
3 What is Hamlet's reaction to the grave-diggers' behaviour as he and Horatio enter?
4 As the skulls are casually thrown out of the ground, Hamlet is forced to confront the stark reality of death. What are his thoughts and feelings at this point?
5 What is Hamlet's reaction to the discovery that the skull is that of Yorick?
6 Hamlet observes the *'maimed rites'* which accompany the funeral of Ophelia. How does Laertes respond to the lack of ceremony? What explanation does the priest give?
7 Why does Hamlet disrupt the funeral?
8 How do Gertrude and Claudius react?

Scene 2

1 What are Hamlet and Horatio discussing as the scene opens?
2 What do we learn of Claudius's plot against Hamlet's life?
3 Hamlet says, *'There's a divinity that shapes our ends'*. Is this an important line: has Hamlet changed?
4 What has happened to Rosencrantz and Guildenstern and how does Hamlet feel about it?
5 What reasons does Hamlet give for arguing that it would be *'perfect conscience'* to kill Claudius?
6 How does Hamlet treat Osric when he arrives, and why does he behave like this?
7 Why do you think Hamlet is so willing to accept the challenge proposed by Claudius?
8 How does Hamlet behave towards Laertes when he appears?
9 What exactly happens in the duel?
10 How is Gertrude killed, and how does Hamlet react to her death?
11 What finally pushes Hamlet to kill Claudius?

12 What news do the ambassadors bring from England?
13 How does Fortinbras respond to Hamlet's death?

Drama

1 Consider the arrival of the funeral party at the graveside. Using
   members of the class, arrange the characters as if they were in a
   photograph. (See PHOTOGRAPHS on page 296.) Concentrate on the
   line *'What ceremony else?'*
       How do the different people feel about the death of Ophelia?
   Examine the arguments put forward by the two grave-diggers earlier
   in the scene to see how complicated the issue of suicide was for
   Elizabethans. How does this argument impinge on the various
   characters present? Is Claudius bothered? What effect has it had on
   Laertes? Has Gertrude considered taking her own life?
       When you have arranged the photograph ask each character to say
   aloud what they are thinking. Consider what difference there might be
   between the thoughts they might share with others and their
   innermost thoughts.
2 Use FORUM THEATRE (see page 297) to explore the moment when
   Hamlet leaps into the grave *'This is I, Hamlet the Dane.'* How does
   everyone react to such a sacrilegious act?
3 Osric
   • Osric is an example of Shakespeare's skill in producing humour at
     the blackest moments. As costume and prop designers, how would
     you deal with this character? Create some designs and ask one of
     your group to act as a model so that you can develop some
     mannerisms as well.
   • In threes, improvise Osric reporting back to Claudius and Laertes
     after his encounter with Hamlet and Horatio. Does he keep up the
     pretentious manner or is it just an act? What is he really like? How
     does he feel about his treatment by Hamlet?
4 After the tragedy
   • Hold a series of television news conferences with the survivors –
     including Horatio, Osric, attendants, grave-diggers and Fortinbras.
   • Produce a variety of articles and reports written in different styles.
     This could include Horatio's statement to the police, the post-
     mortem documents, newspaper headlines and obituaries.

Key elements

In Act 5 these are:
• the graveyard scene
• the duel scene.

Key Scene

The duel scene: Act 5 scene 2 lines 262–363

Keying it in

This scene is the violent climax of the play.
- How does Hamlet behave to Laertes as they prepare for their duel?
- How does he try to excuse his past actions?
- How does Laertes respond to Hamlet's apology?
- Is he sincere?
- Is Hamlet a guilty man at this stage of the play?

The scene itself

1 As Hamlet and Laertes prepare to play, Claudius asks for wine to be put on the table.
   - What appearance is Claudius trying to give here?
   - What are his real hopes and intentions?
2 Hamlet wins the first bout of fencing.
   - How does Claudius react to this?
   - Why does Gertrude drink from the poisoned cup?
   - Why is Claudius unable to prevent her from drinking?
3 The fight becomes more intense and both Hamlet and Laertes are wounded with the poisoned rapier.
   - Why do you think Laertes says he is *'justly killed'*?
   - Do you agree with him?
   - Does the fate of Laertes affect your response to Hamlet himself?
4 Laertes condemns Claudius for the deaths of himself, Hamlet and Gertrude.
   - What do you think is the importance of this public accusation?
   - How does Hamlet react?
   - What does he achieve in this moment of violence? Is it revenge or justice? Look at Laertes's dying words.
5 Horatio pays tribute to the dead prince (lines 361–363).
   - How do you react to his words?
   - Do you agree with his sentiments?

Close study

Act 5 scene 1 lines 186–219
- What was Hamlet's relationship with Yorick?
- How does he react to the realization that this is Yorick's skull?
- What effect does this have on Hamlet?
- How does the language of these lines stress the horror of death?
- What conclusions does Hamlet draw from what he has just seen?
- How would you describe his feelings and attitudes?

Hamlet and revenge

In Act 5, Hamlet is drawn into the conspiracy planned by Claudius and Laertes. It is interesting to note that Hamlet himself makes no active attempt to plot against the life of Claudius.

In the graveyard scene, Hamlet is brought face to face with the gruesome realities of death. At first, he seems to feel a mixture of shock, horror and revulsion and yet, also, a kind of grim satisfaction in the recognition that all is vanity, and that the pretensions of human existence simply end in the grave. However, death is made unbearable by the sight of Ophelia's body, and Hamlet is forced to abandon the theory in favour of a passionate, but tragically belated, declaration of love.

After the graveyard scene he does seem calmer, more at peace with himself. He seems more prepared to accept that there is 'a divinity that shapes our ends' and less frantic in his pursuit of revenge. Perhaps the assertion of love for Ophelia has purged some of the 'evil' from his consciousness. Whether his mood is now one of spiritual enlightenment, fatalism or weary resignation is not easy to determine, but Hamlet seems to come to terms with death and the possibility of death. As he says – 'the readiness is all'.

In the duel scene, Hamlet achieves his revenge, but it is at a terrible cost and it is the result of unpremeditated action. It is perhaps worth asking the question: when Hamlet does finally kill Claudius, whom exactly is he avenging?

When he kills Claudius it is not a secret murder and it perhaps looks more like an act of public justice than private revenge.

Assignments

Essays

1 Look at the graveyard scene. What is the dramatic significance of this scene?
2 Some critics have observed that Hamlet is a changed man in Act 5. How far do you agree with this observation?
3 Do you think that the duel scene brings the play to a satisfactory conclusion?

Explorations

Drama activities

In the Activities sections we suggest a number of ways in which you can explore the play using drama. The notes that follow explain how the different types of activity can be organized. Most of the suggestions in the book fall into one of these groups:

- improvisation
- hotseating
- stopping the action
- forum theatre.

Improvisation

Improvisation is a form of theatre in which the actors do not have a written script, but make it up as they 'go along'. When you improvise, you need to know:

- **who** you are
- **when** and **where** the scene takes place
- **what** happened before the scene takes place
- **why** the scene is happening (for example if there is a conflict between the characters or a problem they are faced with).

How you improvise depends on how much planning and polishing you want to do. Some people like just to launch into the situation without any planning at all. This is a good way of working if you want to find out about the characters, relationships and emotions involved. Others like to discuss the situation and the main things that will happen before they begin to improvise. This is useful if you are working towards a scene, so that it becomes more confident and 'polished' – especially if you are preparing for a performance. Which approach you use depends on the situation you are working on and what you want to get out of it.

Hotseating

This is a good way of examining very closely the thoughts and feelings of one character at a key moment in the play. For example, you might choose Ophelia after Polonius has given her his lecture. If you wanted to explore this situation through hotseating, this is what you would do:

1 Choose one member of the group to be Ophelia.
2 That person sits 'in the hot seat', with the rest of the group around her.
3 Other members of the group ask Ophelia about her actions – why she acted in the way that she did.
4 Ophelia must reply in character, and without pausing too long to think about her answer.
5 The rest of the group keep the questions going, picking up the replies that Ophelia gives.
6 At the end you can discuss what came out of the questioning and whether Ophelia's replies agree with the way other people see her character.

Variations

- The people in the group can become characters themselves: Laertes, Gertrude and Hamlet. Then each one has to ask questions from the point of view of that character.
- The questioners can take on different styles of questioning. One might be sympathetic, while a second would be aggressive, and a third sneering, for example.

Stopping the action

This is a different way of focusing on a particular moment in the play. Instead of choosing a particular character, you choose a particular moment. There are two main ways in which you can do this.

Photographs

A photograph is based on the idea that you freeze a particular moment in the play. You can do it in different ways:
- Have one member in the group as the photographer. The rest of the group act the scene and at the moment the photographer says 'Freeze!', everyone must stay absolutely still.

- Choose the moment in the scene you want to photograph. Discuss how the photograph should look and then take up the positions you have agreed.
- Choose the moment in the scene you want to photograph. Give each member of the group a number. Number 1 takes up position as his/her character and freezes. Number 2 then joins Number one and freezes. Number 3 does the same and so on until everyone is in the photograph.

Once you have made your photograph you can come out of it one at a time and make suggestions about how it could be improved. You can also build on the photograph by one of the following:

- Make up a caption for the photograph.
- Let each character speak his or her thoughts at that moment in the play.

Statues/Paintings

For these you choose one member of the group to be the artist. Then choose:

- a moment in the play
- a title you have made up
- a quotation.

The artist then arranges the members of the group, one by one into a group statue of the chosen subject. Different members of the group can take it in turn to be the artist.

Forum theatre

Another way of exploring a key moment in the play is called 'forum theatre'. The group divides in two:

- A small number of actors to take on roles
- The rest, are theatre directors.

You then work as follows:

1 Chose the moment in the play you are going to work on. (For example, when Claudius rises and leaves the play.)
2 Choose someone to be Claudius.
3 Arranging the space you are working in, agree where the characters are, where people enter and exit and so on.

4   Start by asking Claudius to say what he thinks about
     where he should be and how he should move.
5   Then the rest of the group, the 'directors', try out
     different ways of presenting that moment. For
     example:
     •   they can ask him to speak his lines in a particular
          way
     •   they can suggest he uses certain moves or
          gestures.
6   The short extract from the play can be tried in
     several different ways until the group have used up
     all the ideas.
7   Then you should discuss what worked and what
     didn't work and why.

Character

Questions about character are common in A-level examinations, although they very rarely invite a simple 'character-sketch'. Usually you will be asked to explore the 'importance' or 'dramatic function' of a character or to give your personal evaluation and response.

Judging a character is not simply a matter of accumulating the evidence of the written word and drawing conclusions. It is more complicated, and requires some selection and evaluation to allow you to reach a coherent response to the character.

The evidence 1

Characters are revealed by:
- what they say
- what they do.

Problems

1 Unfortunately (for examination purposes) characters are not always consistent. Major characters are subject to change because the events on which the action is based are significant enough to affect the main protagonists: the more important the character, the closer to the action and the greater the reaction to events.

   You must always be aware of how, and why, characters are developing and be prepared to explain and trace the changes.
2 Characters might say or do things for effect. They might be seeking to impress or mislead someone else and not mean what they say at all.

   You must always consider whether the character is being sincere or if s/he has an ulterior motive.

The evidence 2

Characters are also revealed by:
- what others say about them
- how others behave towards them.

Problems

As in life, whether you accept A's opinion of B depends on how you feel about A. If you believe that A is untrustworthy or has a perverted sense of justice, then A's criticism of B might be interpreted as a glowing character reference! Alternatively, an opinion might be based on false information or might be deliberately misleading.

It is essential that you do not simply accept one character's opinion of another at face value.

The evidence 3

Characters are also revealed by:
- soliloquies
- asides.

These are often the most reliable evidence on which to assess a character since s/he is sharing his/her thoughts with the audience. All pretence is dropped because the soliloquy and the aside are devices which allow characters to express their thoughts and feelings directly, and solely, to the audience.

Critical moments

At critical moments in the play you can begin to gain a better insight into a character by seeking answers to certain questions. Sadly, there is no formula which will apply to every situation, but you need to identify the key scenes and speeches which relate to a particular character and then ask these questions to start you off and perhaps prompt questions of your own.
- What has the character said or done here?
- Why has the character said or done this?
- What will happen as a result of this speech or action?
- How do you feel about the consequences of this speech or action?
- What does this incident tell us about the character?
- How does the character change or develop as a result of it?

The CRITICAL MOMENTS' approach can be used to highlight key points in the development of a character. For example, it is possible to do this with Hamlet himself.

1 Ophelia refers to Hamlet before the drama itself, to the young man she loved whom we never see:
   '*Th' expectancy and rose of the fair state*'
   (Act 3 scene 1)

2 However, our first glimpse of the prince reveals bitterness and hostility:
   '*A little more than kin, and less than kind.*'
   (Act 1 scene 2)
   '*I have that within which passes show*'
   (Act 1 scene 2)

3 In soliloquy, Hamlet reveals profound despair and disillusion:
   '*How weary, stale and unprofitable*
   Seem to me all the uses of this world!'
   (Act 1 scene 2)

4 He denounces his mother, and women in general:
   '*O most wicked speed, to post*
   With such dexterity to incestuous sheets.'
   '*frailty, thy name is woman.*'
   (Act 1 scene 2)

5 The Ghost's revelations produce a surge of passion and violence, as Hamlet is called upon to take action in the name of revenge:
   '*Haste me to know't, that I with wings as swift*
   As meditation or the thoughts of love,
   May sweep to my revenge.'
   (Act 1 scene 5)

6 However, there are signs of misgivings or self-doubt:
   '*And shall I couple hell?*'
   '*O cursed spite,*
   That ever I was born to set it right.'
   (Act 1 scene 5)

7 Hamlet then finds himself baffled, confused and distracted: the world is '*a foul and pestilent congregation of vapours.*' man is '*this quintessence of dust?*'
(Act 2 scene 2)

8 He reproaches himself for his inaction:
' *O what a rogue and peasant slave am I!*'
' *I am pigeon-livered and lack gall*'
(Act 2 scene 2)

9 He improvises a plan, using the arrival of the Players to his advantage:
'*the play's the thing*
Wherein I'll catch the conscience of the king.'
(Act 2 scene 2)

10 However, Hamlet is still subject to violent swings of mood and preoccupied with death and life's futility:
'*To die, to sleep... 'tis a consummation devoutly to be wished*'
'*conscience does make cowards of us all*'
'*the native hue of resolution*
Is sicklied o'er by the pale cast of thought'
(Act 3 scene 1)

11 He is also distracted by his feelings about women and sex:
'*why wouldst thou be a breeder of sinners?*'
'*I have heard of your paintings, too*'
'*To a nunnery go.*'

12 The inner play brings proof of Claudius's guilt, and elation for Hamlet:
'*I'll take the ghost's word for a thousand pound.*'
'*Now could I drink hot blood*'
(Act 3 scene 2)

13 However, he is frustrated in his desire for revenge as he encounters Claudius at prayer:
'*this is hire and salary, not revenge.*'
'*This physic but prolongs thy sickly days.*'
(Act 3 scene 3)

14 In the closet scene Hamlet seems to release some of the emotional pressure inside him as he finally confronts his mother:
'*You cannot call it love, for at your age*
The hey-day of the blood is tame'
'*To live In the rank sweat of an enseamed bed*
Stewed in corruption, honeying and making love
Over the nasty sty.'
'*go not to my uncle's bed,*
Assume a virtue if you have it not.'
'*I essentially am not in madness,*
But mad in craft.'
'*'Tis sport to have the engineer*
Hoist with his own petar.'
(Act 3 scene 4)

15 Hamlet prepares to depart for England but the meeting with Fortinbras's army reminds him that his task is not complete:
'*How all occasions do inform against me,*
And spur my dull revenge!'
'*O from this time forth,*
My thoughts be bloody or be nothing worth.'
(Act 4 scene 4)

16 On his return to Denmark, Hamlet is again confronted by death:
'*Now get you to my lady's chamber, and tell her, let her paint an inch thick, to this favour she must come.*'
'*I loved Ophelia, forty thousand brothers*
Could not, with all their quantity of love,
Make up my sum –.'
'*I'll rant as well as thou.*'
(Act 5 scene 1)

17 Hamlet seems less tortured at this stage of the play. Perhaps he is more balanced emotionally, more resigned to life and destiny or perhaps simply weary of the struggle:
'*There's a divinity that shapes our ends*'
'*the readiness is all*'
(Act 5 scene 2)

18 At the end he does kill Claudius but it costs his own life:
'*I am dead, Horatio.*
Thou livest; report me and my cause aright
To the unsatisfied.'
'*But I do prophesy the election lights*
On Fortinbras, he has my dying voice;'
'*The rest is silence.*'
(Act 5 scene 2)

There will be other events and other quotations to which you will wish to refer but this process of pursuing character development through the whole play is an invaluable exercise.

Claudius

See how many 'critical moments' you can find to illustrate the following characteristics in Claudius:

- charm
- cunning
- hypocrisy
- ruthlessness.

Relationships

You can use the same approach to explore the relationships between characters. The quotations below are all concerned with the relation between Hamlet and Ophelia and they are presented in chronological order. Consider what you think each of them reveals about their relationship and what stage each of them marks in the development of that relationship.

1 '*For Hamlet and the trifling of his favour,*
   Hold it a fashion and a toy in blood.'
   LAERTES (Act 1 scene 3)

2 '*He hath my lord of late made many tenders*
   Of his affection to me.'
   OPHELIA (Act 1 scene 3)

3 '*I would not in plain terms from this time forth*
   Have you so slander any moment leisure
   As to give words to talk with the Lord
   Hamlet.'
   POLONIUS (Act 1 scene 3)

4 '*Yea, from the table of my memory*
   I'll wipe away all trivial fond records'
   HAMLET (Act 1 scene 5)

5 '*He took me by the wrist, and held me hard;*
   Then he goes to the length of all his arm,
   And with his other hand thus o'er his brow,
   He falls to such perusal of my face
   As a would draw it.'
   OPHELIA (Act 2 scene 1)

6 '*Or if thou wilt needs marry, marry a fool for wise men know*
   well enough what monsters you make of them.'
   HAMLET (Act 3 scene 1)

7 '*And I of ladies most deject and wretched,*
   That sucked the honey of his music vows'
   OPHELIA (Act 3 scene 1)

8 '*Lady, shall I lie in your lap?*
   '*Do you think I meant country matters?*'
   '*It would cost you a groaning to take off mine edge.*'
   HAMLET (Act 3, scene 2)

9 '*I hoped thou shouldst have been my Hamlet's
wife.*'
GERTRUDE (Act 5 scene 1)
10 '*I loved Ophelia*'
HAMLET (Act 5 scene 1)

It is possible to build a coherent, methodical approach to
characters and the relationships between them by making
selections of significant quotations and using them as a kind of
'skeleton' structure on which you can build an essay.

There can be irony in actions as well as words. In Act 5
scene 2 the Queen takes and drinks from the poisoned cup.
Claudius, who loves her, cannot stop her bringing about her
death by drinking the wine he has poisoned.

There can also be unintentional irony, as when Claudius,
trying to persuade Hamlet that his father's death is not
unique, speaks of '*the first corse*' (Act 1 scene 2 line 105,
page 21) and so unwittingly invokes the murder of Abel by
Cain, just as he killed his own brother. See also **Dramatic
irony**

Metaphor: A figure of speech in which a person, or thing, or
idea is described as if it were something else:
(1) *'Your bait of falsehood takes this carp of truth.'*
(Act 2 scene 1 line 62, page 73)
(2) *'The serpent that did sting thy father's life
Now wears his crown.'*
(Act 1 scene 5 line 39, page 51)

Onomatopoeia: Using words that are chosen because they
mimic the sound of what is being described:
*'The graves stood tenantless, and the sheeted dead
Did squeak and gibber in the Roman streets;'*
(Act 1 scene 1 line 114, page 11)

Pastiche: A piece of writing done in imitation of the form and
style of another writer or literary period.

Personification: Referring to a thing or an idea as if it were a
person:
*'But look the morn in russet mantle clad
Walks o'er the dew of yon high eastward hill.'*
(Act 1 scene 1 line 166, page 15)

Play on words: see **Pun**

Pun: A figure of speech in which the writer uses a word that
has more than one meaning. The puns on the word '*tender*'
(meaning 'offer', 'look after' and 'present') demonstrate the
self-regarding long-windedness of Polonius and at the same
time ram his point home:
                              *'think yourself a baby,
That you have ta'en these tenders for true pay*

Which are not sterling. Tender yourself more dearly;
Or – not to crack the wind of the poor phrase
Running it thus – you'll tender me a fool.'
(Act 1 scene 3 line 105, page 39)

Simile: A comparison between two things which the writer
makes clear by using words such as 'like' or 'as':

'Make thy two eyes like stars start from their spheres,
Thy knotted and combined locks to part,
And each particular hair to stand an end,
Like quills upon the fretful porpentine.'
(Act 1 scene 5 line 18, page 49)

Soliloquy: Spoken apparently to himself or herself when a
character is alone on stage, or separated from the other
characters in some way. In *Hamlet* the soliloquies are
particularly important because, in the atmosphere of spying
and intrigue where Hamlet constantly has to watch what he
says, and in his assumed madness, it is only when he is alone
that we can hope to learn his true feelings.